D0146410

Confronting the Margaret Mead Legacy

Confronting the Margaret Mead Legacy

*Scholarship,
Empire, and
the South Pacific*

Edited by
Lenora Foerstel
and Angela Gilliam

Temple University Press • Philadelphia

Temple University Press, Philadelphia 19122
Copyright © 1992 by Temple University. All rights reserved
Published 1992
Printed in the United States of America

∞ The paper used in this publication meets the minimum requirements of
American National Standard for Information Sciences—Permanence of Paper for
Printed Library Materials, ANSI Z39.48-1984

Library of Congress Cataloging-in-Publication Data
Confronting the Margaret Mead legacy : scholarship, empire, and the
  South Pacific / edited by Lenora Foerstel and Angela Gilliam.
      p.   cm.
    Includes bibliographical references.
    ISBN 0-87722-886-8 (alk. paper)
  1. Ethnology—Oceania.   2. Mead, Margaret, 1901–1978.
  2. Anthropology—Government policy—Oceania.   I. Foerstel, Lenora,
  1929– .   II. Gilliam, Angela, 1936–
  GN662.C64   1992
  306′.0995—dc20   91-16194

This book is dedicated in loving memory to Eleanor Leacock

CONTENTS

FOREWORD

Peter Worsley

Critical evaluation of Margaret Mead's work is long overdue, particularly in the United States, where I have frequently found it difficult to engage in discussion about Mead, since the slightest breath of criticism commonly evokes a passionate—and to my mind quite uncritical—defense of the entire corpus of her very uneven writings and of her life-career. I am, therefore, glad that the contributors to this book have undertaken an examination of the Mead legacy in a Pacific-wide context.

I myself cannot contribute on Melanesia, as I would have liked to have done, because my efforts to carry out fieldwork there were aborted, the day before I was due to leave for the New Guinea Highlands, by the refusal of the Australian colonial authorities to give me an entry permit to the country (Worsley, 1990). I was forced, therefore, to switch rapidly to fieldwork among Australian Aborigines.

But the intelligence services who had earlier banned me from Africa—on the region on which I had been specializing, following several years of army service and employment on the Tanganyika Groundnut Scheme—finally achieved their objective: forcing me out of anthropology. When I was told I would never get an anthropological post, I decided I would have to turn to sociology. McCarthyism was thus not confined to the United States, even if it was manufactured and exported from there, and for many years after McCarthy's fall from power, I still had to get a special "waiver of Congress" every time I wanted to visit the country.

Any hope of fieldwork in Melanesia having been abandoned, I nevertheless decided to make use of the cultural capital accumulated while in Australia to write a study of "cargo" cults (1957a) as a farewell to the region, of necessity based entirely on library sources.

As a result of publishing that book, I was asked to review Margaret Mead's (1956) study of the Paliau movement. It seemed to me so inadequate a work (unlike the splendid 1962 study by her colleague Theodore Schwartz) that I suggested to the editors that, instead, I write something more general about her work.

In the review article, "Margaret Mead: Science or Science-Fiction?" (Worsley, 1957b), I paid full tribute to her major achievement in putting anthropology on the map and to her commitment to what in my mind is the classic anthropological "project": the demonstration that anthropology is not a purely scholastic discipline, fixated upon the study of exotic cultures and customs "out there," and therefore, to most people, of no relevance to their own lives. Mead's vision, per contra, and her achievement, was to show that the findings of anthropologists about remote peoples were highly relevant to the concerns of Americans about their own society, and that the culture of the United States was only one among very many cultural forms, not necessarily the culmination of human evolution.

Yet, at the same time, I took leave to raise criticisms about the impressionistic and often dubious nature of the evidence she used in these popular works. That she could do work of the most rigorous kind when addressing herself to her professional colleagues, there is no question, as

"Kinship in the Admiralty Islands" (1934), to name no other work, shows. Nor was I suggesting, of course, that she should have written in that way when writing for a popular audience: I simply regretted that the standards that informed her writing for professionals were absent in her popular writings.

I soon found that Margaret Mead did not react kindly to criticism, for she responded with a letter in which she expressed "outrage." She was generous enough to praise *The Trumpet Shall Sound,* only to contrast it with my *Science and Society* review, which was, she wrote, a "sloppy piece of writing," a "lambast . . . which bristles with inaccuracies," and a "rehash of [my] professor's bricks" in which she could not find "anything specially of value." Taken aback by the virulence of this language, I soon discovered that it evidently was not unusual, for I received several communications from anthropologists in the United States who told me that they had been treated to similar withering counterattacks when they had dared, especially in public situations, to say anything critical of her work.

These exchanges about a minor review 30 years ago scarcely matter now. But the evaluation of such influential work does remain important. It was not just the general Boasian message about the importance of culture that brought her a mass readership, but what she had to say about one particular aspect of culture: about the different ways in which the biological facts of sex are converted, in different cultures, into highly varied forms of institutionalized gender. To women in particular, this came as a powerful, liberating idea, because it contained the implication not only that the existing division of cultural labor between the sexes was not a fact of nature, but that it need not be as it was in Western societies. I remember in particular how one of my very first students, who was not unaware of the variability of culture, having experienced firsthand the singularly traumatic experience of the transition from life in middle class Poland before World War II to the extremity of the culture of the Dachau concentration camp, telling me, years later, that the most exciting intellectual experience of her social science course had been reading Margaret Mead's *Sex and Temperament in Three Primitive Societies* (1935).

Uncritical adulation of Margaret Mead is something else. Unfortunately, it is far from dead in American anthropology. Thus, I found it disturbing that most contributors to the 1983 symposium in the *American Anthropologist* on Freeman's *Margaret Mead and Samoa: The Making and Unmaking of an Anthropological Myth* (1983), responded to his detailed and documented critique of her Samoan work not so much by refuting his charges but by denouncing his own theoretical orientation. One does not have to share Freeman's views on the relationship between biology and culture to recognize the relevancy of his critical comments about the inadequacy and inaccuracy of Mead's treatment of the topics of rank, cooperation and competition, aggressive warfare and behavior, pagan and Christian religion, punishment, childrearing, Samoan character, sexual mores and behavior, adolescence, and the Samoan ethos, and of the limitations of the fieldwork. *Tu quoque* is a poor argument.

In any case, the entire discussion (as Leacock argues in Chapter 1), whether focused upon the theoretical debate or the debate about the accuracy of Mead's empirical work, continues a tradition of which both Mead and Freeman are part: the abstraction of supposedly timeless Pacific cultures from a real context of massive rapid social change. During the colonial epoch, the indigenous aristocrats intensified their efforts to extend their power at the expense of the autonomy of village communities. And, during the post-colonial epoch, there has been an ever-increasing involvement of the whole region in the global struggle between the superpowers, notably because of the enormous pressure exercised by the United States upon new and tiny statelets in its effort at "strategic denial" of the region to feared (but imaginary) communist penetration.

These things rarely enter the work of those anthropologists, who concentrate predominantly upon lineage and clan (real enough phenomena, to be sure) and upon big men and intervillage rivalries. To this extent they have contributed to the construction of "primitivism by omission," to the consolidation of stereotypes that they would laugh at were they to find them in the pages of the *National Geographic:* the image of the Pacific as a sexual paradise under the palm trees, and the quite contrary image of a region inhabited by savage cannibals engaged in constant warfare.

To those who live there, the Pacific is certainly no paradise, not because they are constantly threatened by intertribal warfare, but because, as Durutalo notes in Chapter 8, these are islands where there is no work, some of which are used as nuclear testing zones and garbage cans and their inhabitants as nuclear guinea pigs, where old-style direct imperialism and settler colonialism still flourishes in places such as New Caledonia and French Polynesia, where the major sources of wealth everywhere (particularly minerals) are owned by foreign corporations, and where world financial institutions (particularly the IMF) increasingly determine what will be done with that wealth. Hence, Durutalo says, "how to get away" from this paradise—emigration—has become a major preoccupation.

Because these processes affect the entire region and, more widely, the Third World, they have resulted in the emergence of new levels of political consciousness: the awareness that the islands have common problems, that there are oppositions of interest between indigenous elites and the mass of ordinary people, and that these elites manipulate ethnic hostility to consolidate their position and identify themselves with similar anticommunist elites in Malaysia, Taiwan, and elsewhere. A whole set of populist ideologies—*Vakaitaukei* (the Fijian Way of Life), *Fakatonga* (the Tongan Way), *Fa'aSamoa* (the Samoan Way), the Melanesian Way, the Pacific Way—have emerged that seek to deny any fundamental conflict of interest, whether between traditional aristocrats and commoners, between classes, or between modern elites and the ordinary citizenry. And there is a counterposed awareness of radicals who realize that what is happening in their region also happens in other Third World countries and that inequalities in access to resources and hierarchies of power are as much part of Pacific cultures as of any other.

This collection also makes a significant, perhaps even historic, departure from traditional Pacific scholarship, in that—guided by the principles of egalitarianism and advocacy-based scholarship—it includes among its contributors Warilea Iamo, Papua New Guinea's first anthropologist and director of the New Guinea Institute of Applied Social and Economic Research, and John D. Waiko, Papua New Guinea's first Ph.D. in the field of history. There are also interviews with two major women activists, Nahau Rooney and Susanna Ounei. For them, white culture is not what it was for Margaret Mead, the open door to "civilization": it also includes indentured labor, master-servant relationships, the color-bar, and enforced taxation.

More than this, it involves Western cultural hegemony. Today, some 40 Christian missions claim to have converted 40 percent of the population of Papua New Guinea; special attention, backed by massive inputs of money and technology, is paid to the "last tribes." Having experienced life in the village, on mission stations, and in Western universities, Waiko (Chapter 9) finds "life ordered by the ringing of bells" inferior in quality to the culture of the Binandere, which is based on reciprocity and on obligations to others. Though anthropology is by no means dismissed, Iamo (Chapter 4) fiercely rejects the arrogant assumption that theirs was and is a "lesser and simpler" culture. Though they lacked writing, their culture is so complex that it takes a lifetime to learn, something that cannot adquately be done within the short period anthropologists normally have available for their fieldwork. Having attempted a sketch of the principles by which Australian Aboriginal thinkers classify plants and animals (Worsley, 1961), I am aware how much that study was merely an elementary introduction to the subject. A thorough analysis would have required at least the 15 years and the close association with expert Aboriginal informants that Julie Waddy's superb book on the same theme entailed (Waddy, 1988).

Mead's assumption that her professional training enabled her to master the subtleties of a culture within a few months, despite modest linguistic skills, is therefore, rightly challenged by Rooney (Chapter 2), who remarks that Mead "was dealing with people who were in fact her equal" in their knowledge of their own culture. Rooney's own anthropological perceptiveness in her observations about bride price and the involvement of networks of kin in the contracting of marriages are evidence of this intellectual competence. But as a woman, this struggle for her education and for her country's independence called for her to be "exceptionally good," not just Mead's equal.

This respect for the knowledge of his own people explains why Waiko (Chapter 9) insisted that the examination of his Ph.D. from Australian National University be carried out not just in Canberra by whites, but also in his natal village by a panel of knowledgeable elders who listened to tapes of his work in Binandere.

As far as Mead is concerned, the Papua New Guineans are not terribly impressed, certainly in terms of the accuracy and depth of her fieldwork. And in terms of reciprocity, Rooney remarks (Chapter 2), "we gave [her] more . . . than she gave us in return," which was materially little beyond the establishment of a memorial to her fieldwork when they had hoped for a cultural center for their use. Their critical remarks about Mead must, however, make any anthropologists, not just specialists on the Pacific, reflect on their own relationship to their informants.

The nonislander contributors to the volume are usually more cautious. Thus Leacock (Chapter 1)—who died during her attempt to carefully evaluate the rival positions of Mead and Freeman, not in her study, but in Samoa—cites Holmes' view that Mead's characterization of Manua in the 1920s was "substantially correct," and points out that "no Pacific ethnographer . . . has accepted Freeman's description." My own evaluation of Mead's *popular* work, at least, is closer to that of Pospisil (1987), who characterizes it as "creative speculation" but poor anthropology.

As for Mead's political stance, to an outsider, her criticism of Western institutions is always vitiated by her commitment to U.S. foreign policy and by the limits of a liberalism that made her a pioneer of women's rights, but one who stopped abruptly when women started organizing struggles to have those rights actually implemented. It would be a lengthy operation, but careful examination of her innumerable "provocative" public statements on most topics would, I believe, disclose a similar delicacy when it came to seriously confronting powerful institutions within U.S. society.

Abroad, certainly, Margaret Mead's theoretical posture of concern about the danger of global war never prevented her continuing in the service of the U.S. State Department and the military long after World War II was over and after others, such as Gregory Bateson, had withdrawn from working with those organizations. As the editors of this volume point out, Mead's posture of theoretical opposition to nuclearism contradicted her denunciation of U.S. labor unions and others who opposed nuclear power and nuclear weapons, and it never resulted in her participation in anti-war movements. It is both ironic and sad that the world's leading authority on the peoples of the Pacific never raised her voice to protest the explosion of nuclear weapons and the deportation of entire populations by the United States in Micronesia. Durutalo (Chapter 8) and Alcalay (Chapter 7) document the persistence of that policy and of the attitudes that inform the continued refusal of the United States, together with France and Britain, to sign the Treaty of Rarotonga, despite its endorsement by the fifteen South Pacific Forum states. This attitude was classically enunciated by Henry Kissinger in a comment on the Marshall Islands: "There are only 90,000 of them out there. Who gives a damn?", (Hickel, 1971). In contrast, the role of the new statelets in the United Nations, the solidarity they have exhibited toward each other, and the support given by the larger and older, but equally threatened Pacific states, Australia and New Zealand, have been exemplary and heartening.

Anthropologists might find many of these issues outside their field of competence and concern. This is precisely the point of the book.

REFERENCES

Freeman, D. 1983. *Margaret Mead and Samoa: The Making and Unmaking of an Anthropological Myth.* Washington, D.C.: Howard University Press.

Hickel, J. W. 1971. *Who Owns America?* Englewood Cliffs, N.J.: Prentice-Hall.

Mead, M. 1934. "Kinship in the Admiralty Islands," *Anthropological Papers of the American Museum of Natural History* 34 (2), 183–358.

———. 1935. *Sex and Temperament in Three Primitive Societies.* New York: Morrow.

———. 1956. *New Lives for Old: Cultural Transformation, Manus 1928–1953.* New York: Morrow.

Pospisil, L. 1987. Editor's personal communication.

Schwartz, T. 1962. "The Paliau Movement in the Admiralty Islands. 1946–1954," *Anthropological Papers of the American Museum of Natural History* 10, 11(2), pp. 211–421.

Waddy, J. 1988. *The Classification of Plants and Animals from a Groote Eylandt Aboriginal Point of View.* Australian National University, North Australian Research Unit Monograph, Darwin.

Worsley, P. 1957a. *The Trumpet Shall Sound: A Study of "Cargo" Cults in Melanesia.* London: MacGibbon & Kee.

———. 1957b. "Margaret Mead: Science or Science Fiction," in *Science and Society* 21(2), pp. 122–134.

———. 1961. "The Utilization of Food Resources by an Australian Aboriginal Tribe," *Acta Ethnographica* 10, pp. 153–190.

———. 1990. "The Practice of Politics and the Study of Kinship," in the forthcoming festschrift, *Critical Anthropology: The Ethnology of Stanley Diamond*, edited by Christine Gailey and Viana Muller.

Angela Gilliam and Lenora Foerstel

Few subjects of international scholarship are as stereo-typed as Pacific cultures. In travel brochures and in the media, these places are represented either as exotic para-dises or as sites of "clan warfare." Melanesian societies especially have been tainted with the same image of sav-agery, cannibalism, and wanton sexuality that colonialism projected onto African peoples. The widespread nature of such images owes much to the continuing legacy of Mar-garet Mead and later anthropologists. Mead looms large in popular awareness of U.S. anthropology, her name and authority still being synonymous with Pacific ethnography at this level. Even Pacific peoples sometimes find that economic necessity leads them to reproduce their cultures to satisfy the market for the stereotypes. As Delmos Jones once remarked (1987), "Anthropology actually creates a metaculture that people experience."

Because the Pacific cultures are seen as a result of Western scholarship as outside the "civilized world," their ecological, geopolitical, or national concerns, including the struggle to achieve a nuclear-free and independent Pacific, are not taken seriously. Thus, indirectly, much Pacific ethnography has served imperialist strategic purposes.

The participants in this book are taking part in the struggle between two paradigms in scholarship. On the one hand, there is the anthropology created by the conditions of burgeoning empire, developed by the need to dominate, administer, and "understand" the "natives"—the Other.

Such scholarship has notions of superiority and inferiority built in, relativist protestations to the contrary notwithstanding. Much of Pacific ethnography cloaks Pacific peoples in inferiority. It is disturbing that those who describe and define humanity and its direction also place themselves at its pinnacle. As Hsu acknowledged in his classic study of the impact of prejudice on United States anthropology, although not every Western social scientist functions this way, there is an "intellectual *conscience collectif* of White American anthropologists today in the Durkheimian sense" (Hsu, 1973: 2). In other words, most Western anthropologists believe that they are able to scrutinize world cultures more objectively than their non-European counterparts. This belief distorts the accuracy of their observations.

This paradigm is being challenged by scholars from varied backgrounds within a context of a more inclusivist and egalitarian anthropology that recognizes the historicity of the social sciences. That is, anthropology should be conceived of as a social construction—a way of seeing humanity and the world that fits the demands of the particular era and time. Many North American anthropologists and other social scientists have paved the way for the process we are suggesting here. Gough (1968), Hymes (1974), Nader (1974), Jorgensen (1971), Wolf and Jorgensen (1971), Lewis (1973), Nash (1979), Barrett (1984), among others, have called attention to the need to formulate an anthropology that would include "studying up"—specifically local and international elites. The implications gleaned from the contributions of Berreman (1981), Gough, or Wolf and Jorgensen suggest that the anthropologist is contextually and historically situated in relation to power and access to resources, especially while doing "fieldwork."

Such issues also are being raised by contemporary

scholars who have examined Western characterizations of other parts of the world. For Said (1978), the centuries-old concepts of "Orient" and "oriental" are components of European scholarship and have stimulated the creation of the Other. Such representation lends itself to reinforcing a false opposite, that of "occidental" from the "West." Mudimbe (1988) comes to similar conclusions about the "invention of Africa," and Goonatilake (1984) warns that genuine intellectual innovation in dependent Third World countries is often "aborted." Related themes are salient in the work by Bernal (1987), which asserts that the "Ancient Greece" identified as the cradle of "classical" civilization was a fabrication created between 1785 and 1985. To these works is added that of Samir Amin (1989), who maintains that European social theory has reflected the influence of powerful economic forces and is marked by Eurocentrism.

A Collective Tugata

This book is in good measure a collective *tugata*. *Tugata* is the concept of the Binandere people of Papua New Guinea which directly ties the actions of the individual to the well-being of the community. Contributors to this volume not only present "another way of seeing" the Pacific, but most are active supporters of the concept of a nuclear-free and independent Pacific. One objective of this undertaking is to demonstrate that the views and work of an international and interracial group of women and men who are committed to equality present a cogent strategy for addressing the sensitive issues of our times. Because a *tugata* is directed toward advocacy, the participants are described by their activism as well as their research.

Peter Worsley (Foreword) wrote one of the first critiques of Mead, an analysis not cited in the debates over the differences between Mead and Freeman. Worsley also has demonstrated a concern about Western colonialism and the Third World's vulnerability to nuclear proliferation (Worsley, 1977; 1984; Worsley and Hadjor, 1987). Both Worsley (1957) and C.A. Valentine's (1963) explanatory treatments of "cargo cults" influenced Iamo (Chapter 4) and Waiko (Chapter 9) as valid explications of Melanesian cultural responses to colonialism.

Eleanor Leacock's prolific life produced many important writings, including two that aided in the struggle against gender inequality, *Myths of Male Dominance* (1981) and the introduction to the new edition of Engels' *The Origin of the Family, Private Property and the State* (1972). That introduction challenged simplistic conceptions of "stages of development" and pointed out the "political implications of evolutionary theory," thereby suggesting a path for scholars of Pacific cultures who were interested in transforming colonial-centered definitions of "civilized" versus "primitive" societies. It is in that introduction to Engels that Leacock critiqued *Cooperation and Competition Among Primitive Peoples* (Mead, 1937), noting that European expansion had not only affected anthropological theory in general, but that it was a fundamental component of Mead's "culture and personality" theory in particular (Leacock 1972:23).

Of special relevance to this volume is that Leacock (Chapter 1) had undertaken "research on adolescence [and youth suicide] in Samoa in response to Derek Freeman's (1983) criticism of Margaret Mead's *Coming of Age in Samoa*, and his argument that adolescence in the Samoan Islands has always been a difficult period" (Leacock, 1987). Though she had criticized Mead (Leacock, 1981) previously, Leacock believed that Freeman's attacks on Mead suggested a resurgence of biological determinism, making a reassessment of Mead's work advisable.

Nahau Rooney (Chapter 2), referred to as Nahau in *Letters from the Field* (Mead, 1977), is the first woman leader of the Usiai [Nali] Manus. She was prepared for leadership by her father, then the head elder, prior to his death. This role was later expanded to one of national function and prominence, when she became the Minister of Justice in the first Somare government subsequent to the independence of Papua New Guinea in 1975. In 1979, Rooney defied an inherited, colonially-rooted legal system. She lost her parliamentary portfolio and was briefly imprisoned. However, she subsequently was re-elected and by 1986 had acquired the portfolio of Minister for Civil Aviation and Tourism. Rooney is currently an advisor to the People's Democratic Movement Party and to the office of the opposition leader, former Prime Minister Paias Wingti.

In his anthropological dissertation, Warilea Iamo (1986) studied the homeless in the United States, deliberately applying purposeful mutuality and reciprocity in the anthropological method. His model for fieldwork that embraced informants as equals was the thesis and later book of Dr. Bettylou Valentine (1978), his former teacher at the University of Papua New Guinea.

Many people associated with the University of Papua New Guinea have objected to what was written about their country's cultures and the images projected upon their peoples by Margaret Mead (Rooney, Chapter 2; Iamo, Chapter 4; Waiko, Chapter 9). As Papua New Guinean scholars and leaders begin to find access to the media, their concerns and criticism of ethnographic fieldwork are sometimes characterized as biased by the foreign scholar elites.

Iamo, reflecting on "the stigma of New Guinea," points out that anthropologists saw his people as having no history nor any idea of how they came to be. Today, Iamo is the director of the National Research Institute in Papua New Guinea.

For Susanna Ounei (Chapter 6), a nuclear-free Pacific is impossible without an independent Kanaky—the indigenous name for New Caledonia. As a Kanak woman, Ounei has been one of the pioneers of the struggle for independence in the French colony of New Caledonia. Indeed, during the resistance activities in New Caledonia in April 1988, two of Ounei's brothers were killed in the massacre by the French army. Ounei was a founder of Kanak and Exploited Women with the Struggle (Groupe des Femmes Kanakes et Exploitées En Lutte) and a leader in FLNKS, the Kanak Socialist National Liberation Front.

As a Peace Corps volunteer in the Marshall Islands from 1975 to 1977, Glenn Alcalay (Chapter 7) organized an agricultural cooperative in order to teach Marshallese adults about the effects of radiation on humans. In the latter part of 1976, he initiated a compensation bill in the U.S. Congress on behalf of the Micronesian victims of radioactive fallout from the Bikini and Enewetak nuclear experiments. From the British House of Commons to the United Nations, Alcalay has testified more than 30 times on behalf of the irradiated islanders in the Marshalls. Alcalay was aboard Greenpeace's *Rainbow Warrior* during the May 1985 evacuation of the Rongelap islanders in the Marshalls and prior to the bombing of the ship in New Zealand by French commandos. Glenn Alcalay has worked as an advisor to two films about the impact of U.S. nuclear policy on the Pacific peoples: *Half-Life* (1985) and *Radio Bikini* (1987).

Simione Durutalo (Chapter 8), a Fulbright-Hayes scholar at the State University of New York at Binghamton, is a former vice president of the Fiji Labor party and a founding member of the Fiji Anti-Nuclear Group. He is currently teaching at the University of the South Pacific in Fiji. For Simione Durutalo, the crisis of the Pacific intellectual is grounded in the double heritage of nuclear politics and the "happy native" image. Durutalo maintained in an interview with Foerstel that interpretations of Fijian culture and revitalistic movements and return to former religious patterns are often illusions created by anthropologists. "The idea that traditional cultures do not evolve, but remain stagnant and can be pulled out like a plant to be studied and regrown, is obviously a myth. . . . It is important to note that the synthesis which does come about is unique to each culture. . . . The Fijian people have tried to soften the impact of the modern world, and if indeed we are not successful, this impact will be like a fallout which will destroy our landscape, forests, water and whole ecosystem" (Durutalo, 1987).

John Waiko, the first Papua New Guinean Ph.D. in the field of history, is currently Professor in the History Department at the University of Papua New Guinea. Waiko's expertise was central to the documentary, *Angels of War* (1983), a film showing how Papua New Guineans carried World War II "on their backs" and were referred to in racist terms by those who used them as "cargo boys." In his writings, he has attempted to integrate Binandere cultural regulations with the sociology of knowledge (Chapter 9). He has aided his people in confronting the colonial definitions of development imposed by the national government's relationship with a multinational timber company. How could "development" mean cutting down the trees when the term properly signified preserving the forested land base in Binandere? *Man Without Pigs*, the film about Waiko and his Binandere village's relationship to his education that he refers to in Chapter 9, was part of the fourteenth annual Margaret Mead Film Festival in 1990 at the American Museum of Natural History in New York City.

For the editors of this volume, the project began during our preliminary work on a Public Broadcasting Service film about anthropology and anthropologists in Papua New Guinea, titled *Anthropology on Trial* (1983). In that initial discussion we provided part of the concept that was central to the film. Moreover, we furnished the contacts in Papua New Guinea that enabled the film to proceed. Although Foerstel accompanied the filmmaker to Manus and directed a portion of the film, both of us were separated from *Anthropology on Trial* by its final stages. Coincidentally, three other contributors to this volume—Iamo, Rooney, and Waiko—participated in some aspect of the same film.

Foerstel had gone to Papua New Guinea to assist in the making of the film as a way to participate in a reevaluation of her own work with Mead. Though this relationship was begun initially on Manus in 1953 when Foerstel did the major part of the visual documentation of the Manus experience, it continued off and on for approximately twenty-five years. Some of Foerstel's background in this regard has been captured in Howard's biography of Mead (Howard, 1984:298–310).

For Foerstel (Chapter 3), a long period of reappraisal culminated in 1978 when she returned to Manus to confront the Papua New Guinean perception of Margaret Mead's work. Stephen Suluwan (1978), an active member of M'Bunai village, asked why Mead and Foerstel never told him about the racism that existed in the United States. "We shared everything with you," he said, "and you told us very little about your country." Paliau Maloat, leader of the well-documented Paliau movement, was in the process of forming the Makasol Pati [Party], with an emphasis on a return to the collective aspects of an earlier culture. "The white man took our children away, put down our customs, and gave his customs to our children" (Maloat, 1978).

When Foerstel returned to Manus in 1984, she was reminded by Peter Topo, an acknowledged Nali Leader, that his conversations with her in 1953 had never been documented. He had taken care to tell her that after World War II he worked as a servant to an Australian, during which time he was required to bathe the man and endure sexual harassment. Topo also had described the experiences of other fellow servants, experiences rarely if ever recorded as part of the cultural interaction between white and black. Foerstel realized that this aspect of colonial contact had been overlooked or excluded from the ethnographic publications.

Learning from Pacific peoples in their struggle to redefine themselves to the world has also been pivotal for Gilliam (Chapter 10), whose original purpose in going to Papua New Guinea to teach was to witness how Papua New Guineans were engaging in intellectual decolonization. As one of three nonwhite female teachers (B. Valentine was another) in a university where the female student population rarely exceeded 10 percent, teaching meant challenging colonialist definitions of development as they related to language, communication, and scholarly discourse (Gilliam, 1984, 1989). Gilliam's lifelong intellectual and moral pursuit has included learning other languages and from other cultures as a way of understanding shared human values and working toward worldwide equality. Gilliam also organized the first and second international film festivals in Papua New Guinea in 1979 and 1980. Gilliam's visit to New Caledonia in 1978 provided her the opportunity to experience the lives of the Kanak people under French rule. In a speech before the Committee of 24 at the United Nations, Gilliam described the apartheid-like situation in New Caledonia and the people's desire to understand the "comparison and contrast between Martin Luther King Jr., and Malcolm X and their relationships to the state" (1978; 1987). How and why could Kanaks become so sophisticated about the United States, yet most U.S. citizens not know where New Caledonia was?

In defining the challenge of a global anthropology in this way, the participants in this anthology hope to contribute to a more inclusivist study of humankind. It is the duty of social scientists everywhere to expose the problems faced by Pacific peoples as they resist destruction and extinction. And in our collaborative resistance, we help to make possible future life and the emergence of a universally shared civilization. To ignore this struggle for survival in the Pacific is to imperil the civilizing agents within humanity. Above all, it is hoped that this work continues the constructive aspects of the Boasian struggle against biological determinism, an early objective of Margaret Mead that still resounds today.

REFERENCES

Amin, S. 1989. *Eurocentrism*. New York: Monthly Review Press.
Angels of War. 1983. Distributed by Film Makers Library, New York.

Anthropology on Trial. 1983. Produced by Public Broadcast Service (NOVA), WGBH, Boston.

Barrett, S. 1984. *The Rebirth of Anthropological Theory.* Toronto: University of Toronto Press.

Bernal, M. 1987. *Black Athena: The Afro-Asiatic Roots of Classical Civilization,* vol. 1, *The Fabrication of Ancient Greece, 1975–1985.* New Brunswick, N.J.: Rutgers University Press.

Berreman, G. 1981. *The Politics of Truth: Essays in Critical Anthropology.* Delhi, India: South Asian Publications.

Durutalo, S. 1987. Personal communication.

Freeman, D. 1983. *Margaret Mead and Samoa: The Making and Unmaking of an Anthropological Myth.* Cambridge: Harvard University Press.

Gilliam, A. 1978. "Comparaisons et contrastes entre Martin Luther King, Jr., et Malcolm X et leurs relations différentielles à l'état." Parti de Liberation Kanak (PALIKA) Headquarters, November 29, Noumea, New Caledonia.

———. 1984. "Language and 'Development' in Papua New Guinea." *Dialectical Anthropology* 8, pp. 303–318.

———. 1987. "Petition in Support of the International Mandate for the Decolonization of New Caledonia," August 14. United Nations Reference #A/AC.109/PV.1328.

———. 1989. "On the Problem of Historicist Categories in Theories of Human Development." *Conflict in the Archeology of Living Traditions,* R. Layton (ed.). London: Unwin Hyman.

Goonatilake, S. 1984. *Aborted Discovery: Science and Creativity in the Third World.* London: Zed Books.

Gough, K. 1968. "Anthropology and Imperialism." *Monthly Review* (April), pp. 12–27.

Half-Life: A Parable for the Nuclear Age. 1985. Distributed by Direct Cinema, Los Angeles.

Howard, J. 1984. *Margaret Mead: A Life.* New York: Simon & Schuster.

Hsu, F. 1973. "Prejudice and Its Intellectual Effect in American Anthropology: An Ethnographic Report." *American Anthropology* 75(1), pp. 1–19.

Hymes,. D. (ed.) 1974. *Reinventing Anthropology.* New York: Vintage Books.

Iamo, W. *"The Struggle for Justice and Shelter in Mix-Town, USA".* Unpublished Ph.D. dissertation. Berkeley: University of California.

Jones, D. 1987. Personal communication, September 11.

Jorgensen, J. 1971. "On Ethics and Anthropology." *Current Anthropology* 12(3), p. 321.

Leacock, E. 1981. *Myths of Male Dominance: Collected Articles on Women Cross-Culturally.* New York: Monthly Review Press.

———. 1987. "Youth Suicide in Samoa: Relations between Cultural and Socio-Economic Factors." *IWAC* (International Women's Anthropology Conference) *Newsletter,* issue number 9.

Leacock, E. (ed.) 1972. Introduction to F. Engels, *The Origin of the Family, Private Property and the State.* New York: International Publishers.

Lewis, D. 1973. "Anthropology and Colonialism". *Current Anthropology* 14(5), pp. 581–597.

Maloat, P. 1978. Personal communication.

Mead, M. 1937. *Cooperation and Competition among Primitive Peoples.* New York: McGraw-Hill.

———. 1977. *Letters from the Field, 1925–1975.* New York: Harper and Row.

Mudimbe, V. 1988. *The Invention of Africa: Gnosis, Philosophy and the Order of Knowledge.* Bloomington: Indiana University Press.

Nader, L. 1974. "Up the Anthropologist: Perspectives from Studying Up." In D. Hymes (ed.), *Reinventing Anthropology.* New York: Random House, pp. 284–311.

Nash, J. 1979. "Anthropology of the Multinational Corporation." In M.B. Leons and F. Rothstein (eds.), *New Directions in Political Economy: An Approach from Anthropology.* Westport/London: Greenwood Press.

Radio Bikini. 1987. Distributed by New Dimension Media, Eugene, Oregon.

Said, E. 1978. *Orientalism.* New York: Pantheon.

Valentine, B. 1978. *Hustling and Other Hard Work: Life Styles in the Ghetto.* New York: Free Press.

Valentine, C. A. 1963. "Social Status, Political Power and Native Responses to European Influence in Oceania." *Anthropological Forum* 1, 3–55.

Wolf, E., and J. Jorgensen. 1971. "Anthropologists on the Warpath." *New York Review of Books.*

Worsley, P. 1957. *The Trumpet Shall Sound: A Study of "Cargo" Cults in Melanesia.* London: Mackibbon and Kee.

———. 1977. *The Third World.* 4th ed. Chicago: University of Chicago Press. Originally published 1964.

———. 1984. *The Three Worlds: Culture and World Development.* Chicago: University of Chicago Press.

Worsley, P., and K. Hadjor. 1987. *On the Brink: Nuclear Proliferation in the Third World.* London: Third World Communications.

ACKNOWLEDGMENTS

In any project of this magnitude, the debt to those who offered assistance and encouragement is overwhelming. Yet we are especially humbled by those who aided us and have since died. In the days before he succumbed on June 17, 1990, C.A. Valentine made an extraordinary effort to read and make commentary on the manuscript. Similarly, Kathleen Gough's detailed appraisal, done five months before her death on September 8, 1990, helped us to clarify our synthesis. Both of these scholars shared with the late Eleanor Leacock (Chapter 1) the belief that a global anthropology must be advocacy-based.

The assassination of Jean-Marie Tjibaou transformed his words (Chapter 10) into a record of singular importance. The debt to Donna Winslow for helping to translate on that occasion also has increased as a result. And the conceptual contributions by Ralph Karepa and Archie Singham are magnified because they too have passed on.

We are also particularly grateful to G. Evelyn Hutchinson, Del Jones, Nahau Rooney, and Eric Wolf for substantive interviews that reminded us how important it is to continually make linkages between scholarship and ethics.

From the beginning, friends and colleagues, some of whom we only met over the telephone, have shared their time and resources with us. Jim Anthony, William Arens, Lynn Bolles, Jessie Campbell, Sarah Diamond, Manet Fowler, Myrna Goldenberg, Luis Kemnitzer, Marion Langer, Harry Lerner, Charles O'Connell, Louise Thompson Patterson, Leonard Pospisil, Ellen Ray, Irving Rouse, Councill Taylor, Karen Watson-Gegeo, Harold Wechsler, and Robin Winks were especially helpful in providing ideas about the relationship between social context and anthropology.

Words cannot express our gratitude to those colleague-friends who, besides Valentine and Gough, read all or part of the manuscript. Debbie D'Amico-Samuels, Herb Foerstel, Michael Nixon, Ethel Tobach, Bettylou Valentine, and Joyce Wike offered suggestions that greatly improved this project.

Ambassador Renagi R. Lohia (Papua New Guinea), in addition to reading part of the manuscript, offered guidance and support throughout, and Ambassador Robert van Lierop (Vanuatu) also provided valuable materials.

Carol Champion with the McHenry Library at the University of California at Santa Cruz; Richard Hunter of the World Federation for Mental Health, Alexandria, Virginia; Steven Kirkpatrick at the State University of New York, College at Old Westbury; Kevin Profitt of the American Jewish Archives at Hebrew Union College in Cincinnati; Terry Hubbard, Pat Matheny-White, and Randy Stilsom of the Evergreen State College library; Evelyn Hatkin, editor of the Declassified Documents Reference System at Research Publications; and Mary Wolfskill at the Library of Congress extended their generous research skills as well.

Mention must be made of the gracious hospitality that the late Mrs. G. Evelyn Hutchinson extended to the editors, which enabled the interview with G. Evelyn Hutchinson to be memorable.

We also thank Anne Brownell Sloane and the Institute for Intercultural Studies in New York City for facilitating the use of materials from the Margaret Mead and Gregory Bateson collections.

We are also grateful to Sue Buchner and Marie Bower for working with us and typing some components of the document more than once.

Financial and resource support for this project has come in part from Evergreen State College; Maryland Institute of Art; State University of New York, College at Old Westbury; and Rose Catchings, former Executive Secretary (Women), World Division, United Methodist Church.

Most important of all, we thank our children—Onik'a Ilaisaane Gilliam, Jonathan Paliau Foerstel, Helen Foerstel Cooke, and Karen Foerstel—who shared our vision and whose love and support kept us going in the difficult times.

And finally, we express our heartfelt thanks to our editor at Temple University Press, Michael Ames, without whose commitment this book would not have come to be.

Part I

The Margaret Mead Legacy

Part I

ELEANOR LEACOCK

1 Anthropologists in Search of a Culture: Margaret Mead, Derek Freeman, and All the Rest of Us

The Mead–Freeman controversy, as it has come to be called, certainly has its bizarre aspects. Just how many papers can outsiders write about the culture of one small island nation?[1] One can indeed take a cynical view of the entire affair, and see the creation of an attention-attracting issue as simply serving the demands of the academic market place. Dealing with a recognized "issue" makes it easier to publish a paper and thereby add to one's vita, to have a symposium accepted, to obtain a research grant, or to win support for a dissertation topic. In my own case, it enabled me to put on my applied-anthropology hat—for I am no Pacific expert—and conduct reserach on youth problems in Samoa,[2] visit the University of the South Pacific in Fiji, and in the process learn firsthand about a politically important and exciting part of the world.

There is, however, the other side to the deluge of papers that criticized Freeman's book, *Margaret Mead and Sa-*

moa: The Making and Unmaking of an Anthropological Myth (1983b). As Lenora Foerstel illustrates so well (Chapter 3), the issues raised by Freeman's book are deeply ideological. In the context of today's reactionary climate, Freeman's scathing attack on a leading female scholar, and his vitriolic criticism of Franz Boas as a "cultural determinist" who seriously neglected biology, cannot fail to have racist implications. To be sure, in the closing passage to his book, Freeman (1983b:302) avers that he is simply asking for a synthesis that recognizes "the radical importance of the genetic and exogenetic and their interaction," and he disclaims "extreme biological determinism" as unscientific. In the context of his portrayal of Boas as an "extreme" cultural determinist, however, his emphasis on the need for a *new* synthesis of biology and culture calls his seemingly balanced position into question. Freeman deals with Boas in considerable detail, yet from his treatment one would not understand that it is precisely the *Boasian* synthesis of biology and culture that laid the foundation for the "new physical anthropology," which deals with the interaction of these variables both in the course of human evolution and in relation to contemporary problems concerning fertility, population, and health. In this light, Freeman's insistence that a truly scientific anthropology must place greater emphasis on biological factors in human behavior, can only be read as a plug for biological determinism.

Support for biological determinism was clearly the message picked up by the *New York Times* in its unprecedented front page announcement of an as-yet-unpublished anthropology book. In the *Times* story of January 31, 1983, the ethologist Nikolaus Tinbergen commends Freeman's book as "a masterpiece of modern scientific anthropology," and the zoologist Ernst Mayr states that the book "is not only a contribution to cultural anthropology, but it will also have a major impact on psychology and other aspects of human biology." Significantly, statements about the scientific achievements of the book that grace its dust cover are by Tinbergen, Mayr, and two physical anthropologists, rather than by scholars who are knowledgeable about Samoa or the Pacific, or even about cultural anthropology. The *Times* writer aptly states, "Defenders of Miss Mead say that many scholars who have lined up behind Professor Freeman are longtime champions of biological determinism, a doctrine that has gained considerable strength and credence within the academic community during the last decade" (McDowell 1983:C21). It was fitting, then, for anthropologists to launch a strong and consistent counterattack against Freeman's book, although this, of course, was no longer front page news.

The Critique of Freeman

Freeman bluntly argued that Mead's study of Samoa was designed to provide Boas with a "negative instance"— a case where adolescence was not accompanied by the stress familiar in the West—thereby demonstrating the primacy of cultural factors in social behavior, that the inexperienced and biased Mead found what she was supposed to, but that in fact adolescence in Samoa is very stressful and Samoan culture as a whole is and always has been characterized by highly punitive parenting and a strong emphasis on aggression and violence.

Freeman was criticized on many counts. For example, he has been criticized for his misrepresentation of the Mead-Boas relationship and his treatment of Boas' argument with proponents of the eugenics movement of the 1920s as if people such as Madison Grant were disinterested scholars (Weiner 1983), for his ignoring current work on the relations between biology and culture and his failure to offer any formulation of these relations beyond programmatic statements such as that cited above (Levy 1983; Strathern 1983), and for his mishandling of his own asserted scientific method (Patience and Smith 1986). Freeman also has been criticized for the scientifically unjustifiable selectivity of his citations. For instance, he cites every criticism of Mead made by Holmes, who restudied Ta'u, a village in which Mead worked, but never mentions Holmes' overall evaluation of her study as generally sound (Holmes 1983, 1987).

Above all, Freeman was criticized for his harsh, one-sided, and insulting description of Samoan culture. In his view "intense competitiveness" pervades all aspects of Samoan life, and Samoans live in an authority system so stressful that it "regularly result(s) in psychological disturbances ranging from compulsive behaviors and *musu* states to hysterical illnesses and suicide" (Freeman 1983b: 153, 225). Rape is a "common occurrence" that has "long been intrinsic to the sexual mores of Samoan men" and a "major element in their sexual behavior" (Freeman 1983b: 245, 249–50). Some Samoan researchers place the "reality" of Samoan culture somewhere "in between" Freeman's and Mead's pictures (e.g., Shore 1983), while others feel that Mead's characterization of Manu'a in the 1920s was substantially correct (e.g., Holmes 1987). No Pacific ethnographer, however, has accepted Freeman's description.

Freeman also was faulted for ignoring the culture changes that have been taking place in Samoa (e.g., Ember 1985) as well as its problems as a small Third World island nation beset by the difficulties of economic dependence and cultural conflict (e.g., Shankman 1983). A *New York Times* writer visited Samoa after the appearance of Freeman's book and found it to be "a very troubled place, plagued by most of the difficulties besetting developing countries. . . . In general, social tensions are worse in Western Samoa [where Freeman worked] than in the far smaller, highly subsidized American Samoa [where Mead worked]. Western Samoa has the world's highest rate of suicide among young people, a high crime rate, a yawning trade deficit, political difficulties and a strange loss of its historic self-sufficiency" (Bernstein 1983:54).

As a major part of his argument, Freeman cites police records on violence and delinquency among youth in the 1960s as if these logically disproved Mead's account of adolescence in a small, remote village in the 1920s. He does not discuss the possibility that these data may tell us something about the problems of contemporary Samoa. Instead, to Freeman, they simply reveal the "darker side," the "grim realities" of an unchanging Samoan culture (Freeman 1983b:xvii, 85). He buttresses his argument with examples of violence in the ethnohistorical record without any reference to their context, a subject to which I shall return. His accounts of rape and of youth suicide are similarly ahistorical and contextless. Nowhere does Freeman make reference to the kinds of problems some Samoans I talked with discussed: disjunctions between traditional mores and contemporary conditions in a poor Third World island nation, the problem of youth unemployment (meaningless in a subsistence economy but a major problem throughout the Third World today), the tragedy of a *rising* rate of youth suicides (a problem of concern throughout the South Pacific as well as in many other parts of the world), and the new phenomena of teenage vagrancy (impossible in the Samoa of the past) and teenage prostitution (a logical spinoff of vagrancy in a port town and a concern in Pago Pago). Nor does Freeman make any reference to the dilemma of young people who would strive to fulfill both old and new goals, that is, fulfill parental and kin expectations for their contribution to the traditional subsistence economy (in which a fair amount was expected of them, but where the rewards were predictable and certain), as well as expectations for their success at school and in employment, where competition is intense, particularly in Western Samoa, and where effort may only result in failure (Leacock 1987).

A further criticism to be leveled at Freeman pertains to his insistence that Samoan culture as described by Mead constitutes the only known "negative instance" of a sexually permissive and relatively stress-free adolescence, when, in fact, the ethnographic record offers many such instances. One of the best known was documented at the very time Mead was working on her Samoan study. Before Mead ever went to Samoa, Malinowski had referred to the early age at which children "become initiated into sexual life." He wrote, "As they grow up, they live in promiscuous free love, which gradually develops into more permanent attachments, one of which ends in marriage. But before this is reached, unmarried girls are openly supposed to be quite free to do what they like," and he went on to describe intervillage visiting parties where adolescent sexual adventure was expected and accepted (Malinowski 1961: 53).

In a later publication, Malinowski wrote that parental attitudes toward childhood sexuality were either indifferent or complacent. Parents "find it natural and do not see why they should scold or interfere. Usually they show a kind of tolerant and amused interest, and discuss the love affairs of their children with easy jocularity" (Malinowski 1941:56). He described the adolescent group as leading a "happy, arcadian existence, devoted to amusement and the pursuit of pleasure" (64). He saw the induction into work as a gradual permissive process. Boys may participate in adult activities, but

> if they grow tired of work, they simply stop and rest. The self-discipline of ambition and subservience to traditional ideals, which moves all the elder individuals and leaves them relatively little personal freedom, has not yet quite drawn these boys into the wheels of the social machine. Girls, too, obtain a certain amount of the enjoyment and excitement denied to children by joining in some of the activities of their elders, while still escaping the worst of the drudgery. (65)

The Trobriand case does more than add further refutation to the assumption that biological changes during adolescence necessarily produce the Sturm und Drang expressed in youth violence, suicide, and other disorders (c.f. Freeman 1983b:268). This and other instances where teenage sexuality could be enjoyed without shame or guilt by boys and girls alike (Schlegel and Barry 1980), and where teenage induction into work could be pleasant and unpressured, point up a process that has been taking place in many parts of the world where subsistence economies have been engulfed by expanding capitalist relations. This is the process whereby youth is transformed from a period of maturation in the context of an assured future to a period of intense competition for new and highly desired but very limited rewards. In each instance, the intricacies of a unique culture history are woven into the specific pattern of stress experienced by the young, yet in broad outline the pattern as a whole is repeated around the world (Leacock 1987). It is late in the day for an anthropologist who purports to be advancing scientific methods to so totally ignore such general world developments. Although in response to critics Freeman (1983a:116–118) has admitted to some change in Samoa "since the 1950s," he has maintained his position that it is irrelevant to his characterization of Samoan culture.

The irony of Freeman's ahistorical analysis is that, despite his claim to be moving anthropology forward, his concept of culture falls squarely within the outmoded functionalist framework shared by Mead and other members of the "personality and culture" school. Freeman is still caught in the bind that this volume is designed to investigate: that of the Western anthropologist who presumes to interpret life in a Third World country without any reference to its history of colonization or analysis of the structure of colonial domination and its thinly veiled successor, called economic dependence. Thus, the actors in Freeman's book cannot be wholes. They are not portrayed in their active attempts to cope with changing realities as they meld old traditions with new ideas in the *Fa'aSamoa*—the Samoan way—that guides behavior. Freeman's culture is indeed a mold. Samoan society and behavior have changed so little since the 1920s, he argues, that he can use data from the 1960s and as late as 1981 to refute Mead (Freeman 1983b:120).

Freeman, then, despite his frequent protestations of being misunderstood, has only substituted a "negative" for a "positive" stereotype of Samoa and Samoans. As Lelei Lelaulu (1983), a Samoan working in the secretariat of the

United Nations, has put it, it is all very well to unsaddle Samoa from the romantic myth of free love under the stars, but he is not happy about the effect of replacing it with the myth of having one of the highest rates of rape in the world. Sad to say, if Mead's work fed into romanticized Western images of the Pacific, that would infantilize Samoans as "simple happy natives," Freeman's supposed balancing of the record with his emphasis on aggression and violence only helped derogate discriminated-against communities in New Zealand, Hawaii, and the United States west coast, where, taken together, more Samoans live than on the islands themselves. Despite the sharp contrasts in their presentations, both provided images that could too easily be incorporated into idealogies used by the West to ration- alize its claim to world hegemony. Both anthropologists reified Samoan culture as something apart from Samoan history and the efforts of different Samoan groups and individuals to understand and direct it, or at least negotiate their own interests in relation to its course. Some concrete examples of what I mean are called for before I return to Western anthropologists and where we might go in relation to the analysis of culture and cultures.

Culture: Flat and in the Round

A Samoan friend, a very thoughtful woman who had lived abroad and returned, and who was reading Mead's *Coming of Age in Samoa* after talking with me, commented that the behavior Mead described rang true enough to her own youthful experience, but that she hated the way Mead wrote about it. Her comment brought out the difference between two levels of culture—or between the "social" and "cultural" for those trained in that terminological usage—that is, between behavior itself and the ways in which it is typically felt, codified, and evaluated. Mead admiringly described the social skills she observed in Manu'a that kept things running smoothly in a still primarily kin-based society where large numbers of people closely shared both work and space. She apparently took the maintenance of a calm social demeanor in the face of personal trouble to be a direct reflection of feelings and referred insultingly to Samoan emotions as "shallow."[3]

Yet the relations among behavior, value-attitude systems, and personality patterns were a central concern of Mead's throughout her long life. Furthermore, in an appendix to *Coming of Age* she did attempt to locate the Manu'a she studied in the context of Samoan culture history, tyrannical powers of chiefs without destroying the security derived from the "communal ownership of property" (Mead 1973:154). Although her ethnocentric phrasing in the rest of this passage is embarrassing, and her view of the benign influence of the American navy a distortion, the point itself is well taken. So is her forecast of what the future would bring: "Economic instability, poverty, the wage system, the separation of the worker from the land and from his tools, modern welfare, industrial disease, the abolition of leisure, the irksomeness of bureaucratic government—these have not yet invaded an island without resources worth exploiting" (Mead 1973:154–155).

Returning to Freeman, I have already referred to his use of recent data on crime and violence in Samoa as if they were simply direct evidence of these traits in the "Samoan ethos," and his reference to youth suicide as expressing the tensions of Samoan culture when it is a growing tragedy throughout the world (see Leacock 1987). In dealing with the past as well, Freeman does not interpret individual and group actions and their relations to value-attitude systems in the context of particular circumstances. Instead, although he is well aware that Samoans are skilled at the art of hiding their feelings behind the appropriate facade when it is necessary to do so (Freeman 1983b:216–217), when it suits his purpose of contradicting Mead in each and every particular, Freeman refers to particular behaviors as if they directly expressed individual feelings and cultural values. His treatment of conversion and the emotional response of Samoans to missionary activity provides an example.

Freeman treats the introduction of Christianity into Samoa as a simple matter of Western beliefs and their associated rituals being accepted by Samoans. He does not deal with the reactions of Samoans to the church as an institution that, on the one hand, opened up avenues for new interests and opportunities, but on the other directly conflicted with established codes for social behavior and indirectly with patterns of ecnonomic activity. Freeman proposes that new beliefs and practices were integrated with, or replaced old ones rapidly, largely due to similarities in Samoan and Western concepts of deity: "Tagaloa, then was an all-seeing, all-powerful creator god, remote yet ever present, peaceloving yet every ready to punish the disobedient and wayward, who bore a distinct resemblance to the supreme and demanding god of the ancient Hebrews and of the strait-laced Protestant missionaries by whom the pagan Samoans were so rapidly converted during the fourth and fifth decades of the nineteenth-century" (Freeman 1983b).[4]

Holmes (1980) makes clear, however, that the conversion process described in nineteenth-century missionary reports was a prolonged one that met considerable resistance, and furthermore, that Samoans did not simply adopt a Western belief, but took over the church amd made it a Samoan institution. Freeman's knowledge of Samoan ethnography and ethnohistory is formidable, yet for the purposes of his argument with Mead he chooses to ignore the variability and complexity of Samoan relations with the missionaries. For example, Freeman (1983b:213) cites as evidence of Samoan emotionality the loud weeping, the bodily convulsions, and the outpouring of emotion in response to their sermons that astonished and gratified Murray (in Tutuila in 1839) and Harbutt (in Upolu in 1841), but pursues the matter no further. Thereby he sloughs over one of many interesting examples of conflict among the Samoans who were interested in the church and the missionaries, albeit in this case the conflict is a minor one having to do with ritual behavior.

To elaborate on the subject, Slayter's (1841) account mirrors Murray's and Harbutt's descriptions. Slayter's call for a prayer to God to bless his labors for the salvation of their souls was met with "the simultaneous weeping of the whole congregation. Not being able to proceed with prayer I looked abroad in the Congregation and to me it was the most affecting sight I had ever witnessed. . . . About twenty minutes passed away before I could proceed with my sermon" (Slayter 1841).

It was not long, however, before the missionaries challenged this ritual form of group supplication that, among other considerations, interrupted their sermons and transferred leadership from themselves to their congregations. Harbutt (1841) later wrote of a trip to Savaii that he found "a source of great anxiety and grief" in relation to the "work similar to that which is producing such blessed results in Tutuila having commenced in this part of my district." In this visit he noted many things that caused him "to conclude that it is a delusion of the enemy and not the work of the spirit" and that it was his duty "to stop its progress." He continued,

> this threatens to be no easy matter it has taken such root in the minds of many—Several fell down in fits of crying, some apparently in convulsions during each of the services which I held, even during family prayer—but when I questioned them closely they could give no reasonable account why they did so and many things of which I took notice at the time when they so acted convinced me neither the tears nor outcries were real but counterfeit expressions of feelings—I solemnly told them the sin of which I was certain many of them were guilty and charged them to desist. (Harbutt 1841)

Several years later, Bullen (1844) reported having a serious talk with Murray about the abatement of religious fervor and the problem of people who were interested "in the externals of religion" rather than with God. The two men decided to hold a series of special meetings with teachers and their congregations in local districts, in which the teachers "were to seek especially the revival of religion in their own hearts and in the church members." When direct appeals to their conscience elicited "a burst of wailing long deep and loud," Bullen warned the congregation that it was not "outward expressions of sorrow but real love to Christ that will avail on that day when the secrets of the heart shall be revealed." Bullen continued that with respect to "that excess of feeling, I thought it my duty steadily though gently to suppress what rising indications I saw of it, and at the same time to cherish that inward contrition of heart and silent grief for sin, which would be acceptable to God and would give no interruption to the services" (Bullen 1844).

A decade later, Stallworthy (1854) wrote despondently, "The impulse of first love has spent itself. The novelty of Christianity no longer attracts the people." Many who had turned to it with "false impressions and expectations have discovered their mistakes." He added cynically, "They thirst, but not for Christian waters," and that they had taken up again the "narcotics or stimulants which they rejected for a season." About the same time Powell (1853) wrote, using the Samoan expression, "From personal conversations with most of the church members on the subject, it appears that *heart* religion is on the decline among them."

The "teachers" referred to by Bullen were the converts assigned to different villages who were to become the pastors of an independent Samoan Congregational Church. As Bullen's report indicates, the teachers, like their congregations, were by no means simply accepting a new Western belief and all that it presupposed, but instead were adapting it to Samoan mores. The disinterest referred to in Powell's letter was actually in part a form of protest to the departure of Murray, a man who was much loved and respected. In keeping with Samoan ethics, personal ties of loyalty were more salient guides for action than the formal commitment to the church that the missionaries wanted Samoans to put before all else. Furthermore, to the missionaries' dismay, the teachers expressed dissatisfaction with what they saw to be their second-class status; unsuccessfully they went on strike in an effort to win the same kind of financial support from the church that the missionaries received.[5]

Missionary letters also reflect the proud refusal of most Samoans to concede to the far-reaching cultural changes the missionaries sought as they tried to establish the rigid mores of the bourgeois Victorian family. Their strong emphasis on female dependence and the double standard for sexual behavior led the missionaries to be suspicious of the women's work group, the *auluma*, and they tried to break it up (Roach 1984). They also fought what was for a long time a losing battle with the "night dances" and their ritualized celebration of sexuality. In fact, what the historical record suggests—though more research is needed on the subject—is that the formalities of the Victorian family were not so much introduced by the missionaries in the mid-nineteenth century as by the new elite that became established later, consisting of European businessmen and their high-ranking Samoan wives. It was apparently in this new socioeconomic stratum that the role of the *taupou* became the model for the deportment of young women. The gratification with which the mid-century missionary letters tell of individual women who went to live in the mission in order to avoid the advances of men attests to the rarity of the attitude the behavior reflects.

Samoans were attracted to the missions for a variety of reasons. New medicines were important, particularly because new diseases were being introduced. In the early days the mission stations also offered avenues to other European goods and equipment. The missions soon came into conflict with the traders, and the missionaries bemoaned the alcohol and the model for loose living that the sailors provided, and deplored the fact that trade with whaling and other ships reduced the gifts of coconut oil that sustained their enterprise. Of great and lasting interest were the arts of reading and writing, and the new information, literature, and ideas for philosophical debate and oratorical exercise that missionary teachings offered. Despite the decline of zealous devotion on the part of adults that the missionaries reported, the future they gave on school attendance among both boys and girls remained relatively good. In time the village schools run by the pastors became a basic part of village life and a source of satisfaction to those pastors who were deeply dedicated to the service of their parishes.

All told, the ultimate success of the new religion (Catholic and Protestant) lay in the fact that it became grounded in new centers for village life. Unfortunately, the work of their wives with women's groups is but peripherally mentioned in the missionary reports, but Roach's (1984) research has shown that women played a large part in the establishment of the church and integrated it with many of the village activities that they governed. The village churches also provided gratifying careers, for men who were personally ambitious and for those truly committed to religious teaching and other service. Finally, but importantly, churches that were well built and well cared for served to enhance village prestige.

Freeman (1983b:120) cites Keesing on the conversion to Christianity and establishment of traders in Samoa as leading to "a post-contact 'equilibrium of culture' " by 1879. But to characterize the Samoan experience with the church in the limited terms of "conversion" and the adaptation of old beliefs to Christianity is to ignore the range of choices Samoans were making and the kinds of decisions they were implementing, and thereby to distort an important chapter in recent Samoan history. For his part, Keesing (1934:410) quotes a missionary view of the conversion process: "Instead of accepting Christianity and allowing it to remold their lives to its form, the Samoans have taken the religious practices taught to them and fitted them inside

Samoan custom, making them a part of the native culture.
. . . Christianity, instead of bursting the bonds of the old
life, has been eaten up by it."[6]

History, Advocacy, and the Analysis of Culture

I have been making the point that cultural analyses that
focus on what people "are" or "are not," without giving
the historical context in which data on their beliefs and
activities were collected, too readily lend themselves to
stereotyping. The stereotyping does not lie only in the
writing, of course; reading too is located in a social context.
Freeman continues to protest that a negative emphasis of
his book has been misread. Perhaps this is to some extent
true, yet he cannot so easily absolve himself from responsibility. As a social anthropologist and analyst of culture
process, he should have been more sensitive to the impact
the negative thrust of his description would have.

In the case of Mead, her *Coming of Age in Samoa* and
other popular works are written with the purpose of demonstrating the cultural variations possible in human societies, making clear that knowledge of these was important
to the search for solutions to social problems, promoting a
cultural relativist perspective of the world, and countering
ethnocentric bias. Unfortunately, her refusal to deal with
the political economy of colonialism and its impact on the
cultures she described led to the distortions that contradicted her own commitments. Furthermore, Mead did cater
somewhat to the Western romanticized view of the Pacific
Islands. Perhaps she did so in part to mitigate the Western
bias toward nonindustrial societies; the ethnocentrism and
racism involved always pose a dilemma for Western anthropologists. Perhaps in part her romanticization followed

from the other side of the Western coin—the wish for the more cooperative and satisfying life. In any case, it should be pointed out that this romanticization was neither as great as Freeman claims (for his carefully selected out-of-context quotes leave much to be desired by way of accurate presentation), nor as great as the reactions of Mead's readers might appear to illustrate. When using *Coming of Age* in class for the first time, I discovered the extent to which, in their yearning for a more supportive and cooperative society, students can bypass the problems Mead discussed, and dwell enviously on the relative lack of stress experienced by Manu'a adolescents in the 1920s. Small wonder that Mead's book can be so irksome when read as characterizing Samoa of today, rather than as describing a particular facet of Samoan culture history.

There is another historical dimension that both Freeman and Mead ignore, which is where Samoa stood as a Polynesian nation prior to its entanglement with Europe and the United States. Mead alluded to the tyrannical cruelty that could be exercised by Samoan chiefs in the past, in contrast with the peaceful cooperativeness of village life she observed in the 1920s. Neither in *Coming of Age* nor in works where she dealt with competition, warfare, and status striving in Samoan society, did Mead discuss how such contracting social principles could be integrated. As for Freeman, he describes the brutality that could accompany intervillage and interregional warfare simply as exemplifying the violence of Samoan society, in general, and as "one side" of an undefined human nature that thus expresses itself. He then alludes in a brief, hence ineffective, one-paragraph reference to the Samoan "shining virtues" of hospitality, generosity, and kindness, again with no discussion of how these relate to the aggression and competition he has so heavily stressed (Freeman 1983b:278). One focus of the Mead-Freeman controversy, therefore, has been on the extent to which Samoans "are" competitive or cooperative, assertively aggressive or committed to conciliation, freely emotional or controlled, and soon, when the real questions pertain to the socioeconomic underpinning of competitive and cooperative, aggressive or conciliatory, and expressive or controlled behavior; how these are defined and how valued; how expectations vary for different social categories; and how the whole has changed over time.

Speaking in broad, historical terms often subsumed under the rubric of "social evolution," Polynesian society at the time of Western colonial expansion generally was characterized by the active efforts to undercut the communal organization of autonomous village units on the part of rising elites who were striving to establish and consolidate economic and political control (Goldman 1970; Sahlins 1958). Samoa was among the more stratified of the Polynesian nations, but others, such as neighboring Tonga, were more so, and in Samoa the structure of village cooperativeness was stoutly maintained. The potential for an extraordinary range of behavior is a major characteristic of the human species, but this does not explain seemingly conflicting patterns in a given society. Institutional confict was a fundamental part of Samoan social life at the time of European expansion, and a full culture history of Samoa would require analysis of how new relations with Europe and the United States interrelated with and exacerbated this prior conflict, and how they affected expectations about, possibilities for, and influences on various behaviors on the part of the chiefly and nonchiefly, the male and female, the old and young.

To argue for the importance of treating any given culture in full historical perspective, however, is not of itself sufficient. After all, history is approached differently by analysts whose commitments differ. History writ large, or "social evolution," offers a prime example. In the hands of nineteenth-century ideologues who were seeking to justify Europe's drive toward domination, human culture history was phrased in terms of progress from "lower" to "higher," with the pinnacle of achievement the "civilization" represented by Victorian society. In the hands of those who criticized the imperialism and capitalistic individualism of the West, the case was otherwise. Human culture history was presented as demonstrating the unity of the human species, and the cooperative social arrangements that once prevailed throughout the world were seen as relevant to attempts to reshape Western society along cooperative rather than exploitative lines. It should be added, however, that the full implications of the latter view could not be clearly stated nor widely understood until there was a further turn of the historical wheel. It was not until the latter part of the twentieth century that recently independent nations, along with still directly oppressed colonial peoples, could point proudly to their traditions of collective social responsibility as the answer for a world that unrestrained profiteering is driving to destruction.

The historical approach I am urging, then, is an historical approach that is firmly linked with a commitment to cultural pluralism, cultural autonomy, and national independence. These are familiar themes; hardly a meeting of the American Anthropological Association takes place without the passing of one or more resolutions supporting a cultural or national freedom movement that is seeking support. Yet it is not common for Western anthropologists to think through the relationship between such advocacy and scholarly research. Gerrit Huizer is among those who have argued that it is necessary to do so, and he elaborated on the point at a conference on research and development in the South Pacific that brought Western scholars together with scholars from the region. Working as an applied anthropologist in Latin America, Huizer (1978:54) found that "through active participation in the actual struggle of the peasants helping them to build up representative organizations to get their rights and demands respected, it could be empirically demonstrated that peasants are not so apathetic or traditional or resistant to change as many scholars (with spectator knowledge) still believe, but rather the opposite." With respect to the stereotyped view of peasant conservatism, Huizer notes that "resistance to change by the peasants is an expression of distrust which is justified facing the repressive conditions under which they live—real organization is not allowed," and that "peasants can be mobilized for change if it is clear that they themselves will fully benefit" (Huizer 1978:54).

Huizer's statement on the importance of active advocacy was delivered at a conference on research and development in the South Pacific that brought Western scholars together with scholars from that region. Huizer's position as a Western anthropologist was complemented by the contribution to the same conference by the Fijian scholar, Asesela Ravuvu. In his paper, Ravuvu (1978:74–76) summarizes the many problems South Pacific peoples have with outside researchers: that "a great deal of work being done in the Pacific is oriented towards maintaining the status quo"; that many researchers are primarily interested in enhancing their professional status by contributing something "novel" rather than something relevant to the concerns of oppressed people; that researchers are so often "not prepared to *listen* with patience and understanding," but are only interested in information that fits the model they wish to establish, a stance often met by lies on the part of the cross-examined; that most researchers aim "to achieve scientific objectivity by remaining aloof and detached" from the practical problems of people they are studying, an attitude that "produces only distorted and scientifically-biased information"; and that cultural information that might be useful is either presented in an unintelligible manner or altogether unavailable. Ravuvu writes,

> the distrust which exists between researchers and researched can be avoided if researchers display tolerance and a sympathetic understanding of the people's way of life and problems. They must be actively involved in working with the people, and take positive action to improve the situation. This will demand a great deal of zeal, patience, time and effort, but the return—gaining the confidence of the people—are great and very satisfying. Concern for other's welfare must be the central theme of most researchers if they are to be acceptable and more meaningful to those who are being studied. (Ravuvu, 1978:76)

This is not to suggest that taking the "right" stance automatically guarantees the quality of one's research; research always has its own requirements of good scholarship and hard work. It is rather to say that advocacy is the key for the outsider to the "inside" view that is essential for the fully rounded understanding of the culture. Nor is it to suggest that the most appropriate advocacy stance is always self-evident, once one has moved beyond the level of support to broad independence movements or to programs concerned with health, nutrition, and the like. Applied anthropologists are well aware of the important difference between supporting the right of a people to make their own choices and defending the perpetuation of "traditional culture" per se. I am not referring to what used to be criticized as wanting to make museum exhibits of "tribal" cultures; anthropology has grown well beyond that form of romanticism. I am referring instead to two other problems: first, that of defining what the "traditional" is, when traditions have been constantly changing, and second, that of dealing with "traditional" inequalities that call for reform.

With respect to reforming "traditional" inequities, political leaders in the South Pacific are increasingly aware of the need to find a new voice for youth consistent with the new demands being made upon them, and men in leadership positions are increasingly having to respond to women's demands for a public voice and for attention to their needs. Fortunately, the conservative objection to such seeming innovations may well be met by historical analysis of traditions and of the role European influence has had in reshaping and redefining them. To take a mundane and simple example, Samoan women who are criticized for defying the "traditional" *Fa'aSamoa* by cutting their hair might well rebut that they are the true traditionalists, since before the missionaries set about changing Samoan styles, women wore their hair short and men let theirs grow long. Or, to take a broader example, Samoan women who run for public office can point out that they only wish to recreate in a new setting the greater measure of gender reciprocity that existed in daily village life before arenas for village autonomy became reduced by the modern commercial and political structures that, following Western norms, are so thoroughly male dominated.

In sum, then, my argument is that an historically oriented, advocacy-linked anthropology, undertaken in active collaboration with people whose cultures are being documented, treats culture in context as multifaceted and flexible, the embodiment of past history that defines a people, and that they draw on, change, resist, and debate about in relation to the practical problems that confront them. It is this presentation that provides a basis for scientific understanding of the relations between culture and behavior, and not the contextless reified image represented by Freeman's analysis. Moreover, the collaboration of "insiders" and "outsiders" in the study of cultures is possible today to a wholly unprecedented degree. To close with Ravuvu's (1978:73) words on the research enterprise he is proposing: "The present problems of the Pacific Islands cannot be left to the scrutiny of the Pacific Islanders themselves *nor* to the foreign research scholars. It must be a shared responsibility of both, each assisting the other, and each complementing the other's efforts to develop scientific findings in a way most beneficial to the inhabitants of the Islands and all other human beings."

NOTES

1. Though Samoa is politically divided between American Samoa and independent Western Samoa, ties between the two are close; Samoa is one nation.

2. In the spring of 1985, I interviewed professionals working with youth in both American and Western Samoa, among them teachers, school principals, counsellors, psychologists, and health workers. I also attended workshops that were being held on youth problems, and, of course, attended festivities and visited and talked informally with elders and youth. I am indebted to the American Association of University Women for awarding

me the Founders Fellowship that made my research possible, and to the Faculty Research Award program of the City University of New York.

3. The assumption that dispersed parenting and strong extended kin ties would lead to "shallow" feelings was shared by other members of the personality and culture school.

4. The extent to which Samoan ethnohistorians will concur with this phrasing of their original concept remains to be seen. Freeman's account deals only with the Protestant missionaries; the Marist Order was also active in Samoa and some Samoans were converted to Catholicism.

5. It must be said that the missionaries did not have an easy time of it. Their letters reflect their constant problems, not only due to their low salaries, but to difficulties incurred in having additional expenditures reimbursed.

6. That this experience was repeated many times around the world raises the question for research as to what extent the missionary response may have contributed to the liberalization of the church in the West that has since been taking place.

REFERENCES

Bernstein, R. 1983. "Samoa: A Paradise Lost?" *New York Times*, April 24.

Bullen, T. 1844, Correspondence, in Archives of the London Missionary Society (School of Oriental and African Studies, University of London). South Seas, Samoan Islands, Box 17, Folder 7, Jacket A. August 6, Tutuila.

Ember, M. 1985. "Evidence and Science in Ethnography: Reflections of the Freeman-Mead Controversy." *American Anthropologist* 87(4), pp. 906–10.

Freeman, D. 1983a. "Inductivism and the Test of Truth: A Rejoinder to Lowell Holmes and Others." *Canberra Anthropology* 6(2), pp. 101–92.

————. 1983b. *Margaret Mead and Samoa: The Making and Unmaking of an Anthropological Myth*. Cambridge: Harvard University Press.

Goldman, I. 1970. *Ancient Polynesian Society*. Chicago: University of Chicago Press.

Harbutt, W. 1841. Correspondence, in Archives of the London Missionary Society (School of Oriental and African Studies, University of London). South Seas, Samoan Islands, Box 14, Folder 5, Jacket C. April 21, Savaii.

Holmes, L. 1980. "Cults, Cargo, and Christianity: Samoan Responses to Western Religion." *Missiology: An International Review* 8(4), pp. 471–87.

————. 1983. "A Tale of Two Studies." *American Anthropologist* 85(4), pp. 922–35.

————. 1987. *The Quest for the Real Samoa: The Mead/Freeman Controversy and Beyond*. South Hadley, Mass.: Bergin & Garvey.

Huizer, G. 1978. "Applied Social Science and Social Action: Some Experiences on New Approaches." In *Paradise Postponed: Essays on Research and Development in the South Pacific*. A Mamak and G. McCall (eds.) pp. 49–72. Pergamon Press.

Keesing, F. 1934. *Modern Samoa*. London: Allen & Unwin.

Leacock, E. 1987. "Postscript: The Problems of Youth in Contemporary Samoa." In *The Quest for the Real Samoa: The Mead/Freeman Controversy and Beyond*, L. Holmes, pp. 177–188. South Hadley, Mass.: Bergin & Garvey.

Lelaulu, L. 1983. "Coming of Age in Anthropology." *The Periodical Report*, January–February, pp. 1–12.

Levy, R. J. 1983. "The Attack on Mead." *Science* 220 (May 20), pp. 829–832.

McDowell, E. 1983. "New Science Book Challenges Margaret Mead's Conclusions." *New York Times*, Jan. 31, pp. 1 and C21.

Malinowski, B. 1941. *The Sexual Life of Savages in North*

Western Melanesia. New York: Halcyon House. Originally published in 1932, London: Routledge and Kegan Paul.

————. 1961. *Argonauts of the Western Pacific*. New York: Dutton. Originally published in 1922.

Mead, M. 1973. *Coming of Age in Samoa*. New York: Morrow.

Murray, A. 1839. Correspondence, in Archives of the London Missionary Society (School of Oriental and African Studies, University of London). June 10, Tutuila.

Patience, A., and J. W. Smith, 1986. "Derek Freeman and Samoa: The Making and Unmaking of a Behavioral Myth." *American Anthropologist* 88(1), pp. 157–62.

Powell, T. 1853. Correspondence, in Archives of the London Missionary Society (School of Oriental and African Studies, University of London). South Seas, Samoan Islands, Box 25, Folder 4, Jacket C, July 14, Tutuila.

Ravuvu, A. 1978. "Research Responsibility in the Pacific: A Local Viewpoint." In *Paradise Postponed, Essays on Research and Development in the South Pacific*. A Mamak and G. McCall (eds.), pp. 73–77. Rushcutter's Bay, Australia: Pergamon Press.

Roach, E. M. 1984. *From English Mission to Samoa Congregation: Women and the Church in Rural Western Samoa*. Ph.D. dissertation, Columbia University, New York.

Sahlins, M. 1958. *Social Stratification in Polynesia*. Seattle: University of Washington Press.

Schlegel, A., and H. Barry III. 1980. "The Evolutionary Significance of Adolescent Initiation Ceremonies." *American Ethnologist* 7, pp. 696–715.

Shankman, P. 1983. "The Samoan Conundrum." Typescript. Department of Anthropology, University of Colorado, Boulder. Later revised for publication in *Canberra Anthropology* 6(1).

Shore, B. 1983. "Paradox Regained: Freeman's *Margaret Mead and Samoa*." *American Anthropologist* 85(4), pp. 935–44.

Slayter, T. 1841. Correspondence, in Archives of the London Missionary Society (School of Oriental and African Studies,

University of London). South Seas, Samoan Islands, Box 14, Folder 5, Jacket LA, Jan. 15, Tutuila.

Stallworthy, G. 1854. Correspondence, in Archives of the London Missionary Society (School of Oriental and African Studies, University of London). South Seas, Samoan Islands, Box 25, Folder B, Jacket C. December 4.

Strathern, M. 1983. "The Punishment of Margaret Mead." *London Review of Books*, May 5–18, pp. 5–6.

Weiner, A. 1983. "Ethnographic Determinism: Samoa and the Margaret Mead Controversy." *American Anthropologist* 85(4), pp. 909–19.

ANGELA GILLIAM

2 Leaving a Record for Others: An Interview with Nahau Rooney

This interview took place at Nahau Rooney's residence in Boroko, Port Moresby on September 9, 1986. At the time, she was planning a trip to Lorengau in Manus, which has always represented home and the center of her work in provincial government. Present also during the interview was her now-deceased husband, Wes Rooney. For many years, Nahau Rooney was the most prominent woman in national politics, a role that centered around her position as Minister of Justice. When she acquired that ministerial portfolio following independence from Australia in 1975, there were virtually no Papua New Guinean judges, though Bernard Narokobi, Meg Taylor (currently Ambassador to the United States from Papua New Guinea), and others were prominent lawyers. (Narokobi was one of the first Papua New Guineans to earn a law degree, graduating from the University of Sydney in 1972. In 1980 he was appointed an Acting Justice of the Supreme Court of Papua New Guinea.) For Rooney, this was a central issue in the way justice was adjudicated in Papua New Guinea. The questions that Rooney raised by her challenge to the inherited legal structure were embodied in her desire to help Papua New Guineans find the appropriate merger of customary and parliamentary law. In this interview, she demonstrates how all of these questions come together in her personal life.

Gilliam: Could you comment on your background, where you come from, your family?

Rooney: I come from a small village called Lahan on Manus Island in Papua New Guinea. I have two sisters and two brothers in a family of five. I grew up in the village and then went to school at the age of ten. I feel I am very lucky because at my age at that time you were very privileged to go to school. I did not start school early, and most girls my age missed out on schooling. So I had to pack a lot into my primary school days. I then went off to boarding school away from home in the town of Lorengau.

From there I went all the way to grade six in boarding school. And because there was no high school on Manus, I was sent away to Lae in Morobe Province. It was a selective high school for girls only, because in the 1960s there was a big attempt to educate girls. So I went away from the village for another four years to finish secondary school. After that I went to Teachers College and Teacher Graduate School. Halfway through I won a scholarship that took me to Fiji. And that was my first overseas experience.

The day I started school was the beginning of leaving one's community, one's cultural background and education. As my parents saw it then, it was an investment so that I could come back and get a job.

So I returned to Teachers College and completed my teacher's certificate. For my first year of teaching, I went back to Manus, which is my own province, and taught there for another two years at the school which I myself had attended earlier.

By then, the same school had become a high school. Soon after that I won the Winston Churchill Scholarship. The Winston Churchill Fellowship was given specifically to people who had leadership qualities, and it took me to Australia for another twelve months. And I attended yet another Teachers College there at Melbourne University.

Then I came back to teach again in Manus. By that time, I had married in Australia, although I had met my husband while we were teaching at the same high school in Manus. During this period, my husband was transferred to Port Moresby to teach at Pareghawa High School, and it was during that time, while I was having children, that I decided to go to university. That is how I came to spend another three and a half years at the University of Papua New Guinea and received a Bachelor of Arts degree.

Following that, I taught at the Administrative College teaching Community Education and Community Development there. And it was during this time that I served for eighteen months on the Gabriel Gris Committee, which was also known as the University Development Committee. The principal objective of this committee, which the government had set up, was to come up with recommendations as to what the university should be promoting, and to decide what should be the role of the university in a developing country. We produced a report which was presented to the government. Because of government changes, the portfolio of education passed through various hands. And no one ever really put these recommendations into practice.

Just before independence in 1975, I went to work in the chief minister's office. This office was similar to that of a prime minister. The first chief minister was Michael So-

mare. So I became involved in research and formulation of
policy, the development of the constitution, giving advice,
and consultation.

Shortly after, my husband was again transferred back
to Manus. And I had a choice of either continuing the kind
of work I was doing, or going back to Manus with him. At
that time, we had a very young family. We tried to live
apart for five months. But we needed to be together so I
just packed up and followed him back to Manus. It is from
this point on that I got assistance with the preparation of
the constitution of Manus provincial government. In the
mid-seventies, the task of every provincial government was
to prepare their own constitution before national government could allow them to establish their own provincial
government.

For two years, I worked with local government council,
which later became the area authority. As executive officer
to the planning committee on the constitution, my task then
was to travel around Manus. We had to interview people,
and had a well publicized preparation for the constitution.
It was during this time that the people of Manus recognized
what I could do for them. They felt that perhaps I should
represent them in the national government.

So in the 1977 plebiscite it was obvious that people
wanted me to stand for elections. By that time, I had
already been involved at various advisory levels within
national and provincial government. And I felt that representing the people of Manus was a most logical step to
take. And since then I have become very involved in
politics and stood for election. For one thing, I expected I
was going to win. And that was it.

Gilliam: You and I once had a conversation years ago
about the bride-price custom. You maintained that your

family was alarmed because you had never had such a ceremony. You decided after many years of marriage that you still wanted to have it since it was an important part of your cultural background, irrespective of whether your husband was from Manus. Why was that so important?

Rooney: The principle of bridewealth and the exchange of it is very important in the Melanesian context. On one hand some people say that women are not important. But in our own society the woman is very important in the socioeconomic activities that make up the most important elements and features in any Melanesian society. When I first went off to school, especially university, the very concept of being "bought" was based on what I read as to what bride price was all about, and by definition was from an anthropological point of view. And because I had left home very early I had not appreciated, or at least had moved away from the actual exchange of bride price that goes on in the Manus community. I became detached from it and was influenced more by the Western concept that says, "I am an intelligent, educated woman who does not want to be purchased in that context."

But as I went back to teach in Manus and later returned as a family living on Manus, I was beginning to become involved as an adult in the actual conception and behavior of the bride-price exchange itself. After I went back into the community, I was inevitably participating in the exchanges that took place with my own people. And after that, I felt that there definitely is a big misconception as to what bride price is all about.

It was *not* as if I was being bought. The primary concept of the bride price is really as public witness to the bringing of two parties—the bridegroom's and that of the bride— together to accept the principle of marriage. Gradually, I felt that my Western church marriage was not sufficient for me to be perceived fully by my people. This was all the more so since it took a long time for my people to accept my husband who, before independence, was Australian. They just could not understand that this foreign, white man could leave his own people and be part of me, for example. They thought I would have to go and be part of him. When he made the decision to become Papua New Guinean and assume citizenship, it eliminated a lot of doubt by my people on that account.

My parents saw the concept of bride price as affirming that a woman has achieved nothing if she is not valued in the traditional sense. Coupled with the fact that my husband took Papua New Guinean citizenship, I felt that to be culturally accepted by my people, we had to go through what is accepted culturally in our society.

Bride-price exchange really brings many other people to also participate in the marriage. This makes it very difficult to get divorced at the end because you have involved a lot of people in witnessing. Therefore, I had no choice for I believed it was important for me to go through the traditional system.

Gilliam: So, his family paid?

Rooney: Yes. One more thing is important here. My husband said to my people that as far as possible he wanted us to maintain the exchange through traditional commodities rather than having to spend money on trade store goods like rice, sugar, and other imported items. So that was what we limited ourselves to. Normally, we would have just exchanged pigs, taro, and shell money. Now that Manus people have money in exchange for those goods, the woman's side puts up the food, such as pigs, which are very valuable according to the custom. Normally, it would have been shell money, but I did not have much traditional currency. The shell money was also substituted by dog's teeth, which is a traditionally typical Manus currency. So instead of that he used cash money.

Gilliam: It is interesting that traditional currency still has value in Papua New Guinea, and that dog's teeth and shell money still maintain actual means of exchange. Renagi Lohia wrote an interesting article about development in Papua New Guinea about three years ago. One of the things that he affirms in this critique of government development projects—especially with foreign corporations—is that for certain Motuan villages, traditional bride-price ceremonies generated more economic development than many of these foreign-imposed development projects.[1] Would you say that is true for Manus as well?

Rooney: I assume you mean in the exchange that was involved in it. That is a very interesting point. I have noted too that in our own villages, if we call for voluntary assistance, or called on communities to contribute toward building up some community service like the water supply, or a road, or starting a business for that matter, the interest will be very little. The interest of people in coming forward is not as pronounced. But any bride-price festivities, either within our own village or that involve a lot of our people's relations in the other village, will promote a high interest. Everybody will be very keen to contribute.

Now, I myself have observed this and I have concluded that the reason why our people are more interested in bride price is because like any other business it gives quick return. They are confident that if they contribute now, they know that in two days, or even by the end of the same day, they will get something back almost immediately for what they have given. In the other commercial, Western concept in which something is put in, it takes a long time to see a return. Everything is an investment, but I think for this sort of life and the way our people live a quick return is preferable. And that is why the bride price maintains its power and importance.

Gilliam: In a very famous case, you were once Minister of Justice and yourself convicted. What was the background of the issues involved? What were you fighting for, or against?

Rooney: That is now history. It was 1979 and I was then Minister for Justice. What happened was due to a deportation issue of a university lecturer from Guyana. The system was that if someone were to be deported, that person had to appear before a Ministerial Review Committee comprised of three ministers. And if they all upheld the decision of the Foreign Affairs Minister, that meant deportation. If not, and they upheld the appeal, then an appellant could stay in the country. Apparently in this case, they upheld the decision of the Foreign Affairs Minister.

But this person appealed on the grounds of natural justice. He claimed he was not given a fair hearing by the committee. And subsequently, he applied for an injunction. What really annoyed me then and what prompted me to write a letter to the Chief Justice was that the court gave him four weeks to stay in the country in order to lodge an appeal to the Review Committee. However, I felt that four weeks was a long time. If in fact the man was an undesirable, four weeks was time enough for him to do anything. And I still believe that today, that the purpose for having a deportation act is for any given country to be able to protect the sovereign state and integrity of that government. It is the choice of the government of any country to allow a visitor to come in. But if in their opinion, they feel that any visitor from any country is a threat, or undermines the role and function of the sovereign state, then it is government's right to say, "Sorry, we cannot tolerate that kind of person in the country."

This is especially in view of the very strong influences from Western pressure on a developing country. It is that kind of right which must be protected. However, our constitution gives rights to all individuals, citizens, and residents. Therefore, the person felt he had the right to appeal, and did so. My principled position was that he could obtain injunction, but taking four weeks was excessive. The mere fact that by writing a letter expressing this opinion caused all of what occurred to happen is in itself a demonstration that four weeks was not timely.

I felt at that time that the entire Supreme Court was a foreign court. We did not have one single Papua New Guinean court or judge. I therefore felt that there was no commitment to the protection of Papua New Guinea as a sovereign state.

Perhaps because of that, the judges were influenced by the legalities and semantics of the laws that influenced them to provide an injunction that lasted four weeks. That is what prompted me to write a letter to the Chief Justice expressing exactly that. Because I did so while the case was pending, I was charged with contempt of court, as interfering with the administration of justice.

Gilliam: In a sense then you were describing a conflict concerning whose law and whose interest this injunction was serving.

Rooney: Exactly. Then I myself had to go through the court system. The Supreme Court convicted me. They sentenced me to eight months. I, however, had no way of appeal. That was another injustice. It was a system designed to protect the court. The charge concerning the contempt of court is one that can only be heard by a Supreme Court. Thus there is no option to appeal to a higher court. The only way I had to appeal was to the Power of Mercy Committee, which is a nonjudicial committee. Our constitution does allow for that. The committee is composed of nonlawyers who listen to a case, and that court did pardon me. They understood what I did, and felt that what I had done did not constitute a contempt of court.

What was really important was that had the court been genuine about developing Papua New Guinea and upholding the laws that are enshrined in our constitution, it would have acknowledged that I, being Minister of Justice at the time, represented an arm of government. This was the executive branch, the other two being the legislative—which is the assembly or the parliament—and the judicial.

Now this is like any Papua New Guinea leader who looks after a group or organization. I was in one respect representing a clan of the executive. The judicial component is like another clan.

Whenever there is a conflict there must be a way of settling that dispute. At the end of my case, and after all of the hearings had been made, there was a great deal of confusion as to who was right in all of this.

I did not see the right or wrong or the criminal charges made. It may be overstepping and overlapping roles. While the constitution talks about the independence of the judiciary, and the independence of the executive office, somewhere along the line there is going to be an overlap in roles if the government is to exist. You cannot operate totally independently.

Perhaps if instead of writing directly to the Chief Justice, I had discussed the matter at the Judicial Services

Commission, of which the Minister of Justice is the chairperson, that could have been a forum to express my views. But then the role of the Judicial Services Commission as it exists today is really very limited to the appointment of charges. So that was another difficulty. In the end they [Supreme Court] were the prosecutors as well as the jury. This made my position very complicated. I had no choice but to go through the system.

Gilliam: Margaret Mead refers to you fondly by your first name in her book *Letters From the Field* and calls attention to a paper that you had written. Yet, some Pacific people believe that much of her work laid the groundwork for the later emphasis by Western social scientists on a distortion of Papua New Guinean cultures. In view of the contemporary problems of Manus and Papua New Guinea, what is your opinion of Mead's work in Manus?

Rooney: I think most of us concluded that we gave more to Margaret Mead as an anthropologist and to her profession than she gave to us in return. The only value that her work produced, if anything at all, is that she put our little island on the map of the world. People know where Manus or the Admiralty Islands are located. But apart from that, there is absolutely nothing that she contributed as far as we are concerned. By using our culture and writing about us, we felt that she was given the fame, the economic status, and the popularity that she held in her community. As for what she wrote on societal change; well, she came to Manus in 1928 and I do not personally know what Manus was like then. For me to say that she was totally wrong might be misleading. However, some of the things she said were outrageously wrong.

First of all, she never made it clear as to what she was studying. This is true of most anthropologists. Most of them come to study a preconceived idea of what they want to find out. They do not come to record what has happened in a given community. They come mainly for the purpose of a degree which will help them in the Western, economic community. This gives them status. The scholarship that emerges becomes a weapon. Their thesis is cleared out. Their hypothesis is made. If what they find does not fit their hypothesis, then they "make up" the community. They force the description of the community in such a way so that they can collect the data.

From reading Margaret Mead's books about Papua New Guinea, I found out that most of what she wrote was about little Pere village, where she lived. These villagers became guinea pigs. Everything that the Pere people said about another village or community, she took to be the truth. She identified herself with that community. So obviously any prejudice that the Pere people had about the rest of the world or a nearby village, she identified with. That is what became evident in her book, *Growing Up in New Guinea*. Moreover, she did not adequately acknowledge the relationship between the community and herself.

I can excuse a Pere person writing that way, having been brought up in that prejudice. But an academic— somebody who had such training and experience—should know better. The most annoying thing is that because it is documented and read, it has caused a lot of fragmentation when we are trying to build a community in the modern society. Because those prejudices are written in a book and distributed around the world, they are very difficult to undo. This is particularly a problem when we want to progress and bring unity.

I can forgive her for writing these things earlier in 1928, but in her later writing of the 1950s when she came back, she saw our struggle for independence, she witnessed our struggle for economic development and improvement of villages and education and did not acknowledge that.

Gilliam: Perhaps it is because you would seem far less exotic—almost like someone from the United States.

Rooney: It was during the period of the publication of her later book, *Letters from the Field*, in 1977, that was the moment that we believed if Margaret Mead is going to contribute to Manus, now is the time. By that time I had graduated a university and had a degree. This was also true for many other Manus people.

Along with other Manus people, I was in Manus working to make preparations for the provincial government, and for the constitution. When Mead came back to Manus, I went to her and said, "You saw Manus leadership when most of us here did not. We would like to recapitulate some of those times. What did our leaders think? Tell us their weaknesses and their strengths. Now that we are moving from traditional leadership into that of the modern state, we would like to see and hear some of your memories about what you thought was valuable when you came in 1928."

Gilliam: In other words, were you asking for the kind of information that you thought an anthropologist was supposed to know and give?

Rooney: Because we were not around at that time. I was most disappointed because what she gave me was something which was most unrealistic, not progressive, and she missed the whole point in our moving to create a provincial government, which was going to be based on traditional Manus leadership, in any event. Mead's contribution was negligible. After all, we did look to her for consultation in terms of someone who could help us in our task. We hoped she would say, "Remember this is what your parents and your forefathers used to do, these were their strengths, and if you can incorporate them in the modern state, that would be good.''

Also, remember she was dealing with people who were in fact her equal. When we were at the university, we had a very effective Manus student organization. Every year we would go back to Manus during the university break and spend the vacation going around Manus talking about independence. We took Mead out to lunch and asked her for a donation so that we could travel within Manus. We were amazed when she only gave us the equivalent of ten to twenty kina [US $15–$25].

Gilliam: Did she ever provide money for the information she collected from Manus residents?

Rooney: Not to my knowledge. She did, however, take a couple of the elders to the United States, and that was her contribution. We asked, what is she doing? Here we are contributing to her lectures and giving her world status and yet she did not contribute anything. We were making her famous.

It was not until after her death that the leadership of Pere and my area talked about setting up a Margaret Mead memorial, and decided until that time there would not be any more anthropologists coming into their village. Her daughter [Mary Catherine Bateson] initiated a contribution for a Margaret Mead place. It has a tin roof, one room, and photographs of Margaret Mead when she visited Pere in 1928.

Gilliam: What had you wanted to have?

Rooney: What we really wanted was a foundation where we could say that Margaret Mead had fulfilled a duty to establish a cultural center for us. We hoped to have a place to store data, tapes, music, and cultural relics, so that we could use it for further studies of our people. We wanted new anthropologists who came to study to draw a continuity between Mead's early materials collected about Manus, and as things changed in our culture, we could refer back to it. Perhaps even new interpretation by Manus people of the original data could eventually be done. But I was disappointed that this did not happen.

Now, my own community government has asked me to take it up with the American Embassy, because we felt that we had made our contribution and we now wanted a cultural institution. It would be good to have an institution that is funded by her organization. We have not given up that objective and will continue to pursue this, because there is nothing of this kind in Papua New Guinea. Something of that kind in that village would attract a lot of anthropologists.

There are so many people that read about Margaret Mead and know of her. Many of her students still come to us and say, "We are Margaret Mead's students, and she recommended that we come and do such and such a study."

But now we inform people that what Margaret wrote thirty years ago is no longer the case. We say, contribute instead to a cultural institution that we will *all* work to maintain.

Gilliam: This is a complex issue. It *is* important to make anthropologists reflect on the responsibility the discipline has in projecting the image that people have concerning Papua New Guineans. And, in the film, *Anthropology on Trial*, Barbara Holocek interviewed you. Did that film accurately portray your views and perspective about the anthropologist's role in Papua New Guinea?

Rooney: Well, the role of foreign anthropologists in

this country was more applicable some twenty or thirty years ago. If they had not written some of the things that they did, no one would have known about Papua New Guinean cultures. But one could say, "Who cares whether a culture is going to be known or not?" That is another question. But they have played an undeniable role in academic studies. It becomes an issue of what should be studied in a particular area.

Papua New Guinean people were under a misconception about anthropologists at that time. We are very nice, and when people came they were taken as our visitors. They came and wanted to do a given project, and it was fine. But it never occurred to us that what they were doing would later be published. They talked about our private, village gossip at international conferences. Those are the things that people here got offended by. But this was never made clear to us from the beginning by the anthropologists.

I have yet to hear someone honestly reveal that the information is wanted because it will make him or her famous. Nor have I heard someone say that he was applying for a job, and this information will give status. The work behind the purpose of the study has never been told. Of course everyone wants to be written about. People like a bit of publicity from the world. They want the world to know where they are. People like to see their pictures in a book. But often they do not portray good things, and the illiterate person does not know this.

It is only *after*, when their sons and daughters are educated and find these books on the shelves at the University of Papua New Guinea and other institutions of higher learning, that they discover the offensive material written about their community and village. Then they feel offended. Then it is too late.

But on the other hand, we *do* need foreign perceptions. There is some disadvantage of people writing about themselves, because they cannot always be objective.

Gilliam: You seem to be an exceptional woman. Papua New Guinean women often do not speak the language of trade and exchange, nor do they participate in many national discussions.[2] To what do you owe your historical role?

Rooney: People—men *and* women—must know what they want and have a purpose and objective in life. I came from a village background where my father in particular was a traditional leader in the community. That is, he was a *lapan*—our word for chief—in my village. Then when the modern government system came in, he became an automatic *luluai*, which was a person identified as a village leader by the *kiaps* or foreign authority. Then later on, he became a councillor. So I grew up within a family of leadership, where I saw my father being involved in the process of our transformation, from a village traditional community to a local government council, into area authority. The assumption was that I would be a leader. So it was a matter of time before it would be obvious that I would do that type of work. So on the eve of my father's death, I had already traveled outside of Manus and Papua New Guinea. It was during that he said to me, "Your two brothers are not here and I am about to die. Someone must assume the leadership and responsibility of taking care of the community."

I was the elder of two sisters. And in our community, leadership is hereditary in which the father usually picks one of the sons as a leader of the community. But he said that he could not trust anyone else in the community, and I was going to be that leader. From that moment on, although

I had been interested in politics and had been a student activist, the real faith in myself and commitment to provide leadership to my people developed. That was the honor and the trust that my father gave to me. From then on I had the commitment and confidence to be a leader, because my father was respected in the community and everyone knew him. I felt I could not fail such a responsibility which he expected me to carry out. From then on, I did not look back.

There are other attributes. My parents wanted me to be educated and obviously education had a lot to do with speaking the language of trade. Modern leadership needs education. Without it, I do not think I could do what I am doing because of the constant, traditional values which place women in a position where we have to be exceptionally good. This is what they say in Manus. Though they always say that, I was elected twice into parliament, which is an indication of faith and confidence. The minute I had made a commitment to go into government and politics, I saw my role as a leader, whether as a politician or back in the village. Even if I were to be doing something at home, I would be organizing or helping to seed the way for others.

Of course, I must also acknowledge my family and the strength they gave me. My entire extended family system—my sisters, my brothers, my husband—everyone has helped toward my success. They look after my children while I am away, for example. This is important to me because I do not believe in sending my children to a child-minding center. I could not concentrate on my work if I had to drop my children off to someone I do not know. It comes back to the concept that the sisters are the mothers of all the children. By leaving my children with my relatives, I feel they are taking care of their own children and would not mistreat them.

My advice to women is that it is unfortunate, but we must be one hundred times better than men, because a slight mistake is going to be seen as failure. So we must give one hundred percent commitment to the work, and that cannot be done if we are worrying about the children. Of course, I must give credit to my husband, who is understanding and is interested in my personal satisfaction and progress. If you are a working married woman, there must definitely be some understanding from your other half.

Gilliam: Let me ask you a difficult question. Are you involved in preparing other women to replace you or to surpass you?

Rooney: Yes, in one sense. Though I am not directly involved in education, I believe in leaving a track or a personal record for the women who come after me and ask, "How did Nahau do it?" I set myself as an example for women leaders in the future, and say that it is not easy, but it can be done.

It is pleasing to know that there are now women who are interested in politics and participating in real decision making, because they will be able to get to a position where they can influence or shape the destiny of this country. What is difficult is that when you are active in politics, you cannot train others. Your day-to-day activity and political involvement is everything. But when I am no longer in politics or I retire, that is when I will be able to teach—especially discipline.

Politics require very strict discipline, and my advice to girls and to women in politics is that you must discipline yourself. Being vocal at conferences and rallies is not enough to be a leader in politics.

Plan your own part, and decide when you can do what.

If you have not thought about this five years ago, then you are deceiving yourself. It means that you have to do apprentice work. You have to become a member of a party for that is when the real politics begins. If women think they can run for election and become a politician overnight, then they will be disappointed.

For example, I was a councillor for three years in Port Moresby. I was involved in the PANGU Party [Papua New Guinea United] at the organizational level, writing and preparing policy.

Gilliam: What do you believe to be the important issues in Papua New Guinea, today?

Rooney: This week, the 1986 Waigani Seminar is focusing on the issue of ethics. And today in the modern Papua New Guinea, we need honest leadership and hard work. Once you have that, the whole government system will work for the country. In the 1970s, we would talk about being at a crossroads, and whether we could choose a Papua New Guinean or a Western-oriented direction. Today, we are well and truly members of the world community. We are talking about the reallocation of the country's wealth and finances, about the national economy. *If* we are talking about building up the public services and becoming a truly independent Papua New Guinea, then we must have the kind of leadership that will not be so easily influenced by the ready-made institutions that are so common in the Western world at the moment.

That is, we need reallocation of funds into areas of development that will be in the best interest of Papua New Guinea. We have a lot of money in the country at the moment, but three quarters of that revenue are like aid from the right hand that goes right back into the Western world. Very little of the money gets into our communities.

We would be better off saying that any aid—any money that comes from outside the country—should be isolated so that we can see what we really have.

Of course, there are problems of education and health, but I feel all of these problems can be tackled by a committed leadership with a clear vision. We have relied so much on foreign experts, foreign currency, foreign ideas, foreign aid. We are at a point where our rural areas have not changed at all. Manus has not changed a bit in the last ten years. The only aspect of our community that *has* changed is for people like myself, who send a little money home or build a better house in the village. A good government will address those issues and will redirect our national spending more into the countryside.

Our people's participation is on a very superficial level—as labor, not as ownership. The foreign, economic control of the country is the main problem at the moment. We have achieved political independence and are now making decisions in the government. Without the economic control, we are nothing. Because our economy is not controlled by Papua New Guineans, we have very little say in influencing the government of today. Government will survive on business. And if the businesses are not in the hands of Papua New Guineans, then any government will always be influenced by the powerful minority of Western-controlled economic institutions in the country.

So this new government says to people, "Work the land; do not let it be idle, because that is our base." The trade store and all the service industries represent the middle man. One only buys and sells on behalf of the producer—who is somebody else. By the time it gets to us, by the time all the mark-ups are added on, you are nothing. But if you have your primary industry, cocoa, coffee, copra, or cardamon—something that you make yourself as primary producer—you are getting it firsthand. And that in itself is new income for the country. Anything new you make is new money. But if you are just circulating the same commodities that have been produced somewhere else, but are passing our hands ten times, then we are not increasing the economy and not projecting new goals in the country.

After ten years of independence, our assessment is that what is at stake is redirecting that dependency mentality—a mentality rooted in expectation of something from those who have. We must transform an ethos of begging into one that says, "We may have little, but we at least produce it."

Therefore, to return to the subject of Papua New Guinean women, the traditional Papua New Guinean woman is a producer. We women labor on gardens, on coconut plantations, on cocoa, and on coffee. All that we in government would like to see is that these women workers organize themselves. With the new government policy on agriculture, lending, and low-interest and long-term repayment, that should encourage our people to participate in the economic activity. They *can* participate and they *can* reap the benefit.

And if one talks about improved agriculture, inevitably one must also discuss the improved technology that goes with it. I say to women, we have got to stop thinking of gardening with a digging stick—the food production technology for small-scale only. With a surplus, women can have enough for their households and sufficient to sell.

At the moment, we are a part of the world market; we are no longer in isolation. But the mere fact that we have land is wealth itself. We still have a lot of imported potatoes, cabbage, and foods that we could grow ourselves. We just must make that commitment to producing more.

Gilliam: What about the issues that are Commonwealth concerns, like apartheid, or those that are regional, such as the desire for a nuclear-free Pacific?

Rooney: For me, participating in government has day-to-day aspects that take a lot of time. And sometimes, I do not get as involved in these issues, though government's positions are reflective of the people's will. The government took a stand on the Commonwealth Games because we share the concerns about what is happening in Africa. We denounce that [apartheid]. But for us, our leaders must be able to be involved at the right level and at the right time in a manner that is effective. Otherwise, we will merely be making a lot of talk, but without participating in a real sense. Our stand on the Commonwealth Games was a position we were all very proud of. Saying it is one thing, but being able to carry through with what you are saying is another. But we also need to solve *our* problems. It is only when you are healthy and strong that you can also fight for other issues. But as I said, we will support whatever position the Forum or the Commonwealth takes regarding the denunciation of oppressive conditions.

NOTE

1. Renagi Lohia, "Impact of Regional Bride Price on the Economy of Eastern Motu Villages," in P.A.S. Dahanayake (ed.), *Post-Independent Economic Development of Papua New Guinea* (Port Moresby: Institute of Applied Social and Economic Research, 1982).

2. The author is grateful to Mallica Vajrathon for this theoretical formulation.

LENORA FOERSTEL

3 Margaret Mead from a Cultural-Historical Perspective

Margaret Mead was born into Judeo-Christian culture, a culture that produced the two very different philosophies of existentialism and humanism. Existentialism gives a person's biological existence priority over his social conditioning and therefore views individualism as a core for studying behavior. The humanist, on the other hand, considers existence in the context of history and culture in order to understand individual perception.

Margaret Mead was 16 years old when the Russian revolution took place. She recalled with great pride that her mother hung a red flag in the window of their home to celebrate the fall of the tsar and the new power given to the working class. Mead was a witness to World War I, the formation of the Weimar Republic in Germany, the abortive German revolution, and the rise of Adolf Hitler and Nazism. The two ideologies that emerged during this period set the stage for modern world politics. The ideology embraced by Nazi Germany emphasized a biologically determined ultra-individualism, while the Soviet system saw the individual as a product of his social and economic conditions.

Among those who rejected the Nazi view was the anthropologist Franz Boas. Between 1883 and 1887, Boas met with Rudolph Virchow, "who was an opponent of the extravagant race theories of the time, and who became, by Boas' own account, the great single influence in his scientific development" (Gossett, 1973:420). Boas eventually was to favor a humanistic view, and through his lectures and writings he condemned any form of racial prejudice, rejecting the notion of inherited racial behavior in particular. "It is possible," states Thomas Gossett, "that Boas did more to combat race prejudice than any other person in history" (Gossett, 1973:418). It is in Boas' struggle to wipe our racist concepts that we find the seeds for the anthropological approach characterized as "personality and culture," a school that rejects the idea that an organism can be studied in isolation from its environment. "Knowledge of a society or a culture must rest upon knowledge of the individuals who are in that society or share that culture," (Kluckhohn and Murray, 1950:xi) was the basic theme proclaimed by the anthropologists. Members of this school included Laurance Frank, Erich Fromm, Harold Lasswell, Gregory Bateson, Cora DuBois, Karen Horney, Geoffrey Gorer, and its two most famous spokespersons, Ruth Benedict and Margaret Mead. In 1925, Margaret Mead was to test the humanist philosophy in her fieldwork, carried out in Samoa. Boas praised Mead in the foreword of her book, *From the South Seas*. "The results of her painstaking investigation," he states, "confirm the suspicion long held by anthropologists, that much of what we ascribe to human nature is no more than a reaction to the restraints put upon us by our civilization" (Mead, 1939:Foreword).

Yet, despite the humanist movement in anthropology, the threads of existentialism were always lurking within the weave of American culture. This school of thought became even more promiment after World War I, when Sigmund Freud assured an increasingly guilt-ridden society that civilization's discontent grew out of human nature and not from a lack of social responsibility. Modern literature also drew upon Freudian themes, and through writers such as Thomas Mann, James Joyce, Franz Kafka, and T. S. Eliot, the subjects of instinct and frustration were popularized. The period from World War I to the end of World War II was a very challenging and stimulating time for anthropologists, who struggled to bridge the gap between Freudianism and existentialism and the growing views of humanism. History favored the approach of Benedict and Mead, for the United States was drawn into a war against fascism, and the villain became the biological determinist. "The field of national character developed as a wartime measure in which methods based on a combination of anthropological field work and clinical research were applied to attempt to delineate the character of enemies, allies, and native populations" (Mead, 1954:743). Members of the school of "personality and culture" were soon involved in discovering and analyzing the enemy's character through the study of child rearing, communication, feeding, weaning, teaching of control, and so on. Within this research there was the assumption that some cultures produced personality characteristics that were antidemocratic and, therefore, dangerous to the world survival.

Included in the national character studies was a Freudian model, in which Freudian terminology and judgments were assumed to be valid. But Freud's instinctual hypotheses eventually were discarded, replaced by the concept of "pattern," as described by Ruth Benedict in 1934 in her famous book, *Patterns of Culture*. The Gestalt school of psychology lent credence to this new structure for analysis. Margaret Mead and Gregory Bateson were to fashion future research on the idea that clear and consistent patterns could be revealed through the study of any culture.

Fortified with the concept that cultural patterns produced stylized behavior, Ruth Benedict wrote her book, *The Chrysanthemum and the Sword*. This book, primarily a study of the Japanese national character, sought to understand why Japan entered into World War II. Through a psychological-cultural analysis, it described the aspects of Japanese character that the U.S. government would consider in order to create an appropriate and effective peace treaty and occupation of Japan. An examination of this book shows that Benedict had moved from the humanist approach of her earlier work, "Race: Science and Politics," to a Freudian existential view. Benedict ignored the growing industrial revolution occurring in Japan and the increased need for new ports and natural resources. She did not deal with Japan's growing urban population, which produced social protest movements and a cry for constitutional government. Instead, Benedict opted for a psycho-aesthetic analysis in which she stated: "Japan saw the cause of the war in another light. There was anarchy in the world as long as every nation had absolute sovereignty; it was necessary for her to fight to establish a hierarchy—under Japan" (Benedict, 1946:21).

Erick Erickson, another member of the "personality and culture" school, focused his national character study on Nazi Germany. In his paper, "Hitler's Imagery and German Youth," Erickson combined a historical analysis with a psychological perspective. He described Germany as being disturbed by the continual intrusion of foreign aesthetics and ethics, and he recognized that Germany's decaying economy following its defeat in World War I was a factor that led to the rise of Hitler. But Erikson, like Wilhelm Reich, turned to Freudian analysis to ascribe the rise of German fascism to the effects of infantile guilt feelings of Germans towards their fathers. Erickson concluded his interpretation by stating, "It will be one of the functions of psychology to recognize in human motivation those archaic and infantile residues which in national crises become subject to misuse by demagogic adventures" (Erickson, 1950:510).

Like Ruth Benedict and others involved in the study of national character, Erickson treated German culture out of context, separated from a global picture. This may be due to the fact that the study of national character was developed at a time when Western anthropology was a discipline intended to study simple and small-scale exotic villages, without regard for the colonial-imperialist impact.

Placing less emphasis on world events and more on psychocultural theory, the members of the school of "personality and culture" focused their study of Third World cultures through the lens of Western individualism. Between the years of 1925 and 1939, Margaret Mead did an analysis of sex and temperament in three Melanesian societies, basing her research on a Freudian model. It is not surprising that she used a "passive-aggressive" measuring stick to compare male-female behavior, for this is the dichotomy accepted by Western culture.

In her book, *From the South Seas*, Mead (1939) examined the mountain-dwelling Arapesh, the river-dwelling Mundugumor, and the lake-dwelling Tchambuli. Mead stated that both men and women among the Arapesh displayed "a personality that, out of our historically limited preoccupation, we would call maternal in its parental aspects, and feminine in its sexual aspects. . . . We found men, as well as women, trained to be cooperative, unaggressive, responsive to the needs and demands of others" (Mead, 1939:279). Further on she stated, "In marked contrast to these attitudes, we found among the Mundugumor that both men and women developed as ruthless, aggressive, positively sexed individuals, with the maternal cherishing aspects of personality at a minimum" (279). As to the Tchambuli she stated, "We found a genuine reversal of sex attitudes of our own culture with the women the dominant, impersonal, managing partner, the man the less responsible and the emotionally dependent person." In summary, Mead stated that "these three situations suggest, then a very definite conclusion. If those temperamental attitudes that we have traditionally regarded as feminine, such as passivity, responsiveness, and a willingness to cherish children, can so easily be set up as the masculine pattern in one tribe, and in another be outlawed for the majority of women as well as for the majority of men, we no longer have any basis for regarding such aspects of behavior as sex-linked" (279–80).

By challenging the concept that behavior is linked to biology, Mead made a great contribution, not only to Western scholarship, but to Third World people. But overall, was Mead accurately describing the Melanesian culture? In an interview with Ralph Wari, we discussed Tchambuli culture. Dr. Wari began by stating that, considering Margaret Mead's limitations with the local language, she did a fairly good job at describing the way Tchambuli children were brought up. "But," he continued, "she should have stayed in the area for the twelve lunar months in order to understand the full cycle of activities that take place in Tchambuli. You see," Wari explained, "she makes statements which are in error, as for example in her book *From the South Seas* [p. 253] where she states that the people depend upon the fishing of the women, while men only fish when a sudden school of fish appears in the lake, at which time they leap into canoes and spear a few fish. . . . Both men and women do fishing in Tchambuli culture, which is directed by the seasons. The fishing techniques are determined by the seasons, and the seasons also determine the so-called norms of behavior. Fishing is an institution and requires specific knowledge by both male and female."

Dr. Wari continued by stating, "It is during the wet season that men cut the logs which can be floated through the rivers into lakes and to the island of Tchambuli. The logs are used for canoes, fire wood and house building. The men are neither passive or lazy. Both men and women participate in the process of producing food. If Mead had stayed for the full cycle of the year, her conclusions would have been different" (Wari, 1982).

Dr. Wari's statement forces us to reconsider Margaret Mead's use of Western categories in her study of Melanesian people. In seeking to solve the problems of sexual stereotyping in Western civilization, Mead brought with her a model of analysis that overlooked the structures and events that influenced gender shifts within the populations she studied. In particular, the adjustment of sexual roles in order to accommodate the seasonal and economic needs of the people was ignored.

Continuing with the model of Western individualism, Ruth Benedict, in 1941, gave a series of lectures at Bryn Mawr College in which she asked questions such as, "How receptive to individual autonomy and impulse could a society be and still remain whole? How far could an individual put natural inclinations before society intervened?" (Model, 1983:263). It was during this period of time that Benedict developed her theory of synergy. She described low synergy cultures as having a social structure that provides for acts that are mutually opposed and counteractive, and high synergy cultures as having institutions that provide for acts that are mutually reinforcing. "High synergy societies," she told her Philadelphia audience, "resembled corporations and joint stock companies" (263).

Benedict saw independent corporations, which have the right to claim private capital in a civil society, as a model for individuals who wish to claim alternative patterns of behavior outside normal social obligations. That both the corporation and the individual might function as full and responsible citizens of a state was not considered. This is particularly interesting because Benedict, like Margaret Mead and other anthropologists of the day, had studied village cultures where each individual and group is an active participant within the power structure of their society.

By 1953, Mead had returned to the village of Peri to study the Titan (Manus) people, and during this period, Dr. Theodore Schwartz and I joined her to do fieldwork. The year before, Mead had helped to train me to do field photography and administer projective tests. During the 1950s, the discipline of psychoanalysis was highly influential in American thinking, and anthropologists regarded psychological testing as a valid means for gauging a more accurate picture of human behavior. We conducted Rorschach tests, Bender Visual Motor Gestalt tests, Thematic Apperception tests, Mosaic tests, Gessel Infant Development tests, and many more.

The essential criteria for projective testing are based on a Freudian premise that an individual will interpret reality according to his or her individual perception or "projections." Projection as originally defined by Freud, is part of the human defense mechanism in which individuals ascribe traits and contexts colored by their own unconscious motivations. It was assumed that by testing a whole village, we would discover a pattern of thinking not overtly expressed by individual villagers. The concept of cultural relativity, an important theme in Ruth Benedict's *Patterns of Culture*, led to the belief that "each culture was unique and measurable only in terms of itself and that only by recognizing these cultural differences was cooperation between people possible" (Caffrey, 1989:333). This idea was particularly applied to Third World cultures, including those in the South Pacific, where it was assumed that island cultures evolved within their local social and economic context. Mead, influenced by Bateson's study of the Iatmul, believed that each culture favors particular personalities and behavioral characteristics. By promoting these personalities, cultures placed individuals with these behavioral characteristics into an elevated, "popular" status. Considered more attractive than others without these characteristics, these popular individuals tended to reproduce the next generation. In this respect, each culture determined the uniqueness of that culture. Mead, however, did not stress this idea, for as she states, "it seemed clear to us [Bateson and Mead] that the further study of inborn differences would have to wait upon less troubled times" (Mead, 1977:222).

In 1953, all of us accompanying Margaret Mead to New Guinea were aware that the area, and Manus Island in particular, had been a staging point for the United States

Army during World War II. We knew that many of the older men in New Guinea had fought with the Japanese at one time and the Australians at another. We knew and observed that villagers had access to radios and newspapers, and that many of the young men traveled to other islands to work in small European communities. We knew that the villagers were extremely observant and carefully measured the behavior of European people in the towns and communities where they served as a laboring class. As waiters and waitresses in private clubs, in which they were refused membership, the villagers observed the whites' use alcohol, their sexual habits, and the broad range of their cultural propensities. Yet, when villagers told us of their experiences with Australian communities, we chose not to record it, for this would have contradicted our exotic belief that the villager was isolated and hence village life could only be observed in isolation.

The projective test also was introduced with the idea that it was a scientific way of measuring human behavior. Just as scientists work in closed laboratory situations designed to prevent their experiments from external contamination, so the anthropologist sought the villages uncontaminated by culture contact. Mead stated that the answers we would find in these unique cultures "were terribly important to the free world, from the fate of the peoples of New Guinea to the fate of the inhabitants of Sydney, London, Oslo, New York, Paris, Djakarta, New Delhi" (Mead, 1966:202).

There was rarely a day that testing did not take place. Whole hamlets were assigned a time to meet with us and accommodate our needs. Parents with their children would arrive as if going to a clinic, prepared to take motor, visual, and cognitive tests. Newborn babies were tested according to the criteria set up by the Gessel Clinic, and while I conducted the test, Mead and Schwartz recorded and photographed the results. Due to our Western focus on individuality, we would separate a mother and her child from the cooperative efforts of family or neighbors, who traditionally participated in problem solving. Basically, we were observing the culture in the context of Western psychoanalysis, which focused on individual rather than cooperative behavior.

During December 1953 Mead made arrangements to return to the United States, asking Dr. Schwartz and myself to remain in Manus for another year to conduct a series of tests requiring somatotype photographs of the Peri people. Mead convened a village meeting to prepare the villages for this new type of testing, which would require that each male and female be photographed in the nude. Again, the villagers were told that an examination of their physical types would enhance human knowledge.

In the early 1930s, Gregory Bateson, Mead's second husband, influenced by Kretschmer's *Physique and Character*, attempted in his book *Naven* to relate physical types to personality. Mead herself was prone to assign behavioral stereotypes to the peoples she studied, such as the Iatmul, whom she described as "a gay irresponsible, vigorous people always either laughing or screaming with rage" (Mead, 1977:228). In her later years, Mead would moderate her earlier confidence in the results of somatotyping, but she still felt obliged to note that the "Manus are higher on mesomorphy than any recorded population" (Mead 1977:322).

On April 8, 1954, I spoke to the women of Peri village, repeating Mead's claim that a study of their physical types was necessary to enhance human knowledge. The nervous women followed me to an area set up to protect their privacy, but suddenly the woman who led the procession threw off her *lap-lap* and performed a mock dance. This broke the tension and produced general laughter among the women. Two women helped me to arrange the proper pose for the somatotype photographs, but since all were embarrassed to pose nude before an outside observer, it was agreed that everyone, including the two women, would be photographed.

Our criteria for posing was taken from standards established by Jim Tanner, a physical anthropologist who had studied under W. H. Sheldon. Sheldon sought to classify all varieties of the human physique in terms of components of endomorphy, mesomorphy, and ectomorphy. Some psychologists sought to relate human personality to the standardized description of the various human physical types to create a more accurate science of human behavior.

This concept of human behavior placed heavy emphasis on nature rather than nurture, and seemed to ignore the earlier studies made by Franz Boas, who stated,

> It has been known for a long time that the bulk of the body as expressed by stature and weight is easily modified by more or less favourable conditions of life. In Europe there has been a gradual increase in bulk between 1850 and 1914. Adult immigrants who came to America from south and east Europe have not taken part in the general increase . . . presumably because they were always selected from a body the social condition of which has not materially changed. Their children however, born in America or who came here young, have participated in the general increase of stature of our native population. . . . With this go hand-in-hand appreciable differences a body form. . . . These changes do not obliterate the differences between genetic types but they show that the

type as we see it contains elements that are not genetic, but an expression of the influence of environment. (Boas, 1930:44–48).

Eventually, Dr. Tanner was to evolve his research in the direction of studying the growth of children in relationship to health and nutrition.

Mead, Schwartz, and Barbara Heath continued the Manus somatotype studies in 1965 and 1968. The authorization to conduct these studies was given by the Department of Territories of Australia and the Administrator of the Territory of Papua and New Guinea, who was also Australian. Although the Manus villagers were cooperative, their permission for the testing was not solicited. In retrospect, I am somewhat shocked at the submissive compliance with which the villagers accepted their intrusive anthropologists. If villagers complained, we certainly did not hear about it, and perhaps for that reason, we did not question our own behavior.

Western culture during the nineteenth and twentieth centuries was dominated by the paradigm of progress and science. Scholars held to the belief that Europe brought progress to the world, and Western colonialism and neocolonialism in the Third World was rationalized on the basis of this presumed progress. Mead, a true citizen of Western civilization, was not immune to the belief that progress and Westernization went hand-in-hand, and that America, with its advanced technology, would lead the Pacific peoples into the future.

When describing the American presence in Manus during World War II, Mead wrote with great enthusiasm, "The Americans knocked down mountains, blasted channels, smoothed islands for airstrips, tore up miles of bush—all with their marvelous 'engines' '' (Mead, 1966:173). This description, a nightmare for modern ecologists, certainly could not have been a positive sight for a people so dependent on their land for survival. Mead actually believed that their contact with the American military would provide the Manus with "a passionate realization of what it meant to be treated by civilized men, by white men as people, people with individual names like anyone else" (Mead, 1966:173).

During 1953, while we were conducting our fieldwork, the Paliau movement, which had begun in 1946, assumed a new vitality through Paliau's plan to unify the villages of Manus and eventually move New Guinea to independence. Paliau did not trust the Europeans, and he felt that the missionaries lied to the villagers while the Australians were stealing the wealth that belonged to his people. He advocated a policy that would discourage the young men from working for Europeans, using their labor instead to create plantations, new villages, village stores, and independent means of transportation (Foerstel, 1953).

Mead interpreted the goals of the Paliau movement as consonant with, if not identical to, the search for Westernization. She never clearly defined what she meant by Westernization or how it would be accomplished in Manus, except to stress that the Titan were highly flexible and capable of great change. To Mead, the people of the United States represented a civilization built on progressive change, and this characteristic captured the imagination of the Titan. Mead's perception of Melanesia's cultural complexity and diversity convinced her that only through Western democracy, with its associated political, economic, and legal structure and community responsibility, could the Melanesian people unite into a cohesive society. Because of her view of New Guinea as socially unstable, Mead was inclined to rationalize Western military power in the Pacific as a stabilizing force. "Without effective institutions for settling disputes—except by feuds, raids and subsequent ephemeral peace-making ceremonies often with payments in expiation—the British court with the whole sanction of armed might behind it, which could settle things impersonally and see that they stayed settled, seemed a magnificent invention, as indeed it is" (Mead, 1966:291).

In his book, *Lo Bilong Yumi Yet*, Bernard Narokobi describes law as it existed in New Guinea before colonial rule. "A village recognizes itself as an independent, autonomous social unit and legal order. It exists by its own history, tradition and territory. Relations between people of a distinct social unit are of a different order from those of other social units. Self-recognition involves self-assertion of self-identity. The existence of such a unit is autochthonous and is self-executing (in that it does not depend on the state or any other higher authority)" (Narokobi, 1989:21).

The law in Melanesia never existed as a phenomenon that controlled society, but was basically built into the knowledge of the community. If leaders did not meet traditional standards, they were eventually removed. Narokobi explains, "In not recognizing Melanesian institutions of social order, they (the colonizers) unwittingly created the seeds for social disorder and the general 'breakdown' in law and order experienced today in Papua New Guinea" (Narokobi, 1989:13).

Mead believed that the concept of community as an institution was introduced to New Guinea by the Western world. Yet the most powerful tradition held in common throughout all of Papua New Guinea was a sense of community. Traditional Melanesian culture places great stress on consensus and sharing, resulting in the absence of rich or poor classes. With the introduction of a Westernized economy based on laissez-faire capitalism, the rise of entrepreneurship separated individual wealth from village development. In this respect, community life was seriously weakened.

As Mead and other anthropologists encouraged Western education to provide Third World students a window to global understanding, European teachers began to dominate Third World classrooms, bringing with them a philosophy of individualism. New jobs and financial success were promised to those who mastered the English language, and from a generation of Western educated students rose a dominant class, with a philosophy of individualism and competition. This class came to control the economic system in alliance with foreign investors who profit from the new form of government.

Approximately 85 percent of Papua New Guinea's population is engaged in traditional agriculture. Yet, the government does little to provide the main producers of food with essentials such as roads, transportation, schooling, electricity, clean water, banks or postal services. "The government's aim is to accelerate the pace of growth and development, by exploiting the considerable opportunities for mineral sector development, while at the same time developing the potential of the nonmineral sectors so as to lay the foundation for sustained and broadbased growth" (World Bank, 1988:xii).

The government of Papua New Guinea has encouraged foreign investors whose profits are removed form the country. The national government receives the bulk of the corporate taxes on mining projects, while provincial governments pick up the rest. The villagers, whose land and labor are used to develop the mining industry receive barely enough compensation for subsistence.

Villagers have demonstrated their frustrations through protest, such as the convulsive outbreaks in Bougainville (now the Northern Solomons). The villagers and landowners have rejected the unsolicited intrusion of mining technology that gorged a pit 400 meters deep and covering several square miles, while polluting streams and farmland. "The Bougainville copper mine has been a highly profitable venture for Australian-based mining giant, Conzin Riotinto of Australia, itself part of the British mining grant RTZ. The fighting is ultimately about CRA's profits in this case, and the profitability of any future mining. Projects by foreign capital vis-a-vis payment to local landowners" (*Pacific News Bulletin*, 1983:5).

The government of Papua New Guinea is looking forward to receiving revenues from the Misema mine, which is producing 200,000 ounces of gold per year. In Enga Province of the Highlands, the Porgera mine produced 800,000 ounces of gold in 1989. These highly profitable mining interests do not consider the cost of resettling villagers removed from their traditional lands and resources. Nor does the government measure the cost of social dislocation, fractured communities, broken morale, and resultant increases in theft, rape, and murder.

In 1975, Mead became aware of the effects of Western economic interests on Pacific village people. During the Bougainville crisis, she accused the multinational mining company, Bougainville Copper Limited, of creating the condition for popular unrest (Griffin, 1989:28). Although Mead's concept of Westernization may have been motivated by idealism, other anthropologists simply viewed the Westernization of Third World countries as inevitable, something "natives would just have to endure." Bougainville Copper Limited, in its earlier days commissioned anthropologist Douglas Oliver to Harvard University to do a study of the province of Bougainville. "In 1967, he had blandly portrayed to shareholders a primitive and superstitious people, 'who would probably get used to the company's presence' " (Griffin, 1989:28).

Western encouragement of privatization as part of economic development has proven to be a major source of environmental vulnerability in the Pacific. Foreign companies, which do not have the cultural or historical knowledge of the ecosystem within island cultures, continues to deplete and destroy the natural resources needed by the indigenous people.

We are now at the point in history where the views of Western anthropologists are no longer judged by their peers alone, but are being examined by rising new scholars from Pacific islands, scholars whose families and culture had been the subject of anthropological study. These indigenous scholars reject Western racism and remain suspicious of the work of Mead and others, work which propagated and imposed the Western model for progress and change. As Third World villagers find themselves increasingly submerged in poverty which they associate with Western political/economic philosophy, we can expect a growing hostility in the Third World toward anthropologists perceived as coconspirators in neocolonialism.

REFERENCES

Benedict, R. 1946. *The Chrysanthemum and the Sword*. Boston: Houghton Mifflin.

———. 1960. *Patterns of Culture*. Boston: Houghton Mifflin. Originally published 1934.

Boas, F. 1930. "Observation on the Growth of Children." *Science* 72, p. 44–48.

Caffrey, M. 1989. *Ruth Benedict: Stronger in This Land*. Austin: University of Texas Press.

Erickson, E. 1950. "Hitler's Imagery and German Youth." In *Personality in Nature, Society, and Culture*, Clyde Kluckhohn and Henry A. Murry (eds.), p. 510. New York: Knopf.

Foerstel, L. 1953. Personal communication with Paliau.

Gossett, T. 1973. *Race: The History of an Idea in America*. New York: Shocken Books.

Griffin, J. 1989. "Bougainvilleans: A People Apart." *Island Business*, August, p. 28.

Kluckholm, C., and H. Murray (eds). 1950. *Personality in Nature, Society, and Culture*. New York: Knopf.

Mead, M. 1939. *From the South Seas: Studies of Adolescence and Sex in Primitive Societies*. New York: William Morrow.

———. 1954. "Research on Primitive Children." In *Manual of Child Psychology*, Leonard Carmichael (ed.) 2d ed., p. 743. New York: John Wiley and Sons. Originally published 1954.

———. 1966. *New Lives for Old: Cultural Transformation, Manus 1928–1953*. Laurel edition.

———. 1977. *Letters from the Field 1925–1975*. New York: Harper & Row.

Model, J. 1983. *Ruth Benedict*. Philadelphia: University of Pennsylvania Press.

Narokobi, B. 1989. *Lo Bilong Yumi Yet: Law and Custom in Melanesia*. Goroka, Papua New Guinea: Institute of Pacific Studies and Melanesian Institute for Pastoral and Socio-Economic Service.

Pacific News Bulletin. 1989. Vol 4, no. 8 (August).

Wari, R. 1982. Interview, November 28.

World Bank. 1988. "Papua New Guinea: Policies and Prospects for Sustained and Broad-based Growth." Washington, D.C.: World Bank.

WARILEA IAMO

4 The Stigma of New Guinea: Reflections on Anthropology and Anthropologists

Margaret Mead made vital contributions to the understanding of humanity across the face of the earth. Together with her contemporaries such as Kroeber, Lowie, Sapir, and Benedict, Mead's works were guided principally by the leadership of Franz Boas. In addition to social, cultural, and physical anthropology, Mead is also known in social psychology, education, and perhaps sociobiology. Mead's fame and popularity, through studying the so-called exotic cultures of other times and places, has made hers a household name in American society.[1] In Papua New Guinea she lingers in the minds of people. Perhaps she is best remembered by the Manus people and the Pere village, where conceivably she gained the status of the "cult heroine" or a "Madame Ghost." Her *Kula* network (see Malinowski, 1984) is very complex, but in a linear fashion it extended from the United States to Manus, Australia, and to several presidents of the United States. Mead left a legacy that continues. Instead of reviewing Margaret Mead's contributions, as has been done many times over, I will reinterpret, in my own way, her views of New Guinea. In view of the impact these views still hold for Papua New Guineans at home and abroad, I believe this exercise benefits today's anthropology.[2]

My Angle of Vision

The stigma of New Guinea is a theoretical argument from my viewpoint as both a subject of anthropology and an anthropologist. This stigma perceives anthropological "inventions" of New Guinea people and cultures by Margaret Mead, indeed by anthropologists today, as social categories of representation more embedded in Western cultures than they are true depictions of the peoples themselves. I argue that these inventions are no mere imaginations for they now are an integral part of the Western civilization and the interdependent world in which we live.

The stigma of New Guinea arises from comparative anthropology, the specialty of which is the component of human civilization labeled as "primitive" and connoting multiple levels of history, economy, polity, religion, psychiatry, and so on. It is the Western psychological frame of reference to maintain a mirror image of itself projected as the Other, a lesser and simpler person, in order to define itself as "better." This is especially true, because according to Diamond (1974: 119), "without such a model, it becomes increasingly difficult to evaluate or understand our contemporary pathology and possibilities." From my six-year stay in the state of California in the United States, it seems that many Western peoples—particularly Americans—have lost the very essence of primary human potential. That is, what they have lost in their belief system is still well and alive in regional societies such as those in Africa and New Guinea. Therefore, in order to regain the sense of human totality and heal themselves from a deep-seated crisis, a search for and definition of what is human is in order.

If modern anthropology grew from the search for human contrast between Western people and their society, then the anthropologist is a restless person, an agent of those Western societies in search of a restive place. As an agent of a particular society, the anthropologist will find the non-Western social systems therapeutic and comforting for Western social systems. In Africa and New Guinea anthropologists have served colonial administrators (e.g., Malinowski 1929; Williams 1928). Their job was to ensure that the white masters remained in control. Not only are the "natives" in this process sociopolitically, economically, and culturally transformed, but they also have become "things" in Western—for American—eyes. When "natives" are invented and represented in the form of such things as anthropology, artifacts, geographies, museums, politics, and economics, they are perceived as nothing more than these creations when they travel to Western societies. Or they are expected to be these things in their natural environment. As members of a tribe, a people, or as a nation, their dignity and their rights as human beings are denied, because they no longer can survive in their own way and they no longer can represent themselves or their civilization. This is what I call a process of stigmatization, which enhances the power of the Western cultural hegemony. It operates not only when New Guineans travel to the West but also influences the way in which Papua New Guineans at home perceive themselves in relation to the dominant cultures of the world, in relation to their own kind, and in the way they build their society.

Mead's Legacy: A Critique

When Margaret Mead set sail to study Samoa in 1925, Manus in 1928, and Arapesh, Mundugumor, and Chambri (or Tchambuli) in 1931, she went as a scientist and a representative of a culture, as well as a member of a specific class and family in Western civilization. According to the civilization she represented, we Pacific peoples were "a people without history, without any theory of how we came to be, without any belief in a permanent future life, without any knowledge of geography, writing, without political forms" (Mead 1956:45). It was Mead with her scientific discipline and superior cultural understanding that could easily order and discern Manus (or New Guinea) culture within a short time after staying with the people. She could perform this task better than the natives themselves could possibly do. To this, she testified that "An investigator who enters such a society with ethnological training which makes it possible to refer to phenomena of Manus (or New Guinea) culture to convenient and well understood categories, and with immense superiority over the native being able to record in writing each aspect of the culture as it is learned, is in a excellent position for research in a comparatively short time" (Mead 1930:280–81).

Margaret Mead, in another article, "The Rights of Primitive Peoples," goes on patronizingly to cite how the superiority of the advanced civilizations contrasts with the stagnated and backward social life of inferior native peoples. She mentions further that "They can, therefore, be regarded in the contemporary ethic of the mid-twentieth century, as having been treated unfairly by history, as having lacked a location on earth's surface that would have given them an opportunity to accept the culture of more advanced civilizations, and so prove their superiority, or be rejected by it and so prove their inferiority" (Mead 1967:306).

Two great themes—knowledge and power—dominate Mead's remarks about the New Guinea people.

Knowledge to Margaret Mead was knowing the New Guinean by deciphering the knowledge that existed in the memory bank of a few adults, recording this history, surveying the Pacific person's geography, making his polity, teaching him to write, and raising his moral and ethical tone to the standards of her civilization. Although she believes that: "Once they had taken their modernization in their own hands, redesigned their own culture from top to bottom, asserted their full dignity as modern Manus [or New Guinea], the continuity with their personalities as they had been developed in the past was not destroyed" (Mead 1967:416).

It was the burden of the civilized to raise the people who had lived in the "Stone Age" era. It was the white person's responsibility to teach those people to read, write, and think, to clothe themselves, feed and shelter each other, to practice a new economy, politics, and belief system, and moreover, to learn everything there was about white man's civilization. Without the guiding hands of the white man and woman, the native was a helpless soul, like a new born baby.

According to Western civilization the so-called primitive and savage man has no sense of knowledge. He was, as Mead's civilization represented him, the equivalent of a Western madman or neurotic, who had no sense of time, no knowledge of how he came to be, no idea about his surroundings, and never had a chance to survey his own geography. These were familiar assumptions among theorists like Piaget and Freud. In fact, it was just such a curiosity that led Mead in 1928 to land on Manus to study the nature and extent of "animistic thought" among Manus children and adults. Mead (1935) confirmed that the children showed no tendencies of animistic thought but the adult did indeed show such proclivities.

In light of this Western conceptual framework, Margaret Mead believed that the "primitive" trusted his physical condition and belief in "Sir Ghost" so much that he could not even think for himself. She wrote:

> the Manus [or New Guinean] lived, as it were, two lives. Underneath there was the active, zestful physical immediacy of people who trusted their own muscles and their own eyes. . . . They lived with the complete physical self-assurance and the certainty that it was always possible to construct what was needed. . . . But overlaid on this vigorous optimism was a second system, respect for property . . . worried economic effort, first in response to the demands of one's elders who sent misfortune, sickness and death, all of which were attributed to sexual or economic laxity. (Mead 1967:72–73).

Relatively speaking, the Manus or New Guineans had no conception of time and history, and their thought processes were so simple that "The memory of each dimmed as the validating events surrounding them receded . . . it was tacitly assumed that past had always been like this and the future were seen as continuously unpredictable because each depended upon combinations of events, and no combination could be accurately predicted" (Mead 1967:84).

Similarly, Mead felt confident in determining the native

attitudes toward time, which attributes were repeated in their concept of space. "The known world was the world in which they lived. . . . The open sea surrounded them in every direction stretched up to an indefinite horizon, unbounded, unnamed. Other places such as New Guinea, where a few of the men had been, Australia or Germany, where no one had been, simply existed somewhere unmapped, uncharted, unguarded even by mythological sea serpents or gods of the sea" (Mead 1967:84).

It appears to Manus adults, according to Mead, that the past becomes almost like historical amnesia and that even the people's customs could not be recalled. Instead they give a simple answer such as "This is our custom: this is the way we do it now." Moreover, she reiterated that even the Manus could not tell the differences between meat and vegetables and human flesh so that "they were unashamed of selling war captives to their cannibal neighbors."

Manus people and indeed the entire territory of Papua New Guinea, then, were no mere imagination. To Mead the study of Manus people was an integral part of Western civilization. And to Mead, uncovering and representing New Guinea through the science of anthropology was an activity materially bonded to her civilization. The white man's knowledge was more powerful, and they could conceptualize beyond the New Guinean a better way of life that would eventually become interdependent with the West. She wanted the Manus and New Guineans to be transformed by her civilization in a Western image.

To become an integral and vital part of Western civilization meant that Manus New Guinea natives were to discard their evil ancestor worship and accept the Christian God and all the moral virtues associated with it, be subdued to the white's discriminatory "native regulations and laws" having to do with segregated housing, entertainment, vagrancy, curfew, and dehumanized forced labor on plantations, and accept the white's life-style as a model to follow (see Amarshi et al. 1979; Fitzpatrick 1980). But unbeknown to the native is the fact that being interdependent is being ever dependent on the white man's knowledge, religion, polity, economy, and technology. This process plunges the natives into losing their confidence and trust in themselves. In other words, natives give up their creative genius and human potential for white culture, and they look to the West as the mecca for "everything" human.

From her remarks written in 1953, 25 years after her first visit in 1928, one can tell how complacent Mead felt when the past Manus was transformed exactly as she had imagined: "when I returned to visit them in 1953, they had become potential members of the modern world, with ideas of boundaries in time and space, responsibility to God, enthusiasm for law, and committed trying to build a democratic community, educate their children, police and landscape their village, care for the old and the sick, and erase age-old hostilities between neighboring tribes" (Mead 1956:45). This remarkable change in Mead's eyes was so satisfying that she personally saw fit to persuade the Manus people, "if you make as much progress in the next twenty-five years as you did in the last, I'll come back to see the changes" (45).

Indeed, as she promised "her people", when she returned seven years later in 1964, she was quite taken aback to find that, "the whole Territory of Papua New Guinea had taken a great leap ahead and the people of Peri [now Pere], no longer isolated within their small island world, also had moved forward" (1966:12).

These perceptions of Margaret Mead, to me, made New

Guinea appear as a barren civilization left naked by historical accident, with only exotic cultural trappings, with no
history, no geography, no writing, and no knowledge dynamic enough to propel itself in its own way. Therefore, it
was up to Mead and her civilization to guide, reproduce,
and transform New Guinea anthropologically, historically,
geographically, politically, and economically. In this form
of representation, Mead was creating the people and culture
that her civilization demanded. For New Guinean people,
lacking any sense of history and writing, the anthropologist
had to record and collect selected pieces of New Guinean
culture in order to give them a sense of their own history.
Once that was done and order given to those pieces, logically the authentic New Guinea could live on through
academic doctrines and visible art forms. Margaret Mead
was involved in a process Roy Wagner calls "the invention
of culture." That is, "by perceiving them and understanding them in terms of her familiar way of life, her culture,
she invents them as culture" (Wagner 1975:35–36).

This form of cultural representation is further elaborated by Marcus and Fischer (1986) as being a "defamiliar-
ization by cross-cultural juxtaposition," a classic technique
in anthropology for probing different social structures. In
Foucalt's terminology, Mead reconstitutes herself in her
own familiar grounds and repeats herself, recalls herself,
and thus provides identical impressions (see Foucault
1973:70). In other words, Mead's descriptions of the Manus
are nothing more or less than her own perceptions based
on her family values, cultural upbringing, and her culture
and society as a whole.

Margaret Mead first went to New Guinea with specific
projects in mind to validate or disprove, as she had done
three years previously in Samoa. Her representation of Peri

Village in Manus, in "Growing Up in New Guinea" (1930), was a one-sided, static picture of Manus culture. In juxtaposing Manus culture with American life, she brought home to the American public caricature representations of how people in other places lived. This was because, as she stated aptly, "In contrast to our own social environment which brings out different aspects of human nature and often demonstrated that behavior which occurs almost invariably in individuals within our own society is nevertheless due not to original nature but to social environment; and a homogeneous and simple development of the individual may be studied" (Mead 1930:281).

Margaret Mead also presented an image of Manus children leading sullen and gloomy lives without proper toys to play with, who played alone, and ignored and were ignored by their parents. The reader is led to believe that in Manus, as opposed to the American experience, the interrelationship between child rearing and cultural ethos gave the Manus children little or no content for imagination. Yet, both American and Manus children were treated alike. They did not perform adult roles and had an easier life. When they reached adulthood the Manus children were transformed automatically, without resistance, to play their part as adults. They could reject the past and create a new beginning, which demonstrated why Manus people could leap into Western civilization. (cf. Romanucci-Ross 1985:201–8). To Mead, Manus was almost a miniature replica of the quintessential capitalistic society, where the "Sir Ghost" (equal to the Protestant ethic) of the recently dead relative makes the Manus adult restless in hosting festivities, paying up debt, and obligating others to his economic sphere and influence, while observing household etiquette between family members. Social inequality and exploitation appeared to be naturally endowed in the Manus socio-economic system.

Mead also drew idyllic portraits of three New Guinea societies in which her own personality, science, and culture were very much in evidence. Accompanying Reo Fortune in 1931, her project was to study the way different cultures pattern male and female relationships. Her fieldwork situation with Reo Fortune in Arapesh, Mundugumor, and later with Bateson at Iatmul and Chambri (or Tchambuli) facilitated her formulations of culture and personality (Mead 1935). Mead found Arapesh men and women congenial because they were alike in their nurturing and cherishing attitudes, which she believed approximated Western female behavior. The Mundugumor people, whom she loathed, represented men and women who were aggressive and exploitative. Mundugumor men and women behaved most like Western males, while among the Chambri (Tchambuli), the traditional roles of men and women were reversed. Women were brisk and cooperative, and behaved like Western men, while men were more responsive, like Western females.

To Mead the indigenous social system was so stagnant for the Manus (or New Guinea) people that she prescribed the inevitable dominance of Western cultural hegemony through overt inducement. According to Mead, because the Manus social system could adapt, it was easy for them to adjust to Western political, economic, religious, legal, technological, and military institutions. Once Manus people were induced through impressive management by overt displays of superior technology and a better way of Western life, they would be convinced to accept all these things Western. So, when the past order of the Manus economic treadmill was juxtaposed with the new Manus, according to

Mead, such men as John Kilipak were prepared to repudi-
ate their own way of life marked by memories of economic
rivalry, competition, and social prejudice. In the new political economy, adult Manus could no longer suppress the
young aspiring men; instead they were now happy to labor
in coconut plantations and mines under the back-breaking
conditions for little remuneration, or become domestic
servants for their white colonial masters, or be transformed
into peace officers to guard colonial cities. All of these
activities gave the young adults time off from warfare or
economic sanctions.

Margaret Mead idolized Western economy and polity as
the best thing God gave humanity, for through this avenue,
the European was to save the native Manus and New
Guinean. Yet, the natives were to discover upon engagement as laborers on plantations and in colonial towns that
the social conditions were not what they had hoped for and
been led to believe. The agreement to work on plantations
was a forced "indentured labor" system, and although it
was vigorously applied to the Highlands, many coastal
areas also were affected (see Levine and Levine 1979:26;
Amarshi et al. 1979). Natives were in bondage to masters
of plantations for the duration of the indentured labor. The
master-boy relationship in this context was perceived by
the dominant element in this "partnership" as having a
"civilizing" influence on the native laborers. In plantations
the languid character of the native was to be routinized
according to an expatriate's work habits and time. The new
habits of work included punctuality and hard work. Moreover, if one were lazy and absent from work, corporal
punishment was employed by the white master to make the
native obey and acquire the new habits of labor. But the
little remuneration earned was shared between the person's

extended family and as a tax for the maintenance of the colonial administration. Failure to pay tax resulted in sustained *kalabus*, or imprisonment. Moreover, when the indentured labor period was over, a person was given no choice as to where to reside but was shipped back home (see Fitzpatrick 1982, 1980).

In colonial towns as much as the plantations, New Guineans lived in segregated housing quarters, did not socialize in the same places as their "white masters," were not allowed to consume alcohol and dine and wine in same places, and were bounded by curfew and vagrancy laws. To the whites their social relationship extended as far as master-boy or the master-servant social relationship. These discriminatory social and labor conditions made the natives mistrust whites. This point is vividly illustrated by what is still referred to as the Rabaul strike of 1929 in which many *haus bois* (domestic servants), *polis bois* (native police), and native workers from Manus collaborated in a town-wide strike. What shocked the white colonialists was the ability of the natives to effectively organize in terms of solidarity and catch them off-guard until the hour of the strike. As usual the white colonialists responded with draconian punishments inflicted on the leaders of the strike.

The Manus of the past that Margaret Mead depicted in the preceding discussions is juxtaposed with the social conditions that were faced in towns and on plantations. The Manus and New Guinean man was likely to long for his old native village. It appears from the experience of the men, who were away on sustained trips to Rabaul and mainland New Guinea and Papua, that basically their human essence was destroyed. At least back in the village they could return as big men and relate to all, young and old, male and female, as human beings, and not as impersonal things.

The village home, therefore, became the center of the universe for the Manus as it was here that he regained his proper sanity and his person and character. The Paliau Cargo Movement was a reaction against the white colonialists, in part, for the mistreatment of the native. As a former policeman and having had substantial experience in living in colonial towns, Paliau returned to his natal village to launch the protest movement against the mistreatment received from the white colonialists (Worsley 1970).

To demonstrate the whites' power and superior civilization, in 1942 the Manus and New Guinea mainland became a battlefield between the Japanese and Americans and Australians. The natives were led to believe that Anglo-Americans and Anglo-Australians were the "good guys" and the "bad guys" were Japanese. But in essence, they both were fighting for the same basic aim, the annexing of unmapped land, especially for commerce and industry. After the war was over in 1945, the onslaught of the Western civilization began with the imposition of Western schools and institutions. Moreover, the communal political system was replaced by representatives of Western colonial institutions of *luluai, tultul,* police *bois,* and councils. Village communal values and ethos were replaced by Christian ethics and moral values. This discussion demonstrates the conflict within representations of Papua New Guinea culture history.

Thus, I have tried to demonstrate that knowledge is an intricate part of power. Anthropological knowledge means to know the Other. To know the Other is to create the person's history, politics, geography, and culture, to remove the power of imagination, and to make the person dependent. But to know someone else is also to presume to understand ourselves even better. Thus a differentiation and a dichotomy of "us" as the superior and "them" as the inferior develops. And, to know of the Other is to have authority over that person, to represent, and reproduce the person. Such a process will give rise to stigma, where the indigene is not seen in his or her own right but rather from what is made of that individual.

The Stigma of New Guinea: A Personal Critique

New Guinea is a Western invention, a name and a plethora of cultural identities given by European travelers in the 1500s to black peoples, who for millennia inhabited the dragon-shaped island in the Pacific. Their cultures were invented and authorized by a succession of anthropologists, who claimed to have a superior way of life, and influenced the carriers of the invented cultures in perception and behavior. I believe that when cultures are invented by outsiders, there is an active ingredient portrayed to their audience at home that eludes the inventor's sensibility because of their constant search for "other" in order to confirm their own "self." When beliefs about the Other are confirmed through further myths derived by their hosts, a portrait of a culture is painted with unfamiliar and startling characteristics in order to make it interesting and exciting for the home audience.

In the case of New Guinea, such unfamiliar but exciting myths are the stories of "cannibalism" and certain tribal attributes (compare Arens 1979 and Brown and Tuzin 1983). This is also "stigma." Some cultures and subcultures are known best by their stigma outlooks, and we as anthropologists try our best to make some sense out of them to the readers of our work. If such stigmas and attributes are unfamiliar but are inculcated through education and mythical legends, then for those who are presumed to possess them, they are given special treatment by the members of our society.

In a succinct way Goffman eloquently summarized my angle of vision in this matter: "While the stranger is present before us, evidence can arise of his possession of an attribute that makes him different from others in the category of person available for him to be, and of a less desirable kind—in the extreme, a person who is thoroughly bad, or dangerous, or weak. He is reduced in our mind from the whole and usual person to a tainted, discounted one. Such an attribute is stigma" (Goffman 1963:2–3).

Too often in the telling and writing of an ethnography of another culture, famous anthropologists such as Mead (1942, 1977) and Malinowski (1929, 1967), made condescending racial slurs and revealed prejudices against their hosts which they took with them to the field (see Minol 1978; Willis 1974).

In his terminal lecture in September 1979 to the Department of Anthropology, hosted by the Papua New Guinea Sociological Association, Visiting Professor Charles Valentine noted some very important reasons why anthropology in Papua New Guinea has been denounced and despised.[3] It is most important, he went on to explain, "because it is a main source of the racist Western ideas of the primitive. Melanesians along with Black Africans have long been the European's favorite examples of that concept. It refers to all that the Western claims to find inferior in what he is placed to call the lowest levels of humankind" (C. Valentine 1979:4).

That the scientific concept of "primitive" positively defined by Diamond (1974:127) and reviewed and refined again by Goody (1977) is still a common usage in many

U.S. and European universities is an insult to indigenous Papua New Guineans. These anthropological definitions and inventions of another people have been a subject of debate by students, administrators, policymakers, and university academics (see Hau'ofa 1975; Iamo 1979; Lohia 1986; Roleas 1979; Sukwianomb 1983).[4] As a result, anthropologists in the 1980s have been monitored, controlled, and banned from doing social research in the Trobriand Islands, Manus, Morobe, and West Sepik.[5] Even the indigenous people have exploited the word primitive to their advantage to win pride and respect from travelers and anthropologists (Gorecki 1984; Salisbury 1985; compare Mangi 1986), and seek provision of much-needed basic services from the government of Papua New Guinea.

It is not only at home that preconceptions of anthropology and anthropologists are debated and denounced by learned Papua New Guineans. While abroad, indigenous Papua New Guineans confront anthropology as a discipline in its true cultural setting. The very word New Guinea has become so stigmatized, so to speak, that a "live" indigenous person from that region meeting Americans for the first time is barraged with unimaginable questions to confirm what is inculcated at schools and institutions: Are your family members cannibals? How traditional is your family? Are there primitive tribes? Are they Christians or pagans? Is polygamy common? Every now and again, I meet people who, when they hear that I am a Papua New Guinean, associate me with those mythical attributes and want to learn more about them.

Margaret Mead and the anthropology of today are still linked with such myths by the public. And their beliefs are further enhanced by documentary films and travel tales that appear every now and again in the *New York Times,* the

San Francisco Chronicle, and *Rolling Stone* magazine, or even in gossip among anthropologists. Even today we read that cannibalism is practiced, and travelers are advised not to face natives alone, referring to Michael Rockefeller's disappearance in 1961 as proof. It may appear that some anthropologists have become more sensitized to these problems in their writings in order not to label their host cultures. But the image represented of "primitive" cultures has not yet withered away with the passage of time. Mead's New Guinea and Samoa, and Malinowski's Trobriand Islands are very much alive and well in the United States.

Papua New Guinea students and professionals who attend school in the United States and in other Western societies find it common that foreigners see them against the backdrop I have painted. They find it distasteful and demoralizing for their people and culture to be perceived in such derogatory and pejorative terms. In some cases, they maintain an anonymous cultural identity because they wish to remain free of unintelligent questions and not be inhibited. Others, so I hear, educate their less sophisticated audiences about the qualities endowed in what they believe to be a "civilization" in its own right, but one that is denied a viewpoint. At the United Nations, when politically sensitive issues such as the plight of our neighboring brothers and sisters of New Caledonia, West Papua, and other island nations for a nuclear-free Pacific are being proposed, Pacific leaders are often indiscriminately saddled with anthropological paradigms (see Chapter 10).

At home, Papua New Guinea is still anthropologically, linguistically, politically, geographically, and militarily divided. Anthropologists have made people believe they are Trobrianders, Tolais, Manus, Sepiks, Chimbus, and Melpas. Geopolitical and military conditions have made indigenous people believe there are Papuans in the south, New Guineans in the north, and Irian Jayans in the West end, or that there are regional groups such as Highlanders and Coastals. These imposed Western forms and dichotomies convince the people that Papua New Guinea was never united, nor did it have any form of interdependent political system equivalent to the Polynesian type Marshall Sahlins (1963) juxtaposed and contrasted with the Melanesian one. Our world was, and is, always portrayed as a self-evolving and self-regulating entity, whose history and categories can only be uncovered in mythic metaphors. The power of people's imagination and local knowledge is killed and largely replaced with Western institutions through Western forms of inducement.

Some Food for Thought

Anthropologists should never lose sight of the fact that Papua New Guinea culture is not traditional and static. It is just as dynamic as any other civilization. We have no words for tradition and custom. They are introduced and imposed categories to label our way of life. These Western thought patterns have taken their toll on our peoples' minds in that they have been induced to observe their way of life as "traditional" and laden with "custom," while what is imported from western societies is always new and modern.

So when we speak of whether I come from a traditional family or whether my people are still primitives, this is a misconstrued conception, because we are civilized. That is, we have always had gods, history, knowledge, and geography. Literacy and complex technology should not be used as indexes of development, because we had our own forms of recording systems and our people have had a technology that still is universally accepted for its quality. A moment's pause to ponder the superiority of Western technology will sensitize us to the ills of much of this technology. A case in point is what nuclear holocaust may do to our universe and the human race within seconds.

Have we lost sight of the fact that the so-called small-scale societies have always led interdependent political and economic lives that covered oceans and land masses and were never isolated (see Wolf 1982) To imply that Papua New Guinea societies have been self-perpetuating since time immemorial is misleading, and denies the political and economic character endowed in these decentralized and interdependent systems. Despite the plethora of invented evidence that point to the fact that we were divided by oceans, landmass, warfare, and multiplicity of languages, village leaders and individuals were always multilingual, and social and political boundaries were never impediments to interdependent lives. Evidence of this can be recreated in the trade networks that penetrated beyond social, linguistic, political, and military boundaries (see Mangi 1985).

With these hindsights, I recommend that anthropologists in that region known as Papua New Guinea call attention to and perceive of these small-scale societies not as traditional but as civilized in their own right, not as independent and isolated entities but as interdependent and decentralized social systems before their contemporary history was drawn and colonial polity made.

Papua New Guinea must restore the power of the people's imagination and local knowledge. This to me will reconstitute a new order to the society that I will from now on use the name ''Vanua'' in the place of the tainted word ''New Guinea.'' Vanua is the name dialect, Keakalo (also known as Aroma), which connotes at the same time the concepts of a village, a region, a country, or a nation. I will employ Vanua in my writings because I believe by reconstituting Vanua in its own soul and blood it will be revived as a dynamic entity having its own historical past and future, and can always be imagined and carved from the past to the present and into the future.

NOTES

1. In the California community where I carried out my Ph.D. research (Iamo 1986), some white informants knew of New Guinea through their reading of Mead's books, *Growing Up in New Guinea* and *New Lives for Old.*

2. See for example Chapter 10, which poses the question about possible linkage between anthropological perspectives and the interpersonal and political relations between Pacific diplomats and their counterparts in the United Nations.

3. Professor Charles and Bettylou Valentine were visiting professors at the University of Papua New Guinea's Anthropology-Sociology Department from 1978 to 1979, and both had great influence on my intellectual growth and development. C. A. Valentine's paper, entitled "Anthropology is One of Papua New Guinea's Unsolved Problems," was given as a terminal lecture, as both were leaving Papua New Guinea. The seminar was hosted by the then Papua New Guinean Sociological Association (PNGSA) and chaired by Wari Iamo, who was also at that time president of the association. It aroused a strong reaction from the foreign academics at the university, especially from the newly arrived and famed archaeologist, Les Groube from Cambridge. He rebutted with great fury in defense of the discipline and anthropologists.

4. The debate on the making of New Guinea and Pacific cultures and peoples did not end with pioneering students of anthropology at the University of Papua New Guinea, such as

Dr. Epeli Hau'ofa. It continued in the 1970s during my student days. The bitter debate culminated in both IASER and PNGSA sponsoring an important seminar on the theme of foreign researchers in Papua New Guinea. In the annals of Pacific anthropology, scholarly debate on the issue was just as intense among the then university lecturers L. Morauta, A. Gilliam, and R. Gordon.

5. The impact of the debate on anthropologists and foreign researchers was felt after those policy makers who attended directed policy proposals to control foreign researchers at the provinicial level. The first province to have any form of research policy was the Southern Highlands, followed by Morobe, Madang, Milne Bay, Manus, and West Sepik. By at least the 1980s, entry to do research in Papua New Guinea became much more difficult. Several anthropologists were refused and banned from doing research in such places as Madang, Morobe, and Milne Bay.

REFERENCES

Amarshi, A., K. Good, and R. Mortimer. 1979. *Development and Dependency: The Political Economy of Papua New Guinea*. Melbourne: Oxford University Press.

Arens, W. 1979. *The Man-eating Myth*. London: Oxford University Press.

Brown, P., and D. Tuzin (eds.). 1983. *The Ethnography of Cannibalism*. Washington, D.C.: Society of Psychological Anthropology.

Diamond, S. 1974. *In Search of The Primitive: A Critique of Civilization*. New Brunswick, N.J.: Transaction Books.

Fitzpatrick, P. 1980. "Really Like Slavery: Law and Labour in Colonial Economy in Papua New Guinea. *Contemporary Crisis* 4:77–95.

———. 1982. "The Political Economy of Law in the Post-Colonial Period." In D. Weisbrot et al. (eds.), *Law and Social Change in Papua New Guinea*. Sydney: Butterworths.

Foucault, M. 1973. *The Order of Things and Archaeology of the Human Sciences*. London: Tavistock Publications.

Goffman, E. 1963. *Stigma: Notes on the Management of Spoiled Identity*. Englewood Cliffs, N.J.: Prentice Hall.

Goody, J. 1977. *The Domestication of the Savage Mind*. Cambridge: Cambridge University Press.

Gorecki, P. 1984. "The Documented History of the 'Lost Tribes' of the Schrader Mountains." *Research in Melanesia* 8(1):47–56.

Hau'ofa, E. 1975. *Anthropology and Pacific Islanders*. Institute of Papua New Guinea Studies, Discussion Paper no. 8. Port Moresby.

Iamo, W. 1979. "Foreign Researchers in Papua New Guinea." Paper prepared for Pacific Science Congress, Khabarovsk, USSR.

Levine, H., and M. W. Levine. 1979. *Urbanization in Papua New Guinea: A Study of Ambivalent Townsmen*. Cambridge: Cambridge University Press.

Lohia, R. 1986. Personal communication.

Malinowski, B. 1984. *Argonauts of the Western Pacific*. Prospect Heights, Ill.: Waveland Press. Originally published 1922, New York: E. P. Dutton.

———. 1929. *The Sexual Life of Savages*. London: Routledge.

———. 1967. *A Diary in the Strict Sense of the Term*. New York: Harcourt.

Mangi, J. 1985. "On the Question of the Lost Tribes." *Research in Melanesia* 9:37–65.

———. 1986. "The Role of Archaeology in Nation-Building." Paper presented at the World Archaeology Congress, September 1–6, Southhampton, England.

Marcus, G. E., and M. M. J. Fischer 1986. *Anthropology as Cultural Critique: An Experimental Moment in the Human Sciences*. Chicago: University of Chicago Press.

Mead, M. 1930. *Growing Up in New Guinea*. New York: Morrow.

————. 1935. *Sex and Temperament in Primitive Societies*. New York: Morrow.

————. 1949. *Coming of Age in Samoa*. New York: Mentor Books. Originally published 1928, New York: Morrow.

————. 1966. *New Lives for Old: Cultural Transformation, Manua 1928–1953*. New York: Morrow. Originally published 1956.

————. 1967. "The Rights of Primitive Peoples, Papua New Guinea: A Crucial Instance." *Foreign Affairs,* January, pp. 304–18.

Minol, B. 1978. "A Review of the Manus Sections of *Letters from the Field* by Margaret Mead." *Oral History* 6(10): 1–3.

Roleas, P. 1979. "Social Science Research and Issues Related to Its Indigenisation in PNG." *Research in Melanesia* 4(3–4): 28–44.

Romanucci-Ross, L. 1985. *Mead's Other Manus: Phenomenology of the Encounter*. South Hadley, Mass.: Bergin & Garvey.

Sahlins, M. 1963. "Poor Man, Rich Man, Big Man, Chief: Political Types in Melanesia and Polynesia." *Comparative Studies in Society and History* 5(3): 285–303.

Salisbury, R. 1985. "The Myamiya Group of Peoples." *Research in Melanesia* 9:6–24.

Sukwianomb, J. 1983. "The Bamboo Fire: An Anthropologist in New Guinea." *Research in Melanesia* 7:47–49.

Valentine, B. 1978. *Hustling and Other Hard Work: Lifestyles in the Ghetto*. New York: Free Press.

Valentine, C. 1979. "Anthropology Is One of Papua New Guinea's Unresolved Problems." Lecture to Department of Anthropology/Sociology, University of Papua New Guinea, Port Moresby.

Wagner, R. 1975. *The Invention of Culture*. Englewood Cliffs, N.J.: Prentice-Hall.

Williams, F. E. 1928. *Orokaiva Magic*. London: Oxford University Press.

Willis, W. S., Jr. 1974. "Skeletons in the Anthropological

Closet." In D. Hymes (ed.), *Reinventing Anthropology,* pp. 121–152. New York: Pantheon.

Wolf, E. R. 1982. *Europe and the People Without History.* Berkeley: University of California.

Worsley, P. M. 1970. *The Trumpet Shall Sound: A Study of Cargo Cults in Melanesia.* London: Paladin.

ANGELA GILLIAM and LENORA FOERSTEL

5 Margaret Mead's Contradictory Legacy

To understand the impact of Margaret Mead's particular brand of social science on Pacific ethnography and Pacific peoples, it is essential to appreciate the nature of that social science and the influences on her at the historical moment when she was doing anthropology. Margaret Mead was the foremost scholar in the United States who integrated Freudian analysis with studies of culture. In part, that is because she believed in the use of interdisciplinary methods. In an autobiographical essay written near the end of her life, Mead noted that "any one of the human sciences, which now pursue their separate ways in narrow and specialized scorn and indifference to one another, could have evolved into a single human science" (Mead, 1974:317).

Another reason for Mead's interest in Freud was the strength of European, especially German, modes of analysis in U.S. academic discourse. Anthropology gained in importance at the turn of the twentieth century when monopoly capitalism and individualism spawned philosophical tendencies such as modernism, which stressed antirationalism and experimentalism with an emphasis on the inner-directed self. This view of modernism was applied to the philosophy of primitivism and in turn was used by colonial governments to characterize non-western cultures. These concepts were embraced by Sigmund Freud, whose theories of human existence came to prominence in the United States during a period of global expansion. The psychosocial ethos that supported industrial capitalism was rooted in individualism. But even Freud became increasingly uncomfortable with some of the Nietzschean elements of German philosophy that shaped his work (Gay, 1978). One such influence from Nietzsche was primitivism. As primitivism became a major theme in modern thought, some European thinkers sought to understand themselves by searching for man's "primal" state. "Behind the childhood of the individual we are promised a picture of a phylogenetic childhood—a picture of the development of the human race, of which the individual's development is in fact an abbreviated recapitulation influenced by the chance circumstance of life. We can guess how much to the point is Nietzsche's assertion that in dreams 'some primeval relic of humanity is at work which we can scarcely reach any longer by a direct path'; and we may expect that the analysis of dreams will lead us to a knowledge of man's archaic heritage, of what is psychically innate in him" (Freud, 1955).

Mead believed that she was rejecting this analysis. She was to one day state that "we did not make the mistake of thinking, as Freud, for example, was misled into thinking, that the primitive peoples living on remote atolls, in desert places, in the depths of jungles, or in the Arctic north were equivalent to our ancestors" (Mead, 1972:139). Yet, Mead used the Freudian model of linking the psyche to biology in her research on aggression among the Mundugumor and Arapesh peoples of Papua New Guinea, and she sought to correlate bodily configurations with innate temperament among the Tchambuli (now Chambri) as well (Mead, 1935b). The interlocking threads of primitivism and Freudianism in Mead's work was pointed out by Harris in 1968 and later by Torgovnick (1990). Harris (1968:407–421) identified *Coming of Age in Samoa* (Mead, 1928) as pre-Freudian and as a crucial element in what was eventually to become known as the Culture and Personality school of thought in anthropology. Torgovnick (1990:238) saw Mead as a Western primitivist whose ultimate acceptance of Freudianism inhibited a full anthropological understanding of women.

Early on, however, Mead's influential teacher, Franz Boas, warned her to avoid repeating Malinowski's Freudian analysis. "I believe you have read Malinowski's paper in *Psyche* on the behavior of individuals on the family in New Guinea. I think he is much too influenced by [Freud]" (Mead, 1972). Boas was indeed opposed to academic theories that supported biological determinism, but his position emanated more from a concern about racism and anti-Semitism. However, Willis (1974:139), in his insightful classic, "Skeletons in the Anthropological Closet," maintains that the Boasians' intellectual struggle against racism and biological determinism was less a desire to prove equality of humankind across the board as much as it was an effort to win the war against anti-Semitism among U.S. anthropologists. Barrett (1984:227) affirms Willis' contention, noting that Fried (1972:61–63) also recognized Boas' initial view that "big-brained" Asians, Europeans, and [presumably Euro-Americans] were superior to smaller-brained Africans, Australians, and Melanesians (Boas, 1901). Nonetheless, Boas is more identified by his writings that pointed to the fallacy of race (e.g. Boas, 1927). "[Boas] spoke out again and again in the 1920s against racists like Madison Grant, Henry Fairfield Osborn, and Lothrop Stoddard. In the 1930s, and until his death in 1942, he was one of the most active of the American opponents of Nazi race theories" (Gossett, 1963:424). The views that Boas transmitted to students such as Margaret Mead were those that ran counter to the influential racist theories of the period.

Cultural Influences

A description of the science in 1920s New York City and Columbia University, where Mead received her Master's and Ph.D. degrees, and where Boas was the head of the anthropology department, can deepen the understanding of the context of Mead's early work. Columbia University and the American Museum of Natural History had an unusual relationship with each other. The biological sciences had become very important at the turn of the century and had been linked to the need to define who and what was "advanced" or "backward" through evolutionary theory. It was Henry Fairfield Osborn, whose joint appointment as head of the new biology department at Columbia and curator of mammalian paleontology at the museum reinforced the linkage between these two institutions. "The connection with the museum was the first step not only toward making collections, but also laboratories, expeditions, and curatorial staff available as university facilities, resources, and faculty. Within a few years the university reaped the benefits in biology, and with that precedent, developed an anthropology department" (Sloan, 1980:56).

Osborn, like the trustees of scientific institutions such as the museum, was part of the ruling elite. He was a "wealthy scion of New York railroad magnates and [J. P.] Morgan's nephew, [and] a full-fledged member of the very class that governed his museum and university" (Sloan, 1980:59). In addition, Osborn's racial view of history marked his efforts at both institutions, where he had abundant freedom to define the intellectual terrain. Indeed, he was president of the museum for 25 years, until approximately 1933, 8 years after Mead began as assistant curator in the Anthropology Department in what was to become a 52-year career at that institution. Osborn's creation in the museum, the Hall of the Age of Man, was a racialized definition of human progress that placed the European human at its pinnacle. As Haraway elucidates, the racial doctrines of the museum were not publicly criticized until the 1940s (Haraway, 1989:58). It is thus significant that when Mead was later curator of ethnology, she "supervised the creation and installation of the Hall of Peoples of the Pacific at the Museum," basing the exhibit on the art, artifacts, and products of Pacific cultures (American Museum of Natural History, 1978). This was an orientation that placed primacy on the social aspects of a culture, as contrasted with the emphasis on human body type as the central factor, and is one of the positive Mead legacies.

The New York professional world included other scholars who believed that race was the key to civilization (Gossett, 1963:398). Madison Grant, himself both the president of the Zoological Society and member of the Board of Trustees of the Museum of Natural History, claimed to wield influence over U.S. government policy in its development of immigration policy. "*The Passing of the Great Race,* in its original form, was designed by the author to rouse his fellow Americans to the overwhelming importance of race and to the folly of the 'Melting Pot' theory.

. . . This purpose has been accomplished thoroughly, and one of the most far reaching effects of the doctrines enunciated in this volume and in the discussions that followed its publication was the decision of the Congress of the United States to adopt discriminatory and restrictive measures against the immigration of undesirable races and peoples" (Grant, 1921:xxviii). Osborn had affirmed the "superior force . . . of heredity, as being more enduring and potent than environment" in the preface to Grant's book (1921:vii).

Meanwhile, the American Museum of Natural History was sponsoring the second international meeting of eugenicists entitled, "Eugenics in Family, Race, and State." It was a meeting in part intended to influence policy, and the elected officials overseeing policy were sent portions of the exhibit that dealt with immigration (Haraway, 1989:58). It was a time when restrictive immigration laws and quotas that divided the world's peoples into desirable and undesirable immigrants were being reinforced by new legislation, and when groups such as the Ku Klux Klan, which was actively involved in lynching African-American men, women, and children, had a national membership of three to five million people. The world in which Boas taught, and Mead learned and later worked, was one in which racist ideas were commonplace in society and even legitimated by scholarship.

Columbia University was located in Harlem, yet was not of it; there was little interaction between the institution and the surrounding community, even during the Harlem Renaissance in the 1920s and 1930s. The pervasive ideology of primitivism among U.S. intellectuals likely conditioned their approach to African-American countercultural expression during this period. "Thinking that a trip [to Harlem] meant a safari into an exotic jungle . . . Harlem became an aphrodisiac, a place where whites could discover their primitive selves" (Hemenway, 1978:27). Scholars such as Boas encouraged different approaches to the study of culture. Indeed, Boas encouraged Zora Neale Hurston, member of the Harlem Renaissance and the only African-American student ever to study under his tutelage at Columbia, to study the folkways of her community in the South.[1] Boas' burgeoning interest in folkways and the social construction of culture was in sharp contrast to the hereditarian and racial studies that were popular among academics at the time. Because they "were genuinely convinced that races [varied] greatly in innate intelligence and temperament" (Gossett, 1963:373), many of Boas' contemporaries saw the intelligence test as an appropriate instrument of analysis.

This is the context of Mead's Master's thesis entitled, "Intelligence Tests of Italian and American Children" (1924), which demonstrated the importance of culture and learning and directly confronted the eugenicists in their advocacy for controlling the immigration and birth rates of certain population groups. Mead was part of a growing number of scholars who linked socioeconomic status and acculturation to intelligence test results (Rosenberg, 1982:219). She studied the Italian-American community in her home town of Hammonton, New Jersey, and compared the I.Q. test scores of those children who spoke Italian at home versus those who spoke English. Mead found that English-speaking children performed better and was therefore able to demonstrate that "cultural factors, not differences in innate ability, accounted for differences in measured intelligence among various groups of people" (Cassidy, 1982:131). Her findings were in opposition to those who wanted to use intelligence tests to argue the inferiority of Southern Europeans and Eastern European Jews in order to restrict their entry into the United States.

For many years, these contentious issues were a part of the environment at Columbia and Barnard College, its adjacent affiliate for women where Mead completed her undergraduate degree. Annie Nathan Meyer, a founder of Barnard and one of Boas' associates, attempted to have Grant removed from his position as an academic affiliated with the city government. "Here are to be found Hitler's fantastic claims of superiority for the Nordic race; his insane hatred of the Jews, of the Italians, of all people who are not blonde and blue-eyed; his contempt for all who are inclined towards peace rather than war; his willingness to ascribe every crime to those humans who happen to be brunette and short of stature. . . . It is somewhat astonishing that in the city of New York . . . that no citizen has before this arisen to question how it is that a man of such extreme intolerance could have remained for many years at the head of a society which is so immensely indebted to the taxpayers" (Meyer, 1935). Meyer sent reprints of her article to many organizations and individuals and appealed to Mead for assistance. Mead's response was brief and hand-written, noting merely that "all of us here [at the Museum] are only too cognizant of the point you mention" (Mead, 1935a). Yet, the request demonstrates the reputation Mead was commanding as someone who offered a consistent alternative to the prevailing biological determinism.

The concept of "undesirable" races was a powerful one that affected the admissions of students to the institutions of higher learning in the United States for many years. The issue of restricted admission to the nation extended to restricted admission to learning at Columbia, with Jews from Germany or of Spanish origin considered desirable, while those from Eastern Europe were not wanted (Wechsler, 1977:135). Two writers from the period anticipated that Nicholas Murray Butler, Columbia University President from 1912 to 1945, would be deemed one of the leaders of the movement for educational restriction of Jews at the institution for a long time. And a nationwide survey by Jewish students during this era revealed that those students believed Columbia to be among the institutions with the most pronounced anti-Semitism in the entire nation (Broun and Britt, 1974:89). Boas, a Jewish scholar of German descent, was often at odds with the college administration because of his "liberal stance," which "created funding difficulties for the anthropology Department" (Caffrey, 1989:100). The power of the Boas persona enabled him to attract innovative students and faculty, especially women, who were also drawn to challenge the prevailing biological determinism. People such as Gene Weltfish, Ruth Benedict, and Margaret Mead also expressed Boas' concerns about the relationship between race and democratic society (Boas, 1945; Benedict and Weltfish, 1943; Mead, 1926).

Women scholars at Columbia often supported each other's efforts, but they did not become the intellectual stars of their professions. One observer, herself a student at Columbia in the early 1940s, makes the important point that because women scholars such as Mead had no formal power at Columbia, they turned to the public for approval, status, and recognition (Wike, 1990). Yet, the immediate fame that Mead garnered after publication of *Coming of Age in Samoa* led her away from her initial intellectual pathway. By 1939, an article written about her would be subtitled "How Margaret Mead Became One of the Foremost Women Explorers; Her Life among Strange Brown

People in the Pacific Islands; and How the 'Primitive Experiment' Revises Our Most Cherished Notions of Human Behavior'' (Barton, 1939). An apparent bifurcation between domestic issues and the so-called field would explain the militancy with which Mead was to participate in the fight against Naziism and some domestic racism, yet at the same time maintain the racist attitudes and notions of superiority with which she was to describe Pacific—particularly Melanesian—peoples (e.g., 1931c). What limited Mead's work was not fully understanding that the researcher's relationship to power and property can influence the scholarly perceptions of a people.

Even as she struggled against racism, Mead in turn was influenced by it. Her principles on U.S. racial problems were frequently absent in her day-to-day life. Bettylou Valentine recalls attending an official reception for Mead in Seattle around 1960, in which Mead's insensitivity to her as the only African-American present came through. "We [graduate students at the University of Washington] were all sitting on the floor at her feet in the houseboat belonging to the department chair while she sat on the sofa talking to us . . . suddenly she commented that American blacks had no self-esteem, pride, or knowledge about how to present themselves in contrast to West Indians, who did. . . . I was stunned and hurt—even more so, because she and the others acted as though her having said this in my presence was nothing unusual (B. Valentine, 1989).

Some years later Mead expressed class bias in another form with a stunning repudiation of inner-city ways of life. Because the communities in question continue to be made up predominantly of people of color, this was also a statement of racism and was made in response to a proposal by C. A. Valentine (1968:173–89; 1969) for testing hypotheses such as the "culture of poverty" by doing extended ethnography while living among oppressed peoples in U.S. cities. Mead said that such a study could not be done. "Valentine's plea for participatory research suffers from a false premise. The anthropologist who lives with a primitive people adds his respect for their way of life to that of the people he studies. The poverty version of a modern culture contains many elements which require repudiation rather than respect; shared repudiation becomes inevitably partisan and requires involvement, an application of anthropology rather than pure research. Where primitive people's dignity is enhanced by objective research, "the poor" often feel further demeaned" (Mead, 1969b:194).

In fact, the planned study was carried out, and the researchers felt they had no trouble maintaining respect for their neighbors through the years (C.A. Valentine, 1990). Results of this work are available in B. Valentine (1978). But Mead's position then was in opposition to what she would later write about doing fieldwork. "Some of the field workers of the 1950s . . . seem to have mixed the demands for good interracial behavior at home with some imaginary demand that one should like, or even love, the people who are subjects of anthropological inquiry" (Mead, 1970:324).

Nevertheless, Jessie Campbell, an African-American activist with the National Negro Youth Congress who helped to desegregate the Young Women's Christian Association, remembers Mead as a model not merely for women, but especially for those women struggling for equality. "In 1938, at the request of some women from the 'black' YWCA in Brooklyn, Mead gave a lecture on the need for racial integration in the northeast and New England to a packed house at the 'white' Y on Third Avenue. When a person from the audience asked her how could she talk that way about New England—especially in view of its role as the cradle of democracy—Mead said, 'Some rocky cradle!' I never forgot the question or her answer.'' (Campbell, 1987).

Eric Wolf remembers Mead playing a similar civic role when he was a student. ''When I was at Virginia, we invited her to come down and lecture, and she gave one of those Margaret Meadian lectures where she insulted the audience about their racism, but in a way that only *she* could do. . . . That admirable quality was one side to the person. But that same talent could also be used in a different way [for] a different cause'' (Wolf, 1987). And who could fault her brilliant concluding remarks in the jointly developed analysis of the relationship between science and the concept of race? ''As long as genetic markers—pigmentation, hair form, facial configuration—are used to identify, stigmatize, or glorify certain portions of the population in ways that give them differential access to education, to economic resources, and to deference, the biological knowledge of the inheritance and significance of such characteristics will be socially and politically important'' (Mead et al., 1968:169).

This clearly stated and cogent linkage of the relationship between physique and access to resources demonstrates the kind of leadership of which Mead was capable. Her demonstrated commitment to the merger of anthropology and civic life away from ''the field,'' which she would one day take to a series of popular articles in *Redbook* magazine, was present early in her career. Letters from African-American civil rights leaders such as Martin Luther King, Jr. (1965) and W. E. B. DuBois (1947) also reveal the respect she commanded for her perceived role as a scientist with responsible positions on race.

Contradictions in the Field Overseas

Mead's contradictory legacy can be seen in her approach to the use of the words "primitive" versus "savage." In another autobiographical essay, she maintained that she used the term "primitive" by choice; her discussion reflects an obvious sensitivity to criticism that she had likely received on the sociological meaning of those words and her usage of them (Gordan, 1976:15). Yet, she used the term "savage" long after it was not considered good form to do so, in a film review of *Dead Birds* (Mead, 1964b). Above all else, she utilized key words such as "sorcerers" (1934), "savage," "cannibal," "headhunter," "native," which triggered specific responses in the reader and helped to define her as a scholar-adventurer. Even when writing about the United States, Mead summoned those words gratuitously as comparative markers for effect (1971:8–9, 215).

William Arens (1987) notes that Mead's relationship to Melanesian people was ensconced within an "I was there" syndrome. This syndrome created danger, thrill, and excitement in the field situation. Just being in a country fraught with danger maximizes the interest in the subsequently published work to come from such an experience. What could be more dangerous to the researcher than to live among cannibals and headhunters? Mead is the one who "becomes the first of a long line of anthropologists to live among people eaters, but never get eaten" (Arens, 1979:97). In addition, in *Sex and Temperament in Three Primitive Societies,* Mead (1935b) compensates for the fact that she never witnessed cannibalism by writing about this presumed past custom in the present tense. For Arens (1987), *Sex and Temperament* is the first popularization in the United States of cannibalism theory. And in 1953, while in Manus, she explained to Foerstel that people do not want to hear about a place that is safe; she must tell them about the crocodiles in the river that make life in the New Guinea field situation treacherous. She was to later describe that 25th reunion at Manus and comment on how the "salt water" Manusians had influenced "cannibal landspeople" (Mead 1954:68).

In his classic critique of Mead's methodology, Peter Worsley (1957) was to ponder the fact that the American and British reading public was introduced to anthropology almost exclusively through Mead's ethnographies of the Pacific. Worsley refers to Mead's work as the "rustling-of-the-wind-in-the-palm-trees" school of anthropology, and maintains the British anthropologists felt she had exploited an unscientific interest in sex.[2] Moreover, she ignored the repression and the impact of colonialism on the Mundugumor, and chose to describe the consequences of oppression as examples of internally generated cultural forms. Hutchinson remembers primarily the sage comments that Mead made in her private reflections of fieldwork. Mead "used to say, 'Decide who the intellectuals are in a group and go towards them for the data, even though they may not be formally such, and that's where you will get your best information' " (1988).

During the period from 1931 to 1933, when she did research on the Mundugumor for her *Sex and Temperament in Three Primitive Societies* (Mead, 1935b, 1963), she was to continue the sensationalist descriptions of where she was in a letter dated 1932 from the Kinakaten, Yuat River near the Sepik (Mead, 1970:312), maintaining that she had seen "mosquitoes, crocodiles, cannibals, and floating corpses." In the same letter, she suggests a dislike for all Melanesians, leaving the reader to ponder why she would select it for inclusion in a book about women in the field. "The natives are superficially agreeable, but we suspect them of being Melanesians nonetheless, with all the Melanesians' natural nastiness. They go in for cannibalism, headhunting, infanticide, incest, avoidance and joking relationships, adultery, and biting lice in half with their teeth. Also their language is simply ridiculously easy—has hardly any grammar at all. *I've hardly had to try to learn it, it's so simple*" [emphasis added].

Mead (1970:294) maintained that she had learned Melanesian languages, but she asserted that "after weeks of speaking and writing and thinking in a native language," coming back to English was almost physically wrenching.

Most linguists will surely question Mead's indirect contention that there is a relationship between the material production of a particular culture and the grammar of the language spoken in that culture. The grammars of languages spoken in many small, kin-based societies are often quite complex. The part of speech that reflects the material condition of a society (that is, how many things a culture produces) is the lexicon or vocabulary. And the ethnographer who reads, speaks, writes, and thinks in more than one language rarely has difficulties returning to the mother tongue, especially if second or other languages are learned in adulthood.

Howard (1984:207) asserts that few of Mead's supporters would make a claim that Mead knew Melanesian languages well. Leopold Pospisil (1987) remembers Mead as a brilliant woman who, however, would not have gotten a Ph.D. had she been his doctoral student precisely because she spoke no Pacific language. Pospisil asserts that after only several weeks among the Tchambuli, Mead could only write "creative speculation" and he reinforces Worsley's contention that her "irrelevant atmospherics" and "vague-ness of the information" were often more science fiction than science fact.

Mead's contradictory legacy is again visible in two articles about the importance of language in the field situa-tion, articles which belie her subsequent compilation of memories from the field cited above. In *Talk Boy,* Mead (1931e) authoritatively described the contact language—Pidgin English, now called Tok Pisin—using herself what today is disparagingly referred to as "Tok Masta." That is, she converted the orthography and discourse of this Papua New Guinean language to English in order to address the foreign reader. She would later justify that practice in the appendix of *Letters from the Field* as being necessary "in order to make certain words and phrases more easily intel-ligible to speakers of English" (1977:325–26). Yet, she missed the generative source of Tok Pisin as being from within the Melanesian population, the proof of which is that Tok Pisin is the lingua franca of Papua New Guinea and its fastest growing language. That "boy" as a term for Papua New Guinean laborer demonstrates the still-existing need to decolonize the lingua franca has been argued in current work (Gilliam, 1984). Mead used this linguistic manifestation of racialism in many of her analyses. "The little bush monkey [*manki* is accepted contemporary usage for a Papua New Guinean male child] naked except for his loin cloth, with pierced septum and ear lobe and scarified back, is sophisticated in the ways of the white man, far beyond the sophistication of many European peasants" (1931e:147).

If Mead's earlier work contributed to a "perennially primitive" image of Pacific peoples, it provoked sometimes quite thoughtful and insightful critiques by those close to her. *Male and Female* (1949) is a case in point. Gregory Bateson's criticism of this work is perhaps the most important coming as it does from a former husband and renowned colleague. "I'm afraid I gagged on the first sentence of "Male and Female" . . . so many implicit value premises. . . . If bluntly put, it could read, 'I say you *shall* think about your sexuality and this is how' " (Bateson, 1949). G. Evelyn Hutchinson, noted ecological biologist, saw this work in another way, namely that one of its contributions was to suggest that the background against which Western culture developed might be illuminated by anthropology of the right kind.[3] And as much as any other scientist of her day, Mead *did* continue the Boasian struggle to elucidate, as Hutchinson (1950) says, that what seems to be biology turns out to be learning.

Anthropology as Intelligence: Mead Joins the War Effort

Perhaps no other aspect of Mead's intellectual life is more fraught with contradictions than her relationship to the U.S. armed forces and the military goals of her country. This is divided between that which has been called "the war effort" of World War II, and the post-war era, starting from the period in which she assumed the position of director of the government-aided research under a navy contract at Columbia University. This was the position previously held by Ruth Benedict until her death in 1948. And according to George C. Foster, "Nobody played a more important role than Margaret Mead in selling anthropology to the government" (Howard, 1984:135). Among others, Mead, Bateson, and Benedict were all involved in intelligence activities during World War II, committed to defeat of the Nazis.

The "war" for Pacific peoples did not, however, begin with World War II. Colonialism was a burden for all Pacific peoples in the nineteenth century and was consolidated at the turn of the century when the United States upheld the principle of external domination upon annexing Hawaii in 1898 and assuming control of the Philippines in 1899. As a result of winning the Spanish American War, the United States had dramatically increased its access to trade routes and commerce in the South Pacific.

From 1899 to 1951, American Samoa was administered by the U.S. Navy. Thus, the Samoan people through their "high chiefs," relinquished their sovereign authority to the United States and became a subject people ruled by naval captains.

Margaret Mead's close involvement with the American military in the Pacific began in 1925, when the U.S. Navy's cooperation simplified and aided her investigations and fieldwork in Samoa. Her positive experience with the navy led her, in an article entitled "Civil Government for Samoa" (Mead, 1931a:227–228), to characterize the navy's rule over American Samoa as being "wise and discriminating . . . without financial axes to grind," and as assisting the Samoan people to develop a more prosperous economy, good health care, and improved education. Many Samoans also hoped to remove the yoke of colonialism by opting for U.S. citizenship, assuming they could thus acquire the same civil rights as Americans (U.S. Congress, 1934).

In 1929, an American Samoan Commission was formed, subsequently resulting in a bill presented by Senator Hiram Bingham, which proposed that the people of American Samoa be granted dual citizenship. Bingham described unrest in American Samoa and the inability of the people to get "a square deal." He stated in his presentation to the

House of Representatives on May 21, 1932, that Samoan rights were only what had been granted by the Navy Department. He characterized the navy as despotic, explaining that the navy made and repealed the laws at will, often abusing their power. Bingham feared that unless the people were given suffrage, there would be a violent uprising, and he stated, "It is a situation which contains a certain amount of dynamite" (U.S. Congress, 1934).

Bingham's bill recommended a reasonable measure of self government for the Samoan people, but it is important to note that the governor of Samoa was to be appointed by the president of the United States, not by the Samoan people. Many Americans saw this bill as a form of benevolent colonialism, and Margaret Mead responded positively to it, considering it a guarantee to the Samoan people that their good fortune under American control would continue. In a letter to journalist Walter Lippmann, Mead asked him to support the bill stating, "I am very much interested in this unique example of successful colonial administration and its preservation" (Mead, 1931b).

Mead thus did not see colonialism as a form of warfare. Mead's belief in the rightness and duty of anthropologists to have a permanent impact on the people they study is woven through her relationship with Pacific peoples. Her determination to have a lasting impact on the development choices and cultural influences of the Manus can be exemplified by her analysis in the film, *Margaret Mead's New Guinea Journal* (1968): The U.S. military occupation of the New Guinea base in Manus was the catalyst for "modernization" and "a civilized way of life" for the people of Pere (formerly Peri). How sad that "the war should fade away." There is no commentary in this film that suggests that she could *see* the effects of the military operations in the

Pacific—namely the destroyed villages, trees, and community life.

Perhaps the most unscientific, yet brilliant, example of negative exotification of Melanesian people occurs in an article that Mead confessed to friends and colleagues in letters she was not initially enthusiastic about writing—an article for the *New York Times* entitled "Not Headhunters, Nor Appeasers, but *Men*" (1941). In this attack on both Nazi storm troopers (headhunters) and United States pacifists (appeasers) the just cause of fighting Nazis reinforces a social distance by the description of another people. "If the New Guinea headhunter, a bone through his nose and a fiendish fighting joy in his eye, and the Storm Trooper gone to War have the same motivation—well, what about this civilization we thought we'd built, that we still hope to build?" (Mead, 1941). In an earlier letter to Lester Markel of *The New York Times*, Mead stated clearly that she primarily wanted to write essays that could have "positive constructive relevance to the present international situation." In other correspondence to him, she maintained to Markel that the vernacular title of her paper could be "He-men, She-men and *men*." But Markel's original request could have led her to challenge the very definitions of "primitive" and "civilized" that Western cultures were then using. "How, then does behavior in tribal states, such as that you have encountered in Bali and New Guinea, contrast with our civilization and the sort of thing that is going on in Germany today? Have we really advanced? If so, how? And can we hold that advance—or is this thing we call civilization a pretty precarious affair, and is the return to the primitive inevitable?" (Markel, 1941).

Though Mead *was* confronting the definition of "civilization" by boldly calling a Western culture primitive, her limitation was in inventing a description of New Guineans without any thought to the consequences this would have for them. Mead's contradictory concepts about Pacific peoples can be seen in her simultaneous call for social change and preservation of cultures. "The yeast of change, brought in by former work boys, by half castes, by all of the hundred and one subtle impacts of Western civilization, will work among them" (1943b:196). The "work boys" were often recruited in the colonial custom of "blackbirding" wherein Melanesian men were forcibly taken to work on plantations, some never to return. Colonial management of labor in New Guinea and how that would affect kinship and social structure was not one of the questions Mead covered in her work.

But in addressing those Americans who supported the right of self-determination for the Solomon Islands people, Mead asserted that autonomy for Pacific peoples was untenable. "In some quarters in America today we hear talk of the right of self-determination of the Solomon Islands, a suggestion which utterly ignores the absence in this entire region of any political form capable of integrating more than a thousand people. Ideas which have flourished in a period of nationalism now already archaic are ludicrously inappropriate when applied to these cultures of 300, 500, 700 members. Preparation for a degree of political maturity in which they could act as wider groups would be a long and tedious and exceedingly expensive process" (Mead, 1943b:193–194).

She was to make a similar assertion to renowned African-American writer James Baldwin 28 years later, *after* her return to New Guinea in 1953, and the publication of *New Lives for Old* in 1956, affirming that "New Guinea had no kingdoms and no great traditions . . . [and] couldn't hold more than five hundred people together politically" (Mead and Baldwin, 1971:21). Thus, her original views did not evolve over time. During wartime, Mead discussed how the islands could even help the world to see the potential of the field of anthropology in colonial administration. "If these small, isolated cultures were used as training schools for the future international civil servants . . . whose professional competency must depend upon their understanding of cultures . . . [these people] would be contributing to the world the costs of *protecting them from each other* and providing them with a gradual supply of materials for adjustment" (Mead, 1943b:195); emphasis added). In his response to Mead's contentions in this article, Whiting points out the missing element in Mead's concern for "these isolated groups"—acculturation—and wonders whether Mead would prevent the type of cultural changes that are introduced into societies by contact with other groups. Whiting was more preoccupied with the administration of processes of change and how anthropologists "can advise those who will be responsible for organizing the world after the war" (Whiting, 1943:196).

In many ways, these two perspectives represent simultaneously the distinction and unity between Yale University and Columbia during World War II and even for scholarship in the United States. A perusal of the Yale college newspapers during this period demonstrates that higher education was totally marshalled for the "war effort," with 281 colleges named by the government to participate (*Yale Daily News,* 1942, 1943b). Graduate schools across the country transformed their curriculum in order to become centers of training in "international" or "overseas" administration to prepare men to help reconstruct wartorn lands. Student residences were used as barracks, and college credit was granted for work in the armed forces. Furthermore, foreign area studies and internationally focused education emerged within this context. "The purpose of [foreign area studies] is to give those entering upon active service abroad a practical knowledge of the languages, people, customs, economic and social conditions . . . of the countries in which it is expected the Armed Forces and civil agencies will come into contact both during and after the war" (*Yale Daily News* 1943a). As Winks (1987a) demonstrates, Yale as an institution was critical to the formation of the Office of Strategic Services (OSS), the forerunner to the Central Intelligence Agency (CIA). The "OSS really formulated area studies, which got more legitimacy after the war" (Winks, 1987b). The development of interdisciplinary approaches to gaining "cross-cultural" expertise was justified for strategic reasons. In February 1949, Yale, Harvard, and the universities of Pennsylvania, Oklahoma, and Washington joined together to form the initial Human Relations Area File (HRAF) (Ford, 1969). For Murdock, the HRAF represented a "cross-cultural" indexing of many of the cultures in the world. "After the entry of the United States into World War II, the Cross-Cultural Survey concentrated its efforts largely on areas of probable combat operations, especially in the Pacific . . . it assembled considerable information which proved useful to national war agencies. In addition, from materials in its Files it published a series of seven *Strategic Bulletins of Oceania* on such subjects as meteorology, food and water supply, and the distribution of diseases" (Murdock et al., 1961:xiii). Murdock, as one of the leaders in the organization of the HRAF and its Cross-Cultural Survey, perceived anthropology's purpose as inextricably bound to potential military application. While giving a history of the HRAF at a meeting in 1942,

Murdock was to relate how the Strategic Index grew out of the Cross-Cultural Survey. "When the Second World War began, the question arose as to how the Cross-Cultural Survey could prove practical and useful. We determined, therefore, that during the period of the war, we could concentrate on those areas where material assembled by us would be of most value. We decided to work primarily on the Pacific Area. . . . We have not practically completed work on the Marshall Islands and have made a good start on other island groups. . . . Work is likewise being done on Melanesia" (Murdock, 1942). Thus, social science discourse and terminology often masked the military potential of studies that were often labeled cross-cultural, intercultural, transcultural, and concerned with group or human relations (e.g., Mead, 1959). In his memories of the period, Yale professor Irving Rouse (1987) points out that "the three Yale Pacific specialists were anthropologists Murdock, Clellan Ford, and John Whiting—all officers in the Navy."

Yale and Columbia faculty had little regard for each other and were really "two different tribes" (Wolf, 1987), but both schools were involved in development of materials for war. If Yale had the Cross-Cultural Survey and the HRAF, Columbia developed the "national character" and subsequently the "Culture and Personality" methodologies, all of which were framed within the model of social control of potentially hostile populations in a post-war era. The continuing power of Freud in Mead's analysis became an instrument in the consolidation of the Culture and Personality school. It is what led Mead (1943a, 1947) to influence greatly the developments in the field of psychiatry and psychology, and to especially link the study of war psychology to anthropology.

Reflecting on Mead's Freudianism, Hall and Lindzey (1954:171) wrote that "the Columbia University Research in Contemporary Cultures described by Mead (1951a) is perhaps the most ambitious present day attempt at the interdisciplinary application of psychoanalytic theory to cross-cultural data." The themes and orientation of this school of thought were to persist in Mead's preoccupations long after the war was over.

Thus, World War II had posed international problems, which Mead thought anthropologists could help solve in the interest of the Allied Powers. In 1940, the creation of the National Character research program served the war effort. Mead explained, "It was of considerable military importance to know to just what extent the behavior of an U.S.-born Japanese can provide any clues whatsoever to the behavior of a Japanese soldier, to his special strengths and weaknesses" (Mead, 1943a:139). Her emphasis on studying Japanese-American civilians later led to research on other U.S. immigrants. Mead's rationalization of national character studies demonstrates the relationship between this methodology and militarism. "The study of national character by anthropological methods can throw much light upon problems of immediate military importance in both direct and psychological warfare, contribute to the establishment of smoother cooperation with allied nations, and prepare personnel for problems of relief, reconstruction and world reorganization after the war" (Mead, 1943a:137).

Although it is in the union of psychology and anthropology that Mead's war effort merges with her study of culture and war, she avoided the important struggles *within* the United States during the war. For example, in spite of apparently disagreeing with the internment of Japanese-Americans during World War II in the United States, she never took a public stand against this racist policy (Mabee, 1987). And years later, in response to Baldwin, she would remark that Japanese-Americans "weren't interned in Hawaii, where they were far more dangerous" (Mead and Baldwin, 1971:56). Why Americans of Japanese descent were "more dangerous" in Hawaii, she never said. She told an uncustomarily adulatory Baldwin that she had no responsibility for the atom bomb, for had she been asked, she would have advised against dropping it on Japan (Mead and Baldwin). But in her 1942 paean to war, which is sometimes viewed as a study of "American national character," she *did* call for bombing Japan, using the racial epithet of the times. "We may not win the battle—that will depend on transport and on material and numbers of men—but we can take the initiative, bomb Tokyo rather than wait for the Jap to bomb San Francisco (Mead, 1971:160). Following Mead into the study of National Character was Ruth Benedict, who joined the Office of War Information in 1942. Her research, like Mead's, would be used for psychological warfare.

In Gregory Bateson's case, his OSS role in helping the Allied Forces use anthropology in war psychology against the Japanese came to trouble him. In his application for retirement from government service, Bateson was to one day note that the main reason for leaving the OSS was simply that the war had ended (Bateson, 1967). In the letter to Mead (August 28, 1949), he reflected how not only "we worked ourselves into a dislike of the 'Japs' and Germans" but he also mourns Mead's continuing "commitment to 'good works' and militarism." As Mabee (1987:8) notes, "Even though both Mead and Bateson were disturbed by the use of deceit in psychological warfare, Mead was not as upset by it as Bateson was. . . . These differences between them were reflected in the breakup of their marriage just after the war." Hutchinson (1987) also remembered political arguments between the two when they visited his home in Connecticut during this period. The passion with which Bateson (1946) would attempt to come to terms with his role in the OSS in light of the nuclear destruction at war's end is perhaps best exemplified by a letter to *The New York Times,* in which he ponders the "relation between the new techniques of destructive warfare and life insurance" [for his daughter].

The type of work that the U.S. army perceived Mead would do comes in an OSS memorandum dated January 31, 1944, from Major Harley C. Stevens to Edgar Salinger on Japanese propaganda, and was declassified in July, 1985. "On the subject of 'evil omens' which could be incorporated in our propaganda . . . I suggest concocting stories . . . [about] unheard-of colors in . . . rice fields . . . monstrosities . . . tremendous increase in . . . men and women who have been bewitched . . . anger of the gods . . . it would be well to consult any of our anthropologists, such as Mr. Embrey [*sic*] or Margaret Mead" (Stevens, 1944:29). Knowledge about peoples and their cultures in this context could not be other than strategic. One year after the explosions at Hiroshima and Nagasaki, the United States executed its first nuclear test in the Marshall Islands. As Winks points out, Murdock worked with other Yale staff to combine "knowledge to produce short case studies on how best to get Polynesians to cooperate with the military on, for example, building an airfield on an atoll" (Winks, 1987a:47). Thus, the cooperation between the social sciences and the military during the war made it possible for a new kind of research to emerge afterwards.

Mead (1947) would justify this type of work and continue "the application of anthropological techniques to cross-national communication" after the war ended. Mead's work in the Pacific was partly framed by her perception of the region as a "laboratory . . . in the study of cultural evolution" (Mead, 1957). Another reason was to assist in the continuing occupation and the training of armed forces and civil "personnel for international cross-cultural service" (Mead, 1959). Both Dillon (1980) and Yans-McLaughlin (1986:213) suggest that the reality of the atomic bomb greatly affected Mead's commitment within anthropology.

The work on psychological warfare during World War II was transferred to the cold war, focused instead on Eastern Europe and the socialist countries. As noted before, Mead's enemies during World War II were German Nazis *and* United States pacifists. After the war, this focus was modified to include pacifists and communists, with organized labor a central component of the "pacifists." In 1957, at a meeting of the Danish subcommittee of the World Federation for Mental Health and the Executive Board on Mental Health Aspects of the Peaceful Uses of Atomic Energy in Copenhagen, she revealed her total preoccupation with defeating antinuclear elements at home. The "trade unions are conducting a violent campaign against the dangers of building an atomic reactor," she argued, and she described this as a result of "negative" or "subterranean irrational propaganda" put out by "political groups, either Pacifist or Communist . . . in the Western world agitating against test explosions" (World Federation for Mental Health, 1957). In addition, in describing U.S. citizens' fear of nuclear contamination, she cited a newspaper article about a man who was reported to have been exposed to radiation, calling it an example of this propaganda. In her presentation in Copenhagen, her lack of knowledge about radiation exposure was undoubtedly shared by many atomic experts at the time. "The man himself was advised to change all his clothes and to have his family all bathe and change their clothes, so the newspaper said. They then got a rumor round the neighborhood that the whole family were contaminated and the house was contaminated . . . the family . . . could not sell the house . . . none would sit next to the children in school . . . and there was a type of definite hysterical response that ran throughout the community. . . . I am quite certain each detail of this is wrong, and you could say that nothing could happen to an individual that would make them at least as contagious as this" (World Federation for Mental Health, 1957). Hence, Mead's views seemed to cast any concern about testing in the Pacific as being against the national interests of the United States.

Yet, Mead's public posture was as a steadfast opponent of nuclear war. In 1960, she was instrumental "in the American Association for the Advancement of Science in shaping a public manifesto insisting that all scientists, including social scientists, must warn the public of dangers that their competence as scientists enables them to see" (Mabee, 1987:10). In a comparative study of the different cultural characteristics pertaining to war, she wrote about the necessity of controlling violence and preventing nuclear war (Mead, 1968:227). But the government's orientation of psychological warfare remained the same as during the war.

The task of psychological warfare is to present policy as persuasively as possible to the audience for which it was intended with the goal of bringing about changed behavior in that audience. Policy may be diplomatic, economic or ideological as well as military. The audience may be Home, Allies, Neutrals or Enemy. . . . An understanding of different cultural groups' social perceptions and organizational structure should contribute insight into their vulnerability to disruption. Knowledge of a group's concept of authority and responsibility and its members' sensitivity to expression fear and aggression are for example, vital to an understanding of such susceptibility. (Page, 1951:1)

The Navy's Report lists scholars from universities throughout the country who cooperated with the project, including Mead, and explicitly mentions the HRAF.

Mead may have had second thoughts about her significant contributions to psychological warfare. A direct continuum between Mead's focus on the South Pacific islands and their use as experiments in understanding social change had become militarized. In conceptualizing Pacific peoples as her laboratories, Mead (1956:38) established a paradigm for an analysis of Pacific peoples that was adopted by the U.S. military in order to control and manipulate leadership towards a specific and desired direction.

For example, in 1965, the "Conference on Behavioral Science Research in New Guinea," like numerous other conferences involving anthropological research, was supported by a grant from the Army Research Office. This particular conference focused on changes taking place in New Guinea, which the participants felt was "greater than any other area on the earth" (National Research Council, 1967:5). It is difficult to imagine that these conference participants did not take this concept directly from *New Lives for Old*. "They [the Titan Manus] know that I came back because I had heard that they had changed more remarkably and more drastically than any other of the peoples of the Pacific" (Mead, 1956:34). Hence, as the conference participants stated, "New Guinea therefore represented a good laboratory for studying the processes of social and cultural change and development" (National Research Council, 1967:5). Among the themes suggested for further research was the political development under way in New Guinea. "Studies of leaders and their exercise of leadership roles in the introduction of change" were proposed. With reference to New Guinea it was noted, "Such cultures tend to have a life of their own, producing changes, but often not those changes desired by Europeans." So-called cult movements were given as one example of "undesirable" change. Conference participants agreed that "the psychological processes involved in such cults, the reduction of dissonance between cultural features, the degree of felt participation and felt peer-group support, all need study" (National Research Council, 1967:39). The recommendation for the study of cult movements was in reality an expression of Western desire to mold indigenous movements that defied colonial rule. Such movements were in fact a threat to colonialism because they comprised a unique cultural pattern for protest, not easily decoded and therefore more difficult to control.

Mead and the Ethics Question

From a struggle against the Nazis during World War II, Mead gradually began working with the Office of Navy Research as a cold war intellectual. In part, what transforms Mead's scholarship after the war is the quandary that affected many United States intellectuals of the period and since: the question of the nuclear reality. Participation in government research as a cold war scholar changed the definition of the work she did to "applied anthropology," an epiphenomenon that she would later defend, affirming that most of the anthropologists of her era worked with the government during World War II (Mead, 1979:431).

As Mead moved inexorably closer to the government's positions, it is the issue of space exploration that put her closer to the military and its objectives in the social sciences. A project initiated by the research center she helped to found, the Institute for Intercultural Studies, began as a study of "man in space" (Mead et al., 1958). Four years later, Mead would attend a meeting at Air Force Systems Command that not only reflected a transformation of the theme to "military man in space," but, as revealed in the minutes of that meeting written by Colonel Ray Sleeper, demonstrated a concern about affecting the ideas and beliefs of U.S. citizens. Discussion along such lines as "how to break the phrase *space is for peaceful purposes*," "tackling this problem in gaining American acceptance of military mission in space," and "should we identify the '10 most-wanted men' in the Government who are blocking adequate military space programs" predominated (Sleeper, 1962). That Mead apparently envisioned no contradiction between militarizing space and being against nuclear war is the conclusion reached in assessing these documents. Moreover, she took a militarist or progovernment position on the Peace and Disarmament Resolution that was of concern to the American Anthropological Association at this time. "One of the very serious misunderstanding[s] that exists in our search for new forms of national protection is the persistent mistrust with which many liberals view all members of the military. It ill-behooves those social scientists who are working on military problems to aggravate this distrust in any way" (Mead, 1962).

Undoubtedly a friendship with Sleeper was an element

in the consolidation of this direction. In the latter part of Mead's life, she would write a related document in which it appeared that she was indeed attempting to represent that single planetary community. "At this conference we are proposing that, before there is a corresponding attempt to develop a 'law of the air,' the scientific community advises the United Nations (and individual, powerful nation-states and aggregations of weaker states) and attempt to arrive at some overview of what is presently known about hazards to the atmosphere from man-made interventions, and how scientific knowledge coupled with intelligent action can protect the peoples of the world" (Mead and Kellogg, 1977). But in the same written proceedings is an appendix written by Sleeper within the cognitive constraints of the cold war, which begins by defining *air control*. "In 1952, in the Air War College at Maxwell Field near Montgomery, Alabama, a study of 'air control' was begun. . . . It was a British concept which stated that aircraft, through the control of the air, could affect the behavior of people on the earth. . . . The study drew on research just completed at the Harvard Research Center under Dr. Kluckhohn, a social anthropologist of considerable renown, which had developed a 'working' model of the Soviet air control system" (Sleeper, 1977:125). Thus, more than one social scientist maintained a close association with military concerns after the war (Wiener, 1989). Kluckhohn had in fact been in charge of an intelligence unit in the Pacific during World War II (O'Connell, 1989; dissertation in progress).

Moreover, during the period of nuclear testing in the Pacific, Mead did not once demonstrate that she identified with Pacific peoples, as some were shifted from island to island in the wake of radiation poisoning and contamination of their home regions.

Mead's allegiance to military goals became explicit in the debate in the American Anthropological Association's (AAA) response to the war in Vietnam. In 1966, David Aberle and Kathleen Gough introduced a resolution at the AAA's business meeting that condemned the use of napalm and other antipersonnel weapons by U.S. forces in that war. The chairperson, Frederica de Laguna, ruled the resolution out of order, "and de Laguna and Mead spoke vigorously against introducing it, on the grounds that political resolutions did not advance the science of anthropology" and were not in the interests of anthropologists (Gough, 1990). The chair, however, was voted out of order when Michael Harner rose to state, "Genocide is not in the professional interests of anthropologists," and the "resolution was presented, amended, and passed" (Berreman, 1981:30).

As Mead's peers sought to identify with human welfare everywhere, they also became more sensitive to the fact that anthropologists were the ones making the decisions for villagers on what studies were to be made. The AAA's statement on problems of anthropological research and ethics (adopted in 1967 and amended in 1976) clearly affirmed: "Anthropologists should not lend themselves to clandestine activities. . . . Constraint, deception, and secrecy have no place in science. Actions which compromise the intellectual integrity and autonomy of research scholars and institutions not only weaken those international understandings essential to our discipline, but in so doing they also threaten any contribution anthropology might make to our society and to the general interest of human welfare" (*Professional Ethics,* 1967). Yet in 1967, Mead herself moved a resolution at the annual meeting of U.S. anthropologists that is germane to the call from Pacific people concerning a nuclear-free Pacific. "Reaffirming our 1961 resolution, we condemn the use of napalm, the torture and killing of prisoners of war and political prisoners, and the intentional or deliberate policies of genocide or forced transportation of populations for the purpose of terminating their cultural and/or genetic heritages by anyone anywhere" (Weaver, 1973:44). In view of her equivocal public stance on such issues, Mead's occasional support for them represents an uneven commitment. The consolidation of Mead's pro-military positions was brought to the fore in 1970, when an article questioning the ethical behavior of anthropologists appeared in *The New York Review of Books* (Wolf and Jorgensen, 1970). The commentary was stimulated in part by documents received from the Student Mobilization Committee to End the War in Vietnam, which contained information "detailing the involvement of social scientists at a dozen universities in a counterinsurgency program directed against revolution in Thailand" (*The Student Mobilizer*, 1970:1).

Eric Wolf, then chairman of the Ethics Committee of the AAA, and Joseph Jorgensen, a member of the committee, announced at one of the professional meetings that in Thailand, "anthropologists are being used in large programs of counterinsurgency. . . . These programs comprise efforts at the manipulation of people on a giant scale and intertwine straightforward anthropological research with overt and covert counterinsurgency" (Wolf and Jorgensen, 1970:26). The Executive Board of the AAA created an ad hoc committee to evaluate the judgments made by the Ethics Committee, and examined the surrounding controversy. Mead chaired this ad hoc committee and prepared a report that minimized the importance of the documents presented by the Student Mobilization Committee (SMC).

The "report warned that anthropological data should be safeguarded from use in warfare, but it exonerated civilian anthropologists of involvement in counterinsurgency" (Shenker, 1971:78). "The latter term—counterinsurgency—soon became the label under which funds were given, just as 'communication' and 'mental health' had been previously" (Davenport et al., 1971). In the past, Mead had openly acknowledged the possible military application of her work (Mead and Metraux, 1953:v). In retrospect, this adds another dimension to Mead's interest in "mental health." Mead seemed reassured by the fact that the organizations that hired the anthropologists, the Academic Advisory Council for Thailand (AACT) and the South East Asian Development Advisory Group, were backed by the United States Government and funded by the United States Agency for International Development.

Mead's report therefore concluded that the anthropologists had not engaged in any secret clandestine research and denounced the members of the Ethics Committee for unfair and unfounded accusations against their colleagues and the two organizations which hired them. In removing responsibility from AACT scholars, however, Mead came under attack from the AAA membership, which voted—at its 1971 meetings—to reject the committee's report (Klare, 1972:87; Shenker, 1971).

The SMC documents regarding AACT had indeed revealed that the organization was assisted by the Advanced Research Project Agency, an agency of the U.S. Defense Department and part of Project Agile, the Pentagon's worldwide counterinsurgency program. Similarly, the South East Asian Development Advisory Group, the other organization hiring anthropologists in Thailand, was shown to be the parent group for AACT, functioning as an appendage for AACT's counterinsurgency activities.

Thailand was used to establish headquarters for a U.S. Air Force base, employed not only against Vietnam but also for U.S. intervention in Indonesia. For the powerful Thai elite, having American military and economic support provided the weapons to quell the growing peasant insurgency. The U.S. policy was to create a counterinsurgent movement by providing aid to poor villagers, and a military force that would maintain a Thai regime compliant with U.S. interests. "U.S. strategic policies, bolstering military regimes, were, of course, contrary to the interests of the majority of Thai people—including workers, farmers, students, small shopkeepers, minor officials and professionals" (Girling, 1981). Contrasted with the impetus to protect those people who were working with anthropologists in an area of military contention was the propensity by some scholars to cooperate in counterinsurgency tactics against the Thai people they were studying. Speculating on how this could be, Wolf and Jorgensen suggested that "The researcher would get the chance to carry out field work with a heady sense of engagement in a global welfare operation, punctuated by occasional participation in an international meeting, followed by a dry martini at the airport bar in Bangkok or Dar es Salaam. . . . Many signed their contracts, unwittingly or otherwise, in return for fellowships, research grants, and jobs. Others more reticent, subcontracted"(Wolf and Jorgensen, 1970:26).

In a 1987 interview with Gilliam and Foerstel, Wolf stated that he believed that Mead had her mind made up before she started the investigation about the issue. "She thought we [Wolf and Jorgensen] had done the wrong thing. She said to me that anthropologists, in taking part in the protest of the 60s, were also doing the wrong thing. Instead of acting as advisors to people who made decisions, we were out there pounding on the pavement, and that was a stupid way to go about it." Wolf went on to surmise that Mead's convictions, while "one-dimensional" also "must have been part of her strength. I think she acted out of what she thought was right. . . . I think that she thought she knew what the score was and once she made up her mind, that was that." In response to a question about the possible intersection of foreign policy, anthropology, and intelligence work, Wolf suggested that many types of ethnographic information could serve that purpose. "This can range all the way from general information such as the study of the language a people speak, how they file their teeth, or carry a burden of x pounds, to that of a more specific nature such as where villages are located, what are possible lines of fire, to who the village headman is, and does he have a contact with China." And though he could not "verify it absolutely," he maintained that he had "it on fairly good authority that in a certain period, every proposal submitted to the National Science Foundation had to be submitted in 12 copies, one of which was sent to the Intelligence Agency." Wolf still thinks that his and Jorgensen's stand on ethics was not fully appreciated by fellow colleagues. For him it was "not very easy talking about the entire matter . . . everyone involved lost a lot of friends in the process" (Wolf, 1987).

Commenting on the same controversy, Delmos Jones came to the conclusion that the 1960s and 1970s represented a "sad period" in anthropology. "We exposed a problem, and then it was covered up. As a member of the Ethics Committee of the Society of Applied Anthropology, I wanted to point out that applied scientists who work for institutions of the state/or state institution within stratified societies are often working on behalf of stratification. I helped to revise the statement on Ethics which was sent to Mead. Her response to the document's preamble was to send a blistering letter stating that, 'Anthropologists do not oppress people' '' (Jones, 1987).

Anthropologists have been questioning the ethical standards of anthropological research since the early twentieth century. In 1917, Franz Boas received information that several anthropologists had engaged in espionage activities in Mexico while conducting ethnographic research. Boas was extremely disturbed by these revelations, and on October 16, 1919, he wrote a letter to *The Nation* under the title, "Scientists as Spies." He stated, "The point against which I wish to enter a vigorous protest is that a number of men who follow science as their profession, men whom I refuse to designate any longer as scientists, have prostituted science by using it as a cover for their activities as spies" (Boas, 1919). His letter created a bitter dispute within the AAA, eventually resulting in a vote of censure against Boas, removing him from office. It is perhaps an ironic reversal of history that 50 years later Mead, a devoted student of Boas, led the attack on two members of the ethics committee who had denounced the involvement of anthropologists in Thailand's counterinsurgency.

The debates in this era produced numerous articles and books covering ethics and anthropology. One of those that intimated a connection between methodology and ethics challenged Margaret Mead directly. "Margaret Mead's attempt to apply her positivist anthropological cultural relativism in the American Anthropological Association itself to justify the application of the cultural relative formula 'one anthropologist vs. ten guerrillas' in exotic Indochina proved unacceptable to that august body during the Thailand scandal, but the function of the theoretical patterns of Mead's cultural ideology, and that of her teachers and students, has proved much more culturally resistant both in the profession and among the public at large" (Frank, 1975:63). The Vietnam War, unlike World War II, forced social scientists to take a closer look at colonialism, and its effect on Third World cultures. Issues of poverty, injustice, and inequality could no longer be separated from the studies being conducted on Third World people. The Vietnam War was a turning point for American foreign policy, because it symbolized a demonstration of American willingness to counter any economic order which challenged its international hegemony. The war in Vietnam was also a symbol of the U.S. domestic conflict embodied in assuming that colonial mantle. Vietnam became the great symbol of containment, particularly against Asian communism.

The nineteenth-century philosophy of manifest destiny embraced an identity of U.S. people as a chosen people with the right to extend their society and institutions from the Atlantic to the Pacific coasts. A thesis of Hayes et al. (1987) is that after World War II the belief in manifest destiny was extended across the Pacific and especially into Southeast Asia.

Mead, like many anthropologists, confronted the problem of ethics in anthropological research. She saw applied anthropology as a field that "acts to change conditions in some way, either as commentators on the social scene, as an expert witness, or as a consultant to a government agency, a tribal council, or a voluntary association" (Mead, 1979:437). She stated, "Ethical problems revolved around the ways in which we reported our findings, respect and protection for individuals, caution in reporting practices which might bring individuals and communities into conflict with the laws of the superordinate colonial and colonizing powers, and the extent to which we should engage in struggles dictated by our knowledge of the culture and our human concern for the peoples whom we came to know better and differently than did other outsiders'' (428).

Although Mead's statement shows sensitivity to people under colonial rule, her major focus was on the ethical relationships between individuals. She suggests that subjects be treated as collaborators, stating that ''the position of those with whom an anthropologist works then becomes a highly important one, and one which at the present time in congruent with the demand that students, patients, and clients have more of a role in any activity in which they are involved, rather than continuing their past role as passive recipients on whose behalf power is delegated to the specialist practitioner'' (Mead, 1969a:371).

When Lenora Foerstel went with Margaret Mead to Manus in 1953, permission to study in Pere or M'Bunai was given by the colonial government. Permission by the villagers was not required or sought, and though the villagers asked why the anthropologists were there, they had no control over the nature or location of the research.

Moreover, Mead and Foerstel entered into the most private sectors of village life, photographing birth, death, conflict, political, and traditional events. Nothing the villagers did was off limits for investigation or perusal, and they never challenged the authority of Mead or Foerstel to question and observe them. This cannot be considered collaboration.

Conclusion

Margaret Mead's heritage has been a mixed one. On the one hand, her participation in U.S. culture as a Boasian scholar helped create a critical pathway in the struggle against racism and sexism, and for equality. Mead's work in Samoa led her to ask, "What is human nature?" She returned from Samoa with a conviction that human nature was not universal, inherent, and unalterable, but varied and highly adaptable. She helped to discredit behavioral theories based on race and biology, encouraging serious study of the influence of culture on human behavior. Mead offered U.S. citizens a consistent alternative to the prevailing biological determinism. She and her teacher/colleagues were critical participants in the defeat of the eugenics movement in the United States, a concept that had been an important component of the lapse into barbarism in Germany in the 1930s with the extermination of six million Jews and others deemed to be biologically unfit.

Mead maintained her reputation as a member of the antiracist community until the end of her life. "I remember the day I went to the Waldorf-Astoria Hotel to attend a fundraising event sponsored by Andrew Young [when he was Ambassador to the United Nations] for Morris Dees and the people in the Southern Poverty Law Center. I walked in and was pleased to see Margaret, at the center of it all" (Langer, 1990).[4] On the other hand, Mead's inability to link those domestic struggles to her ethnography of the Pacific contributed to an ahistorical representation of Pacific peoples. Margaret Mead did not set out to leave an academic heritage that would stereotype Pacific peoples when she initiated her career, but it is nonetheless a tenacious byproduct of her more popular works. Pacific students at tertiary institutions find that they have to read the so-called classics about themselves, written by Mead and others, in order to pass social science courses. The values of Mead's own culture inspired the belief system she used when she set to describe other peoples. Those values were constrained by the hegemonic role of the United States within the Pacific. And neither Mead nor most of the social scientists who have assessed her work looked at the socioeconomic situation of Samoa in relation to the other states in the region.

From a Pacific viewpoint then, Mead's intellectual heritage is an outgrowth of empire. Pacific societies are locked in a struggle with powerful foreigners, not merely in terms of the scholarship about them, but also over who will control the lands and waters of the Pacific region. The control of the Pacific was shaped by dropping the atom bomb on Hiroshima and Nagasaki. Moreover, the Pacific region has continually been the theater of experimentation with nuclear weaponry in order to prepare for permanent military and geopolitical preeminence. And, in part due to Mead's populist anthropology, many U.S. citizens still have a definition of "primitive" and "civilized" rooted in colonial ethos. That Mead saw Western societies as superior is evident in the fervor with which she sought to influence Manus people, encouraging them to copy as much of United States society as possible. Ted Schwartz, commented in the film *Taking Note* (1979), that Mead brought the Manus people "from the Stone Age into the present . . . [actually guiding] Pere's modernization."

Moreover, the work in "culture at a distance" and the "Culture and Personality" school of thought worked to reinforce the notion that the New American, the immigrant, could be suspect, as studies about that person could be used for psychological warfare in the country of origin. Stocking provocatively suggests that this school of thought became "in a sense the functional anthropological equivalent of 'race,' explaining the same sorts of (presumed) psychological uniformities in very different terms, as 'culture' took over the sphere of determinism that had been governed by 'race' " (Stocking, 1986:5).

Mead also retained her Freudian definitions of masculinity and femininity, which had been juxtaposed with an imperial interpretation of "national character." "Whether one's country is conceived as masculine, as in Germany, or feminine, as in France and Russia; whether men are more willing to fight to hold fast a boundary against invasion, or to maintain their right to sail the seas, or to uphold some abstract value like freedom threatened somewhere else in the world—these differences can all be shown to be systematic and explicable" (Mead, 1951a:85).

The more Mead became involved with psychoanalytic theory, the more removed she became from the greater variety of information needed for studying human behavior. For example, Mead ignored the impact of colonial history on the people she studied. Thus, she was unable to fully reject the role of individual biology in determining culture. Mead saw innovation as the product of superior individuals in response to their environment, and she concluded that "the actual combination of particular individuals must also be involved if the processes of cultural evolution are to be understood" (Mead, 1964a:230). The questions that she could have posed to the world were lost in her belief that "contact" meant modernization. How was custom affected by colonial rule? How were gender roles for women and men altered by the presence of foreign military?

For Mead, progress in the Pacific meant accepting "Westernization," regardless of how it was imposed. The effect of nuclear testing on Pacific people was not an issue considered by Mead or other Pacific specialists until quite recently, even though testing in the Pacific has long been part of the public record. By ignoring the devastating consequences of continued testing, the nuclear states have broken the moral commitment declared to the world during the Nuremberg trials after World War II, that experimentation on human beings does not reflect a truly civilized society.

Mead's deep commitment to Westernization and laissez-faire capitalism also influenced her uncritical support for the Vietnam War. In opposing Mead's position on the war, the members of the American Anthropological Association reaffirmed their pledge to protect the survival of all of the world's peoples and their cultures.

Although Mead gave the Western world a new sense of culture-consciousness, her uncritical assumption that U.S. society represented the cultural standards to which Pacific people must aspire prevented her from functioning as a credible advocate of cultural autonomy.

NOTES

1. Hurston, like Mead and the other women students of Boas at Columbia University, called him "Papa Franz." In connection with this paternal sobriquet, Boas, for whatever reason, once called Hurston a "misstep" (Hurston, 1971). For Louise Thompson Patterson, Hurston's colleague and associate, the unasked question was why Boas could go to scientific organizations for financial support for his other women protegés, yet felt it necessary to ask a "struggling" Carter G. Woodson (founder in the 1920s of the Association for the Study of Negro Life and History) for resources for Hurston (Patterson, 1990). Though Boas agreed to oversee Hurston's work, "Columbia University had no money for Hurston" (Hemenway, 1977:89), and "Woodson in fact donated $1,500 for Hurston's first data-gathering trip to the South" (Patterson, 1990).

2. Worsley informed the editors of this volume that he first heard this phrase from British anthropologist E. E. Evans-Pritchard.

3. Hutchinson was a friend of Gregory Bateson and his brother, since their childhood in England. They remained best friends through their undergraduate days, when they both joined the Biological Tea Club, which was founded by Joseph Omer-Cooper (see Lipset, 1980:103–5).

4. Marion Langer is Executive Director Emeritus of the American Orthopsychiatric Association, which in 1978 awarded Margaret Mead (who was on the board of directors) the first annual Blanche Ittelson Award. According to Langer, "Ortho" was primarily concerned with the ways in which the psyche interacted with the social environment, and as such was an interdisciplinary organization.

REFERENCES

American Museum of Natural History. 1978. Press release, November 15. Office of Public Affairs, New York.

Arens, W. 1979. *The Man-Eating Myth: Anthropology and Anthropophagy*. London: Oxford University Press.

———. 1987. Personal communication, October 11.

Barrett, S. 1984. *The Rebirth of Anthropological Theory*. Toronto: University of Toronto Press.

Barton, D. 1939. "Exploring Human Nature: How Margaret Mead Became One of the Foremost Women Explorers; Her Life Among Strange Brown People in the Pacific Islands; and How the 'Primitive Experiment' Revises Our Most Cherished Notions of Human Behavior." *Natural History* 64:246–56.

Bateson, G. 1946. "Protecting the Future." Letter to *The New York Times*, December 6.

———. 1949. Letter dated August 28. Papers in McHenry Library, University of California at Santa Cruz.

————. 1967. Papers in McHenry Library, University of California at Santa Cruz.

Benedict, R., and G. Weltfish. 1943. *The Races of Mankind.* Public Affairs Pamphlet no. 85. New York: Public Affairs Committee.

Berreman, G. 1981. *The Politics of Truth: Essays in Critical Anthropology.* Delhi, India: South Asian Publications.

Boas, F. 1901. "The Mind of Primitive Man." *The Journal of American Folklore* 14:1–11.

————. 1919. "Scientists as Spies." *The Nation* 109:797.

————. 1927. "Fallacies of Racial Inferiority." *Current History,* February 25, p. 681.

————. 1945. *Race and Democratic Society.* New York: St. Augustine.

Broun, H., and G. Britt. 1974. *Christians Only: A Study in Prejudice.* New York: Da Capo Press. Originally published 1931, New York: Vanguard Press.

Caffrey, M. 1989. *Stranger in This Land.* Austin: University of Texas Press.

Campbell, J. 1987. Personal communication.

Cassidy, R. 1982. *Margaret Mead: A Voice for the Century.* New York: Universe Books.

Davenport, W., D. Olmsted, M. Mead, and R. Freed. 1971. Report of the Ad Hoc Committee to evaluate the controversy concerning anthropological activity in relation to Thailand, to the Executive Board of the American Anthropological Association. September 27.

Dillon, W. 1980. "Margaret Mead and Government." *American Anthropologist* 82(2):319ff.

DuBois, W. E. B. 1947. Letter to Margaret Mead, September 16. Mead Papers, Library of Congress, Washington, D.C.

Ford, C. 1969. *Human Relations Area File 1949–1969: A Twenty-Year Report.* New Haven: Human Relations Area Files.

Frank, A. G. 1975. "Anthropology = Ideology; Applied Anthropology = Politics." *Race and Class* 17(1):57–68.

Freud, S. 1955. *The Interpretation of Dreams*. New York: Basic Books.

Fried, M. 1972. *The Study of Anthropology*. New York: Thomas Y. Crowell.

Gay, P. 1978. *Freud, Jews, and Other Germans*. London: Oxford University Press.

Gilliam, A. 1984. "Language and Development in Papua New Guinea." *Dialectical Anthropology* 8:303–18.

Girling, J. 1981. *Thailand: Society and Politics*. Ithaca, N.Y.: Cornell University Press.

Goldenberg, M. 1990. Personal communication, March 7.

Gordan, J. 1976. *Margaret Mead: The Complete Bibliography, 1925–1975*. The Hague: Mouton.

Gossett, T. F. 1963. *Race: The History of an Idea in America*. New York: Schocken.

Gough, K. 1990. Personal communication, April 7.

Grant, M. 1921. *The Passing of the Great Race*. New York: Charles Scribners.

Hall, C., and G. Lindzey. 1954. *Handbook of Social Psychology*. Cambridge, Mass.: Addison-Wesley.

Haraway, D. 1989. *Primate Visions: Gender, Race, and Nature in the World of Modern Science*. London: Routledge.

Harris, M. 1968. *The Rise of Anthropological Theory*. New York: Thomas Y. Crowell.

Hayes, P., L. Zarsky, and W. Bello. 1987. *American Lake: Nuclear Peril in the Pacific*. London: Penguin.

Hemenway, R. 1978. *Zora Neale Hurston: A Literary Biography*. Urbana: University of Illinois Press.

Howard, J. 1984. *Margaret Mead: A Life*. New York: Simon and Schuster.

Hurston, Z. N. 1942. *Dust Tracks on a Road*. Philadelphia: J. B. Lippincott.

Hutchinson, G. E. 1950. "Marginalia." *American Scientist* 38(2):282–289.

———. 1987. Personal communication, November 7.

———. 1988. Personal communication, January 18.

Jones, D. 1987. Personal communication, September 11.

King, M. L., Jr. 1965. Letter to Margaret Mead, February 6. Mead Papers, Library of Congress, Washington, D.C.

Klare, M. 1972. *War without End: American Planning for the Next Vietnams.* New York: Alfred Knopf.

Langer, M. 1990. Personal communication, March 13.

Lippmann, W. 1931. Lippmann Papers, Vol. 2, Series 3, Correspondence 1931–1974, Folder no. 1479. Manuscripts and Archives, Sterling Memorial Library, Yale University, New Haven.

Lipset, D. 1980. *Gregory Bateson: The Legacy of a Scientist.* Englewood Cliffs, N.J.: Prentice-Hall.

Mabee, C. 1987. "Margaret Mead and Behavioral Scientists in World War II: Problems in Responsibility, Truth, and Effectiveness." *Journal of the History of the Behavioral Sciences* 23, January, pp. 3–13.

Margaret Mead's New Guinea Journal. 1968. Distributed by Bloomington, Ind.

Markel, L. 1941. Letter to Mead, July 24. Mead Papers, Library of Congress, Washington, D.C.

Mead, M. 1924. "Intelligence Tests of Italian and American Children." Master's thesis, Columbia University, New York.

———. 1926. "The Methodology of Racial Testing: Its Significance for Sociology." *American Journal of Sociology* 31(5):657–67.

———. 1928. *Coming of Age in Samoa: A Psychological Study of Primitive Youth for Western Civilization.* New York: Morrow.

———. 1930. "Social Organization of Manu'a." *Bernice P. Bishop Museum Bulletin* 76. Honolulu. Reissued 1969 by Bishop Museum Press Reprints.

———. 1931a. "Civil Government for Samoa." *The Nation* 132(3425).

———. 1931b. Letter to Walter Lippmann. In Walter Lippmann Papers *2*, series 3, Correspondence 1931–1974. Folder #1479. Sterling Library, Yale University, New Haven.

————. 1931c. "Living with the Natives of Melanesia: How Ethnological Work Is Carried on by Representatives of the American Museum among Primitive People of the South Seas." *Natural History* 31:62–74.

————. 1931d. "Stevenson's Samoa Tody: Its Sensible Government by the United States Navy." *World Today* 58, September, pp. 343–50.

————. 1931e. "Talk-Boy." *Asia: Journal of the American Asiatic Association,* March, pp. 144–51.

————. 1934. "Where Sorcerers Call the Tune." *Asia: Journal of the American Asiatic Association,* April, pp. 232–35.

————. 1935a. Letter to A. N. Meyer, May 20. Meyer Papers, American Jewish Archives, Hebrew Union College, Cincinnati.

————. 1935b. *Sex and Temperament in Three Primitive Societies.* New York: Morrow.

————. 1939a. *From the South Seas.* New York: Morrow.

————. 1939b. "Native Languages as Field-Work Tools." *American Anthropologists* 41, April–June, pp. 189–205.

————. 1941. "Not Headhunters, Not Appeasers, But Men." *New York Times,* November 30.

————. 1943a. "Anthropological Techniques in War Psychology." *Bulletin of the Menninger Clinic* 7(4):137–140.

————. 1943b. "The Role of Small South Sea Cultures in the Post-War World." *American Anthropologist* 45(2):193–196.

————. 1947. "The Application of Anthropological Techniques to Cross-National Communication." *Transactions of the New York Academy of Sciences* 9, series 2, pp. 133–52.

————. 1949. *Male and Female: A Study of the Sexes in a Changing World.* New York: Morrow.

————. 1951a. "The Study of National Character." In D. Lerner and H. D. Lasswell (eds.), *The Policy Sciences.* Stanford: Stanford University Press.

————. 1951b. "Research in Contemporary Cultures." In H. Guetzkow (ed.), *Groups, Leadership and Men: Research in Human Relations,* pp. 106–18. Pittsburgh: Carnegie Press.

————, and R. Metraux. 1953. *Studies of Culture at a Distance*. Chicago: University of Chicago Press.

————. 1954. "25th Reunion at Manus." *Natural History* 63:66–68.

————. 1957. "Introduction to Polynesia as a Laboratory for the Development of Models in the Study of Cultural Evolution." *The Journal of the Polynesian Society* 66(2):145.

————, D. Michael, H. Lasswell, and L. Frank. 1958. "Man in Space: A Tool for the Study of Social Change." *Annals of the New York Academy of Sciences* 72:165–214.

————. 1959. "The Factor of Culture in Cross-Cultural Work: Review of U.S. Selection Procedures." Project on Selection of Personnel for International Cross-Cultural Service. Margaret Mead Papers, Library of Congress, Washington, D.C.

————. 1962. "Reply to Suggs and Carr." *Fellow Newsletter* (American Anthropological Association) 3(7):4.

————. 1964a. *Continuities in Cultural Evolution*. New Haven: Yale University Press.

————. 1964b. "A Savage Paradigm: Film Review of *Dead Birds*." *Film Comment* 2(1).

————. 1966. *New Lives for Old: Cultural Transformation—Manus, 1928–1953*. New York: Morrow. Originally published 1956.

————, T. Dobzhansky, E. Tobach, and R. Light. 1968. *Science and the Concept of Race*. New York: Columbia University Press.

————. 1968. "Alternatives to War." In M. Fried, M. Harris, and R. Murphy (eds.), *War: The Anthropology of Armed Conflict and Aggression,* pp. 215–28. New York: Natural History Press.

————. 1969a. "Research with Human Beings: A Model Derived from Anthropological Field Practices." *Daedalus,* Spring, p. 373.

————. 1969b. "Response to C. A. Valentine, *Culture and Poverty: Critique and Counter-Proposals*." *Current Anthropology* 10, pp. 181–201.

————. 1970. "Field Work in the Pacific Islands, 1925–1967." In P. Golde (ed.), *Women in the Field,* pp. 293–335. Chicago: Aldine.

———— and J. Baldwin. 1971. *A Rap on Race.* Philadelphia: Lippincott.

————. 1971. *And Keep Your Powder Dry: An Anthropologist Looks at America.* Freeport, New York: Morrow. Originally published 1942.

————. 1972. *Blackberry Winter.* New York: Morrow.

————. 1974. "Margaret Mead." In G. Lindzey (ed.), *A History of Psychology in Autobiography.* Englewood Cliffs, N.J.: Prentice-Hall.

———— and W. Kellogg. 1977. *The Atmosphere: Endangered and Endangering.* Fogarty International Center Proceedings no. 39, National Institute of Environmental Health Sciences. Washington, D.C.: U.S. Government Printing Office.

————. 1977. *Letters from the Field, 1925–1975.* New York: Harper & Row.

————. 1979. "The Evolving Ethics of Applied Anthropology." In E. M. Eddy and W. L. Partridge (eds.), *Applied Anthropology in America,* pp. 425–37. New York: Columbia University Press.

Meyer, A. N. 1935. "A Little Hitler in the New York Zoo: A Communication." *Opinion: A Journal of Jewish Life and Letters,* May, p. 27.

Murdock, G. 1942. Meeting of the Advisory Board of the Strategic Index of Latin America, Murdock Papers, Yale University Institute of Human Records (YRG37-V), New Haven.

Murdock, G., C. Ford, A. Hudson, R. Kennedy, L. Simmons, and J. Whiting. 1961. *Outline of Cultural Materials* (4th rev. ed.). New Haven: Human Relations Area Files.

National Research Council. 1967. *Conference on Behavioral Science Research in New Guinea.* Publication no. 1492. Washington, D.C.

O'Connell, C. 1989. Personal communication, December 20.

————. "Soviet Studies at Harvard: Social Science in the Service of the Cold War." Dissertation in progress. University of California at Los Angeles.

Office of Naval Research. 1952. "Psychological warfare themes suggested a psychocultural analysis of the Chinese." Report based on materials of the Research in Contemporary Cultures Project, under contract to the Office of Naval Research. Margaret Mead Papers, Library of Congress, Washington, D.C.

Page, H. 1951. "Human Relations Research Supports Psychological Warfare." Reprint from Monthly Research Report of the Office of Naval Research, July (Washington, D.C.: Office of Naval Research, Department of the Navy). Mead Papers, Library of Congress, Washington, D.C.

Patterson, L. T. 1990. Personal communication, February 18.

Pospisil, L. 1987. Personal communication, November 6.

Professional Ethics: Statements and Procedures of the American Anthropological Association. 1967. Statement on problems of anthropological research and ethics, adopted by council of the AAA, March.

Rosenberg, R. 1982. *Beyond Separate Spheres: Intellectual Roots of Modern Feminism.* New Haven: Yale University Press.

Rouse, I. 1987. Personal communication, November 6.

Shenker, I. 1971. "Anthropologists Clash Over Their Colleagues." *New York Times,* November 21.

Sleeper, R. 1962. "Memo for Record, Visit of Dr. Margaret Mead, January 3, 1962, Air Force Systems Command Headquarters." Margaret Mead Papers, Library of Congress, Washington, D.C.

———. 1977. "Some Thoughts on Control of Aerospace." In W. Kellogg and M. Mead (eds.), *The Atmosphere: Endangered and Endangering,* pp. 125–28. Fogarty International Center Proceedings no. 39, National Institute of Environmental Health Sciences. Washington, D.C.: U.S. Government Printing Office.

Sloan, D. 1980. "Science in New York City, 1867–1907." *Isis: The Journal of the History of Science* 71(256):35–76.

Stevens, H. Major. 1944. "Evil Omens Which Could Be Incorporated in U.S. Propaganda to Reach Japanese Troops Who Are Fighting in Burma." *Declassified Documents Quarterly Catalog: 1985,* vol. 11, no. 4, October–December, fiche #2399. Woodbridge, Connecticut: Research Publications.

Stocking, G. W. 1986. "Anthropology and the Science of the Irrational: Malinowski's Encounter with Freudian Psychoanalysis." In *Malinowski, Rivers, Benedict and Others: Essays on Culture and Personality,* pp. 13–49. Madison: University of Wisconsin Press.

The Student Mobilizer. 1970. "Counterinsurgency Research on Campus Exposed." *Student Mobilizer* 3(4).

Taking Note. 1979. Distributed by Documentary Educational Resources, Watertown, Mass.

Torgovnick, M. 1990. *Gone Primitive: Savage Intellects, Modern Lives.* Chicago: University of Chicago Press.

U.S. Congress. 1934. *Samoan Organic Act.* (The bill, discussed March 19, carried out the recommendation of the American Samoan Commission Bill S1574 to provide a government for American Samoa.) 73d Congress, 2d session, Calendar no. 531, Report no. 500. Congressional Record, Washington, D.C.

Valentine, B. 1978. *Hustling and Other Hard Work: Lifestyles in the Ghetto.* New York: Free Press.

———. 1989. Personal communication, December 20.

Valentine, C. A. 1968. *Culture and Poverty: Critique and Counter-Proposals.* Chicago: University of Chicago Press.

———. 1969. "Culture and Poverty: Critique and Counter-Proposals." *Current Anthropology* 10:181–201.

———. 1990. Personal communication, April 15.

Weaver, T. (ed.). 1973. *To See Ourselves: Anthropology and Modern Social Issues.* Glenview, Ill.: Scott, Foresman and Company.

Wechsler, H. 1977. *The Qualified Student: A History of Selective*

College Admission in America. New York: John Wiley & Sons.

———. 1990. Personal communication, June 1.

Whiting, J. 1943. "The Role of Small South Sea Cultures in the Post-War World." *American Anthropologist* 45(2):193–97.

Wiener, J. 1989. "Bringing Nazi Sympathizers to the U.S." *The Nation,* March 6.

Wike, J. 1990. Personal communication, May 20.

Willis, W. 1974. "Skeletons in the Anthropological Closet." In D. Hymes (ed.), *Reinventing Anthropology,* pp. 121–52. New York: Vintage Books.

Winks, R. 1987a. *Cloak and Gown: Scholars in the Secret War.* New York: Morrow.

———. 1987b. Personal communication, November 7.

Wolf, E. 1987. Personal communication, September 11.

Wolf, E., and J. Jorgensen. 1970. "Anthropology on the Warpath in Thailand." *New York Review of Books,* November 19, pp. 26, 27, 33.

World Federation for Mental Health. 1957. Meeting of the Danish Subcommittee of World Federation for Mental Health Executive Board, on Mental Health Aspects of the Peaceful Uses of Atomic Energy. May 25, Copenhagen. Margaret Mead Papers, Library of Congress, Washington, D.C.

Worsley, P. 1957. *The Trumpet Shall Sound: A Study of "Cargo" Cults in Melanesia.* London: MacKibbon and Kee.

Yale Daily News. 1942. "Harvard Grad Schools Converted to Vital Military Training Centers." August 22.

———. 1943a. "Foreign Studies Courses Begin; Enrollment 77; European, Far Eastern Languages Presented for Study." February 2.

———. 1943b. "Yale Among First Colleges Selected to Train Engineers for Army, Navy, Air Force; Definite Time, Extent Unknown." February 8.

Yans-McLaughlin, V. 1986. "Science, Democracy, and Ethics:

Mobilizing Culture and Personality for World War II." In G. Stocking (ed.), *Malinowski, Rivers, Benedict and Others: Essays on Culture and Personality*, pp. 184–217. Madison: University of Wisconsin Press.

Part II

Empire and Independence

6 For an Independent Kanaky

This chapter is an edited speech by Susanna Ounei, which was delivered in Nairobi, Kenya, in July 1985 at the nongovernmental forum segment of the World Conference to Review and Appraise the Achievements of the United Nations Decade for Women: Equality, Development, and Peace. It was presented to an audience of women with varying levels of education from all over the world, most of whom knew relatively little about New Caledonia and its history.

Susanna Ounei is a founder and former president of the women's organization within the FLNKS (Front de Libération National Kanak et Socialist), the GFKEL (Groupe des Femmes Kanaks et Exploitees en Lutte). This organization recently has been affected by the theoretical conflicts about gender in an anticolonial struggle.

The idea for GFKEL was born in prison after Ounei was arrested and beaten in 1974 for opposing the celebration of the September 24, 1853, colonization of New Caledonia. It was there that she and other women such as Dewe Gorodey—who in 1978 was the only Kanak woman to have received a college education after 125 years of French colonization—began to raise the question about how to address the issue of women's equality *within* the national liberation movement.

The following statement is historical in that it represented the first major outreach of a Kanak woman at an international meeting of women, and to a primarily English-speaking audience. The importance of this critical meeting itself was often minimized, as coverage became relegated to style or fashion pages in Western newspapers, in part to downplay the political, economic, and geopolitical focus of most of the presentations.

This presentation represents the chronicle of the evolution and changing values of a dominated Melanesian people, who move from fear and historically imposed feelings of inadequacy to internalizing and operating with a presumption of equality and their worth as a people. Hence, this is also a brilliant synthesis of the history of the Kanak struggle for independence, and for whom the ethnographic inventions of "Melanesian" and "Polynesian" have singular, day-to-day significance.

Before I start to speak, I would like to say thank you on behalf of the Kanak people, and particularly on behalf of the Kanak women and the FLNKS. FLNKS is a coalition of all the movements for independence in New Caledonia, but especially for a true independence—the control of the wealth in our country. We want the control of the resources in an independent Kanaky.

The story of the resistance of the Kanak people does not begin now. Today, when I heard from our black sisters in Brazil and South Africa, I found the story of our country through their words.[1] For example, when it is said that the

South Pacific is a paradise, where beautiful beaches and white sand and blue skies can be found, that is superficial. There in the Pacific, the Kanak people, the Melanesian people, have been dying every day since 1853. When the French people and their government came in 1853, they colonized our country without asking our permission, or if they could stay in our home.

We have had many troubles since then. We suffered massacres in 1853, and we continue to die from massacres by the French. The colonial government claims that in 1853 we were only 75,000 people. We Kanaks say we were more than 200,000 people at that time. But after the massacre and the murders, the population was only 26,000. A massacre touches every Kanak because most of us are related by family.

Then we became isolated because our grandfathers and grandmothers were really scared. And they stayed like that. But we had several revolts and two national uprisings. In 1878, a great chief named Atai led the first insurrection. The colonists came to him and said, "The leaves of your taro disturb our cattle." And Atai answered, "You know the leaves of my taro do not eat your cattle, but your cattle eat my taro every day." There was a big fight, and they killed Atai and several thousand Kanaks.

The problems we had then are the same as the ones we have now. We had no weapons, just our own arms. But we were isolated then—not like now. Now we have international contact and can go outside New Caledonia and talk about our own issues.

In 1917, there was another insurrection—a big uprising also, this time led by Noel. Remember that during the World War I, the Europeans called up many of the world's blacks to be put in the front lines. In the French language, we call that *service de char a canon*—cannon fodder—put the blacks in front so that they are the ones killed first. They took our people from New Caledonia and sent them to France to protect the French land from the Germans. Noel asked why must he go with his people to die in France for the French land, while the French had stolen our land at home.

So Noel refused to go to France, and they killed him. He was beheaded and his head was sent to a museum in France. And after doing something like that, they call *us* savages and terrorists. Now the head of our chief is in France, and we want it back.

That was the life of our grandfathers and grandmothers, and until 1946 we did not even have the right to go outside the reserves. Our grandparents—and parents, too—did not have the right to leave. If they wanted to go into town, they had to ask permission of gendarmes—the police—who had to write on the permit giving them permission.

Our parents and grandparents began to talk about the creation of the first movement for liberty, which was limited to just wanting some reforms. This was in 1952, and only in 1952 did the Kanak people have the right to vote. Before that they did not have the right to vote or go outside. After 9 o'clock at night, there was a curfew. And if Kanak people found themselves outside of the boundaries, they were killed just like deer or the pigs are slaughtered.

So in 1952, our parents organized a new political movement called the Union Caledonienne (UC), and its creation was helped by the church. The UC was limited to reforming colonialism, but that was alright. It was acceptable because at that time we were only children, still needing our parents to give us food, some clothing, and to pay for the doctor. And so we grew up like that, hearing the story of our grandparents and their struggle.

When the French say they send a lot of money to New Caledonia, in reality they send nothing. The money they send home is coming from the wealth of our country. We are the *third* largest producer in the world of nickel. Nickel is a very important mineral in arms manufacturing. The extraction of it has involved incredible environmental destruction. They just rip the top off whole hillsides. The industry is almost entirely foreign-owned and is the basis for about 90 percent of New Caledonia's money from export earnings. Even though the world market for nickel is not very strong at the moment, France would not like to lose all of "its" nickel. Some Kanaks wonder if the nickel has something to do with French determination not to grant independence.

Also, French undersea mining technology tells them that we have manganese, chrome, zinc, cobalt, gold, copper, and iron, and that our sea is three times richer in minerals than our land. All of these minerals are called "strategic." That means that they are used to make weapons.

We also have coffee, copra, and tourism. So when they say they send money home, that is not true. It is *our* money. And when they send some money from France to home, it is coming from *our* minerals, from the wealth of *our* country.

But from this money that France sends home, we get no benefit. It goes to the white settlers who live in New Caledonia. They have the rights to it, not us. This is also true for the Tahitians, the Wallisians, or whatever.

When they introduce a picture of New Caledonia overseas, they always introduce the picture of New Caledonia with beautiful beaches and a *wahine*—a Polynesian woman—who dances the *tamoure*. But they never show the

picture of the Kanak people. The Kanak people are us—
the black people—who live there. That is why when we
hear the sister from South Africa, we can find our story,
too. On one side there is us—the black people—and on the
other side is the white settlers. Everything is for them. For
us, nothing. That is our life. But in spite of the obstacles,
we are beginning to rise up. One of the obstacles is the
situation of our people in the labor market.

Out of 60,000 Kanak people, only 7,000 have jobs. The
rest of the people live on reserves. We are lucky that our
sea is so rich that it gives crabs and other food, but that is
on a good, beautiful day. When it rains, we just eat our
manioc without anything. That is the life of a Kanak. When
a Kanak becomes involved in a political way, it is almost
impossible to keep a job. Scores of our people have their
baccalaureates, yet do not have a way to earn a living. The
few who do work have the worst tasks.

But when we talk about that, they call us communists—
pro-Russia or pro-Cuba. That is what we are called at
home. They wrote several articles about our struggle, and
they say overseas that we are inspired by Cuba or by Libya.
But as we say, we are isolated. We do not know where
Cuba and Libya are located.

When we were young, we suffered because we were
called names by our teachers. In front of whites at school,
I was called "dirty *kanak*" [nigger] by our teachers. Dirty
kanak. *Kanak* was a pejorative word at that time. And our
grandparents and parents were ashamed as well as scared.
They were ashamed of the name of *kanak*. And as young
people, we grew up in that name-calling environment—
kanak, kanak, kanak—kanak everywhere.

So in 1969 we created the Red Scarves. We created it to
make the word *kanak* valuable, to make it so we do not

have to be ashamed of being Kanak. We have to be proud. We do not have to deny our rights, our skin, our ethnicity. At home, they teach us to deny our skin color. They teach us that our ancestors came from Gaul. You know Gaul; it is old France. So, our ancestors came from Gaul with blue eyes and blonde hair. A big contradiction, you know. When I was 10 years old, I, like others, began to say by heart, "My ancestors come from Gaul, with blue eyes and blonde hair." But that is not our story. That is the story of France.

We asked our teachers if *our* ancestors came from France, with blue eyes. Well, we learned the whole history of France, about Napoleon, Louis the Fourteenth, and the geography of France, but nothing about our country.

So you see, I never had any real opportunity to study because I was thrown out of many schools in my youth for various forms of insubordination. None of the struggles about our people are in the books we read in school. So, it is necessary for me to write as many articles as I can in order to tell the reality of our people, because Kanak young people are taught that they are not worth anything. One of the history books I remember reading said that we Kanaks are the lowest of the black Melanesians, not like Polynesians, who are like whites.[2]

So in 1969, when we created our own group, we made our own Kanak world valuable. We are proud to be Kanak, so we renamed ourselves with a word the French had used to make us feel bad. But our parents got scared and said to us, "What do you want? We worked for 75 years without wages to build up our country, and now you have gone to school, and you have a little bit of knowledge. Aren't we doing alright?"

And we said, "No." We have to talk again about your— *our*—past, because it is not just. We are ignorant of our past, and the only past that we know is you; that is really recent. Our grandparents did not have the right to go outside after 9 PM until 1946, and our parents grew up with that. We say that we have to make *everything* valuable again. Us, our culture, and ask for the return of our land without conditions.

Then, many of our people, like Nidoish Naesseline, went to jail three times. He was our leader at that time. Our people in the countryside began to think again about our story, our own history.

The date of our colonization is 24 September 1853. So every September 24 at home there is a big celebration to commemorate when the French arrived to take possession of our country. In 1974, we refused. We said, "No!" We have to tell our people that they must stop celebrating the death of our people. That holiday represents the blood of our people, and we do not have to celebrate the date of our death. For us, it is a big funeral. So on 24 September 1974 we demonstrated while the army was coming with their guns. We were only 30 or less. We demonstrated with our banner—our opposition to the army. And of course, you can imagine what happened afterwards. They just beat us, and there was blood on the road. They arrested 20 of us on that day in 1974. And I was one of them. That was in 1974.

It was good, because lots of our people were everywhere, and they witnessed that. They began to wonder and to ask themselves why. Why? So that our people would not feel they had to celebrate with the white settlers.

The day after, the Kanak people went to court to demand the release of all the prisoners, and by then the group numbered 50. They gave the prisoners a sentence of eight days. We said, "No," we want a release of all the prisoners now. The French refused. So the Kanaks sat, just like we are sitting now in this room. And that is how we started to evolve. People were asking questions now inside of themselves. Not just the women but also the men. They had a debate. And they talked together, in cooperation.

We began in 1969 and 1974 to ask these questions, and we come back now to see how they have evolved, moved forward—and in front of the army now, because there is a curfew with increased militarization. Everywhere in our tribal lands, they would go every day to beat our people. This time, when they beat our people, not only the men but also the woman fight back.

Do you know what we fight with? Only stones. But with the stones, we have made a big destabilization in our country, in the countryside.

And when they see how the women fight . . . oh, when I think how we have evolved together. We have progressed. We do not fight just the white settlers, but we also fight to change the place of women for the future. I believe that this is an internal problem. We have to be *inside* to ask these questions. We have to be inside the struggle with the men. We do not want to make something that is separate from them, because we live inside with them. We do not have one world with only us, and another world for the men. No. So we women have to raise questions together with them.

I think our Kanak brothers have really evolved in this way now. When I came back in 1974, they told me, "You are full of theory now." Now I see their mentality is changing, and how the people at the grassroots level ask new questions and talk in the big congress. In the big General Assembly of the FLNKS, when men ask questions about the issues of women, then I think we have won a point.

But as for us, that is our problem, from inside. We have to ask them questions, but they are not our enemy. They are our brothers. As for me, I did not identify my struggle with the white woman who had her man to kill my people. Even if we have the same problems as white women, I cannot identify with her. You see I know the right wing at home also talks about the problems of women. But in these social issues, we Kanaks have *nothing*. Everything is for the white woman. They have a better situation than us, because the French woman lives in better conditions.

Let me tell you what I mean. When they killed a lot of our people as they did this year, they killed one of our leaders. He was Eloi Machoro. Eloi Machoro was my brother in the struggle against colonialism and for true independence. And what did white women do? They went all over the town of Noumea—because the town of Noumea is a white town—and they cried, "We won, we won," because they killed him. How could I identify with a woman who does not identify with my brother? But as we say, we are 60,000 Machoros today.

Let me tell you another example about how the French women see Kanaks. Right here in Nairobi, I attended a workshop on the nuclearization of the Pacific. It was being run by the French women, and there were women from Tahiti in the room. A woman I do not know asked the French women what links they saw between denucleariza-tion and decolonization in the region. After they avoided the question, I asked it again. I said that you cannot understand the nuclearization of the Pacific without know-ing what the French government is doing in Kanaky and Tahiti. Finally, they said they were not there to talk about colonialism. The women at the workshop wanted to hear someone from the Pacific talk about the problems there, and so I spoke. Then I asked the Tahitian sisters to speak as well. At the end, the French women told me that I was very arrogant and not like other women from the Pacific, who are much nicer and gentler than me. I replied that it was hard to be nice and kind when your people are getting killed by the French colonial army and settlers.

And so, it was the white women with their men, and even some of the Tahitian and Wallisian women with their men, who helped to say, "We won" that day Machoro was killed. We do not identify our struggle with them. If they have a problem with their men in their homes, it is their problem, as it is our problem when we struggle inside our movement to say, just with our stones, "We almost won."

[Taking chalk and making a map of New Caledonia on the blackboard] Australia is here and New Zealand there. Right here is Noumea, the capital. We have three major islands, including Ile Belet and Ile des Pins, and several islands called the Loyalty Islands. Here is the capital, the white town. Before, in 1979, for 40,000 Kanaks there were only 374,000 hectares [2.47 acres]. Only 4,000 white farmers had 432,000 hectares. So they put us on the mountain. [Pointing to the map on the blackboard,] we are here, here, and here. This is the Kanak area. They put us on the mountain with the mimosa—trees with prickly leaves. How can we grow our yams or vegetables here?

And they have most of our land for their cattle. So now, with just our stones, they are all in Noumea now. All 85,000 whites are in the capital. And we are growing in our strength in many regions.We are everywhere now.

On the 7th of May, 1985, they sent a nuclear submarine to prevent Kanak independence. Since the nuclear submarine arrived, a big struggle has been going on in Noumea because they just hate us now, because we have pushed them away. They do not understand what we are doing in town, because for them Noumea is a white town. We say Noumea is Kanak land. It does not belong to Paris, and we are going to try to stay there now.

Now there is a lot of tension because of the struggle in Noumea. In the countryside, when we came back from our mountain, our people said, "Before, they put us in the mountains, and now we have come back to stay." When they came back to take their cattle, we said that the cattle are ours. When they killed our people, their houses burned.

Our current situation is really, really tense. But if they kill our people, we no longer have to love them. I do not believe in turning the other cheek. They came with the Bible in front of them, in the hands of the Catholic missionaries, and the army behind them. And when we woke up, it was us with the Bible in our hand, and they had our land.

Of all the churches, only the Protestant church believes in our struggle and helps us. But not the Catholic church, because not many Kanaks want to go to the fathers. So the majority of the fathers in the church are the French.

But we Kanaks who oppose participating in French elections are in the majority. We are 80 percent and we boycotted elections last year. Why should we vote when the people who they think will decide the future of Kanaky are those who have lived in New Caledonia for three years? This includes people who have come from Algeria (called the *pieds noirs*), from Tahiti, Wallis, and Futuna, wherever. They all are offered better jobs. Maybe next month it will be even more tense, because it is just getting worse.

We are going overseas by ourselves, to call for solidarity from the international community. We believe in international links, in international help, because we are only 60,000. We are not millions. And we cannot do something clandestinely you know, because of our skins. This is the life of our people. We want international solidarity, but I think our people are so determined they will go to the end. I do not think we will go back.

But France is planning to strangle our struggle by creating a Kanak middle class that will help them. The French have realized that their apartheid-like policies of putting our people out of the white towns and onto reserves is going to be a problem for them some day.

Yet they send all kinds of armies to our home villages now. We have 11,000 mercenaries, CRS [a type of special police force], Red Berets, parachutists—all this for 60,000 Kanak people.

Last year I went to the Philippines, and when I went back home I thought I had missed my plane and was back in Manila. It was the same—everywhere there is curfew, everywhere the guns are ready to shoot.

Since they go to the reserves to beat our people, just as I was leaving the country one of the gendarmes was killed. It is not a crime to defend our lives. On the television, they interviewed the mercenaries and asked them if they were sad to lose one of their friends. They answered, "No, we are not sad, but we just hate them." "Them" is us. I know all of us were in front of the television, and heard how they said that they hate us. And when they said they hate us, we realized that we do not have to love them. We can hate them too.

NOTES

1. The session was entitled, "The Impact of Racism and Class Oppression on the Scholarship about Women," and was

organized and chaired by Gilliam. Here Ounei is referring to other participants of the panel such as Lindiwe Mabuza, currently chief representative of the African National Congress mission to the United States, Mamphela Ramphele, South African co-author (with Francis Wilson) of *Uprooting Poverty: The Challenge in South Africa* (New York: Norton, 1989), and Lelia Gonzalez, Brazilian anthropologist. The sixth member of the panel was Rose Catchings, then executive secretary of the Ministry of Women and Children (World Division) of the United Methodist Church, under whose auspices and travel-funding support Ounei, Gilliam, and 70 other women from around the world were enabled to attend this historic meeting.

2. The full quote is the following: "The natives, too, are poles apart from the merry Polynesians. They are the lowest of the black Melanesians, infinitely more archaic and repulsive, and more like the negritos than the gentle tawny Polynesians, who are almost Caucasians." Stephen H. Roberts, *History of French Colonial Policy (1870–1925),* vol. 2 (London: P. S. King and Son, 1929), p. 517. An excellent critique of this historical ethnology can be found in Nicholas Thomas, "The Force of Ethnology: Origins and Significance of the Melanesia/Polynesia Division," *Current Anthropology* 30(1):27–42. Of particular interest is the published response to the article by Friedrich Valjavec.

GLENN ALCALAY

7 The United States Anthropologist in Micronesia: Toward a Counter-Hegemonic Study of Sapiens

The [trust] territory had been a sort of a government "museum" in which only authorized persons were allowed to make visitations and tours. Those allowed to visit were usually anthropologists or nuclear scientists. The anthropologists came to study the customs and culture, the scientists to conduct research and atomic tests.
— *Carl Heine*, Micronesia at the Crossroads

Having emerged from the intellectual wellsprings of the Enlightenment, anthropology's evolution paralleled the exigencies of European expansionism. Referring to anthropology as "a child of Western imperialism," Kathleen Gough has devised the classic statement for our discipline (Gough, 1968:12). So-called "applied anthropology" provided im-

perial powers the ethnographic wherewithal to penetrate—
and better colonize—the nations of the Third World.

Curiously, the historic liaison between anthropology
and empire has received only cursory attention by the
practitioners of the trade. As Talal Asad observed in his
important 1973 neoclassic *Anthropology and the Colonial
Encounter* in reference to the cozy relationship between
British social anthropology and the state, "there is a
strange reluctance on the part of most professional anthropologists to consider seriously the power structure within
which their discipline has taken shape" (Asad
1973[1985]:15).

This chapter demonstrates how anthropologists—some
naively caught up in the cold war and others more con-
sciously all-too-willing collaborators—helped to lubricate
the machinery for America's immediate postwar colonial
enterprise in the remote and strategic reaches of Micronesia
in the western Pacific. Further, the essay—following a
discussion of some historical arguments about anthropology and the state—contributes to the vital discussion of
positing a decolonized and counterhegemonic anthropology
in the wake of being a largely complicit enterprise for the
stratagems of aggrandizing nations against the indigenous
peoples of the Third World.

Anthropology, Colonialism, and the State

To begin, some notable exceptions of the failure to
scrutinize social science vis-à-vis the power structure mentioned by Asad are worthy of discussion.

Perhaps the earliest and most conspicuous articulation
of the subject emanated from none other than the "father
of American anthropology," Franz Boas. In his famous

letter to the *Nation* in 1919, Boas lamented the fact that "a number of men who follow science as their profession . . . have prostituted science by using it as a cover for their activities as spies" (Boas, 1919). In his *Nation* letter, Boas went on to bemoan, "A person, however, who uses science as a cover for political spying, who demeans himself to pose before a foreign government as an investigator and asks for assistance in his alleged researches in order to carry on, under this cloak, his political machinations, prostitutes science in an unpardonable way" (ibid.).

For this, Boas was hastily censured from the organization he helped establish (AAA) and was severely rebuked for his unorthodox questioning of the darker and dirtier secrets of the anthropological craft at work in close cooperation with the larger imperial stratagems of the time. However, Boas remains an unassailable voice in forecasting the dangers associated with a complacent and compliant social science in service to the state.

In this light, it is disturbing that Boas's most famous disciple, Margaret Mead (an icon of American anthropology popularly known for her compassion and understanding of other cultures), succumbed to tacit racism vis-à-vis the Japanese (along with Gregory Bateson, Ruth Benedict et al.) in the Office of Strategic Services (OSS), the forerunner of the Central Intelligence Agency (cf. Mead's role in World War II, in Dower, 1986).

"Project Camelot" of 1964 resurrected a more contemporary version of the debate on the often close collaboration between ethnographers and those pursuing perceived national interests. In his well-known "expose,"[1] Irving Horowitz laid bare the proposed plan to engage social scientists in Latin American counterinsurgency research.

Initiated in the summer of 1964 and funded by the

Departments of Defense and State and coordinated through the Special Operations Research Office (SORO) of the American University in Washington, D.C., Project Camelot was slated to operate in Chile, Nigeria, and India. By enlisting the support of social scientists, Camelot was created to produce "a better understanding of the processes of social change and mechanisms for the established order to accommodate change in an effective manner" (Kim, 1968:64–65). Project Camelot was canceled in the summer of 1965 amidst U.S. intervention in the Dominican Republic and in the wake of anti-American protests in Chile following the public disclosure of the counterinsurgency program.

One "bright" spot that emerged from Project Camelot came in the person of Johan Galtung. A Norwegian sociologist, Galtung was working in Chile at the time of Camelot and refused an invitation to participate in the project. Among the reasons for rejecting the Camelot offer, Galtung criticized the inherent imbalance of the project whereby Latin American counterinsurgency would be stressed at the exclusion of "counterintervention"—conditions where the nations of Latin America might intervene in the affairs of the United States (Horowitz in Weaver, 1973:140). Aside from his major contributions in the methodology and philosophy of the social sciences, Galtung has since become a renowned and respected force in the international peace and disarmament movement.

Further debate about the role of social scientists and the state followed the publication of a 1966 investigative article in *Ramparts* magazine about the collaboration between Michigan State University and the CIA for the training of secret police for the Diem regime in South Vietnam (*Ramparts,* April 1966). Horowitz again picked up the gauntlet with an essay about the MSU-CIA connection entitled "Social Scientists Must Beware the Corruption of CIA Involvement" (in Kim, 1968).

In an important 1971 paper by the Mexican social scientist Rodolfo Stavenhagen (and in the midst of the general controversy about U.S. involvement in Southeast Asia), another salvo was fired in the anthropology and empire debate. Speaking about "applied" social science in the most bare-knuckled manner, Stavenhagen intoned, "I am personally of the opinion that the difference between social scientists who wittingly contribute to counterinsurgency programs in Southeast Asia or Camelot-style projects in Latin America and elsewhere, and the doctors who experimented on human guinea pigs in Nazi concentration camps is one of degree and not of kind. The end result is genocide" (Stavenhagen, 1971:340).

Citing the "Declaration of Barbados" signed by eleven concerned anthropologists, Stavenhagen advocated that "the role of the applied social scientist in national development cannot be neutral; he cannot remain true to the ethical principles of his science and at the same time refuse to take a stand on the wider ideological and ethical issues of the social processes in which he is involved as a practitioner" (ibid.:343).

In one of the numerous responses to Stavenhagen's 1971 challenge, anthropologist James Silverberg concurred by stating, "I don't think it is paranoia to point out that even the most innocuous-seeming item may be made to play a part in some war scenario of the Rand Corporation or the Institutes for Defense Analysis type—e.g., a description of village house types is potentially useful in planning the weapons and tactics of their destruction" (Silverberg, 1971:345).

In his discussion of colonialism and anthropology, Abdel Ahmed refers to a salient passage from E. E. Evans-Pritchard concerning the colonial enterprise: "The value of social anthropology to administration has been generally recognized from the beginning of the century and both the Colonial Office and colonial governments have shown an increasing interest in anthropological teaching and research" (Ahmed in Asad, 1973:265). Ahmed goes on to provide a lucid analysis of the intimate historical connection between anthropology and colonialism: "The feeling among intellectuals of ex-colonies is that though it was not *merely* an aid to colonial administration, it [i.e., anthropology] played, more than any other human science, a major role in introducing to the administration the people of the colonies and in showing ways by which their social system could be controlled and hence exploited" (ibid.:264).

In an interesting 1974 paper, sociologist Arthur Vidich analyzed the ideological undertones of American anthropology. In what was considered a perceptive article for the mid-1970s, Vidich lambasted the discipline for neglecting to reflect upon its own legacy as an integral partner in the colonial past and neocolonial present. In a searing passage about this conspicuous lapse on the part of anthropologists, Vidich spelled out the reasons why anthropologists have willingly assisted in the process of alienation between anthropological observer and primitive [*sic*]:

> So long as anthropology could conceive of the world as a vast laboratory for the science of man, the anthropologist himself did not have to identify either with his own national ideologies or with the processes of Western conquest and penetration of the primitive and tribal world. The ideology of the universal science served as the cornerstone for upholding both the anthropologist's self-image as a disinterested scien-

tist and the image of primitive and tribal society as an entity that could be studied in terms of itself alone. (Vidich, 1974:726)

As insightful as this essay appears, Vidich curiously failed to mention his *own* participation in the CIMA program (mentioned in the next section) whereby his doctoral thesis on political factionalism in Belau was undoubtedly useful for the U.S. Navy during its colonial administration of postwar Micronesia, prior to the Interior Department taking control of the Trust Territory in 1951. Undoubtedly, Vidich would have many second thoughts about the use of his Belau work now.

In Stanley Diamond's trenchant 1974 work, *In Search of the Primitive,* the discussion concerning anthropologists and colonialism is characteristically broadened and deepened. Citing a quote from Levi-Strauss—"Anthropology . . . reflects, on the epistemological level, a state of affairs in which one part of mankind treats the other as an object"—Diamond argues that this reveals only half the truth (Diamond, 1974:93). In Diamond's dialectical critique of Levi-Strauss, "Anthropologists and their objects, the studied, despite opposing positions in the 'scientific' equation have this much in common: if not equally, still they are each objects of contemporary imperial civilization. . . . For in order to objectify the other, one is, at the same time, compelled to objectify the self" (ibid.:93).

Anthropology and the CIMA Program

Shortly after Pearl Harbor, "the entire facilities of Yale University's Cross-Cultural Survey were re-directed toward the collection and analysis" of all available data on the

Micronesian islands (Mason, 1973:2). In 1943 George Murdock, the director of the survey, and two of his associates were commissioned as naval intelligence officers to create a set of civil affairs handbooks on Micronesia to serve as guides for the occupation forces then being trained at Columbia University and elsewhere. These handbooks comprised the first systematic compilation in the English language of anthropological, economic, social, and political data prepared on the islands, and were virtual translations of Japanese materials previously collected (Gale, 1979:74).

In a recently published book about the role of Yale University in the transition of the OSS to the Central Intelligence Agency, a frank account of Murdock's work appears. In the best-selling *Cloak and Gown* about Yale's close encounter with the CIA, author Robin Winks recounts how Yale's Institute of Human Relations "abundantly demonstrated the value of anthropology, and to a lesser extent of sociology, to intelligence work" (Winks, 1987:43). Winks goes on to describe how the institute served U.S. interests in fortuitous ways:

> Less than a week after Pearl Harbor, Mark May (the Institute's director) announced that the Institute would accept contract work from any government agency, and he launched an immediate crash program to study the 'cultural and racial characteristics' of the Japanese. George Murdock, one of the leading anthropologists at Yale, shifted the emphasis of his Cross-Cultural Survey to the collecting and classification of materials on the people of the Pacific, and he began a fresh study of Micronesia. The Institute drew up a list of anthropologists throughout the nation who had firsthand knowledge of the islands and sent it to the Army and Navy departments.

In another revealing passage, Winks again discusses the work of Murdock:

Charles Walker, a research fellow in the social sciences at Yale, was interested in the military uses of anthropology, and he and Murdock elaborated on a data base that became part of the Human Relations Area Files. . . . He and Murdock also combined knowledge to produce short case studies on how best to get Polynesians [*sic*] to cooperate with the military in, for example, building an airfield on an atoll, to help Americans grasp the practical implications of the communal ownership of property, or to remind them that when treating a native chief they must never stand up, since this was an insult while to remain seated showed the proper form of respect. . . . It was wonderful, Walker thought, that Yale could demonstrate how the research of scholars 'with a purely scientific motive and as wholly remote from any practical application, (could) turn out in the end to be a strong weapon for the Navy.' (ibid.:46–47)

During the war, the navy trained over fourteen hundred military government officers at Columbia, Princeton, and other universities to serve in occupied areas. The students were almost all in possession of undergraduate degrees in the social sciences, and their instructors were usually political scientists, economists, or anthropologists. Because many of these newly trained students were reserve officers, they were quickly demobilized after the war, which resulted in a shortage of trained officers for Micronesia (Gale, 1979:74).

This deficiency was corrected in April 1946 when the first postwar class of students began training at Stanford's School of Naval Administration (SONA). Directed by Felix Keesing—one of the few American anthropologists specializing in the Pacific Islands—the school was staffed by a mixture of navy officers with Pacific experience and academics. Relying heavily on role playing, the curriculum was oriented toward localized problem solving instead of a more generalized political or theoretical perspective. In all, 193 officers graduated from the Stanford program following the five-month curriculum (ibid.:75).

As booty for American blood spilled during the island-hopping campaigns of the Second World War, the United States gained control (under an unprecedented "strategic" United Nations Trusteeship) of the twenty-one hundred Micronesian islands formerly known as the Japanese Mandated Islands. With the war's end and the rapid inception of the cold war, it seems clear that the U.S. presence in the region was based upon its location vis-à-vis the Asian mainland rather than any serious notion of potential economic windfall: Exclusive economic zones (EEZs) with fishing rights and potential mining of seabed minerals did not substantially figure into the immediate postwar American calculus.

The United States' position toward its new wards was marked by interagency squabbling: The War Department advocated outright annexation, while the State Department sought a more diplomatic relationship as trustee through the newly created United Nations.

One navy commander was reported to have suggested killing off the populace as the simplest course to take (Bogen 1950:166). Another course was steered by the U.S. government, and under the aegis of the Reconstruction Finance Corporation, the U.S. Commercial Company (USCC) was created. Douglas Oliver, a Harvard anthropologist, administered the Pacific Ocean Area branch of the USCC, and as he stated in his introduction for the completed report, "Shortly after V-J Day the U.S. Naval Command in the Pacific requested the U.S.C.C. to undertake an

economic survey of Guam and the former Japanese Mandated Islands in order to assist the Naval Military Government in its task of administering these islands" (Oliver,
1946[1951]:v).

Further along in his introduction, Oliver provided this
additional rationale for the economic survey, which included twenty-three specialists from various universities
and branches of the federal government: "The Survey
represents the successful pooling of the knowledge and
observations of many different kinds of specialists all working on one highly complex problem. Its subject matter is
the lives and welfare of thousands of innocent victims of an
international rivalry beyond their control. *Its objective in
the sobering one of attempting to prescribe a way of life
for people who have no effective voice in deciding their
own destinies*" (ibid.:vi) [emphasis added].

From the navy's point of view, the USCC's economic
survey of the Micronesian islands was intended to benefit
naval administration of the islands. In a letter dated October 1, 1945, the commander of the Marianas (i.e., the chief
naval officer in Micronesia at the time) informed the chief
of naval operations that

> it is considered that the [Economic] Survey should indicate
> what natural resources might be developed, how native hand-
> icraft could be improved, what is required to re-establish
> copra or other export crops, and an analysis of the food and
> other commodities which it may be necessary to import.
> Further, it is believed essential that the Survey be guided by
> considerations of the probable entrance into commercial
> activities in the western Pacific of private U.S. business firms
> in the relatively near future, and that it be designed to
> facilitate the same. (National Archives, 1945)

During this period (i.e., the summer of 1946) the United
States forcibly removed (recounting Hiroshima and Naga-

saki, and invoking biblical passages) the indigenous inhabitants of Bikini Atoll in the Marshall Islands for the testing
of two Nagasaki-sized atomic bombs known as "Operation
Crossroads." In stark contrast to the pledges made to the
international community under the aegis of the United
Nations Trusteeship Agreement—especially Article 6,
which specified that the United States would "protect the
health of the inhabitants" and "protect the inhabitants
against the loss of their lands and resources"—the legacy
of the nuclear tests at Bikini bespeaks the violation of the
United Nations Trusteeship Agreement and continues to
wreak havoc upon the Marshallese people.

Likewise, in 1947 the United States relocated the indigenous people of Enewetak Atoll to facilitate further nuclear
weapons experiments in the far reaches of the western
Pacific. In a "Restricted—Security Information" report
from 1954 by then staff anthropologist for the Marshall
Islands, Jack Tobin, a second evacuation of the Enewe-
takese was carefully detailed for the army commander of
Joint Task Force Seven prior to the detonation of the
world's first hydrogen explosion on Enewetak in late 1952
(Tobin, 1954). The complicity of American anthropologists
during the nuclear weapons program in the Marshalls was
invariably quite useful for the military commanders and
Atomic Energy Commission as they proceeded to conduct
unofficial nuclear warfare on their Micronesian island
wards. Today, the Enewetak islanders remain a fragmented
and sociologically disrupted people.

Perhaps even more tragic is the experience of the island
peoples of Rongelap and Utirik atolls in the Marshall Islands. Caught in the lethal radioactive fallout of the United
States' largest and dirtiest hydrogen bomb experiment
("Bravo") on March 1, 1954, these communities suffered

the immediate and long-term effects of radioactive contamination, which necessitated their evacuation to other atolls (Alcalay in Worsley and Hadjor, 1987:107–21). The larger question today concerns the great uncertainty surrounding the total number of atolls and populations affected by the nuclear tests. A congressionally mandated Nuclear Claims Tribunal in the Marshalls is currently wrestling with this thorny enigma.

The CIMA Program

Following close on the heels of the USCC economic survey (conducted in the summer of 1946), perhaps the largest American anthropological undertaking ever was carried out. The navy officially requested the Coordinated Investigation of Micronesian Anthropology (CIMA) program through the National Research Council and its Pacific Science Board for the dual objectives of compiling basic scientific information on the islands and to "provide data relevant to the practical problems of administering the area and its peoples" (Marshall and Nason, 1975:25).

Between 1947 and 1949 thirty-five anthropologists (among forty-two scientists all together) fanned out through the approximately one hundred inhabited islands of Micronesia. There were so many social scientists working within the CIMA Program that one of the scientists ironically jested that you could "go anywhere out in the bush on these islands and you'll step on a Ph.D." (Ullman, 1963:81). At this time the U.S. entered into the United Nations Trusteeship Agreement (July 1947) to administer Micronesia under an unprecedented "strategic" trust agreement: The other ten trusteeships created in the postwar period were not so designated, and therefore (unlike the TTPI, overseen by the Security Council) were under the aegis of the General Assembly.

The functions of the CIMA social scientists can be categorized in the following four ways: as information collectors; as trainers and educators of military government officers; as field investigators; and as administrators and political actors. The forty-two social scientists from twenty-three universities and museums took part in what anthropologist Leonard Mason referred to as "a massive ethnographic salvage program" (Mason, 1973:2). The CIMA "salvage program" was primarily funded by the Navy, with some additional financial support from the Wenner-Gren Foundation (Useem, 1947:3).

According to Navy historian Dorothy Richards, CIMA's mandate was to "determine precise trends in the local development of governments and to recognize, if possible, incipient conflicts and socially disruptive patterns for correction" (Richard, 1957:390). George Murdock, as the director of the CIMA Program, described it as "a model for the collaboration of lay scientists and government agencies. . . . The expedition is certainly the largest, and probably the best equipped, in the history of anthropology" (Murdock quoted in Richard, 1957:582).

Notwithstanding the immediate postwar euphoria, it is troubling that anthropologists—given their sociocultural training and supposed sensitivity about indigenous peoples—did not raise more of an objection concerning their role in aiding the colonial project in Micronesia.

The Navy went to great lengths to provide assistance and transportation to the field teams of anthropologists (and other social scientists) and was keenly interested in learning about the peoples under its colonial administration. Anthropologist Ward Goodenough articulated the rather intimate relationship between the Navy and the CIMA researchers:

> Important for the orientation of our study was the Navy's sponsorship of the research and the interest it expressed in using the results to develop an informed administration in Micronesia. While it was made clear from the outset that participating ethnographers were free to study whatever aspects of Micronesian culture interested them, the prospect that our reports would be used as an aid in solving administrative problems *induced considerations which might otherwise have been neglected.* In the study of property organization, for example, it required that a report on land tenure so formulate the principles of native property law that an administrator would be equipped to assess claims and settle disputes in whatever form they might arise, and do this in such a way that the natives would feel that justice had been done in accordance with their principles (Goodenough 1951:10) [emphasis added].

In this regard, an incisive essay titled "Eurocentrism in the Social Sciences" hammers forcefully on this tidy collaboration: "During the heyday of imperialism, the scholar was useful not only in constructing a conceptual framework within which colonial ideology could be defended and extended, but in helping to select problems for investigation which highlighted the beneficial effects of colonial rule" (Joseph et al., 1990:3).

Broadly speaking, the CIMA Program focused upon kinship, traditional political organization, cognitive measurements, economic exchange patterns, and general ethnography. The working agreement between the Navy and the cooperating universities and individual researchers mandated that the Navy was to "define overall policy regarding publishing of written articles of any nature, based on research done under this program," and that it reserved the right to define "matters affecting national defense or general national interests, which may not be published or written about" (Richards, 1957:1269).

Many of the CIMA anthropologists eventually were hired as staff anthropologists for several Micronesian districts, or else became de facto advisors for administration officials. In the words of Felix Keesing, "the many scattered island settings offer something approaching a series of laboratory experiments in human affairs" (Keesing, 1950:3).

Indeed, as the Embree quote beginning this section suggests, American anthropologists seemed all too willing to serve as cultural "travel guides" and decoders for the Navy in the former Japanese Mandated Islands.

Anthropologist Thomas Gladwin characterized the mission of the anthropologist in administration as being to "fill the functional gaps left in their culture by the effect of the previous administrations and our own." In the view of Gladwin, this was a task that should be carried out "whether our presence is disruptive or not" (Gladwin, 1950:23).

Anthropologist John Useem was even more candid in his assessment of U.S. ambitions in Micronesia, and wrote that there was a general consensus among the anthropologists working in the trust territory that the islands were "to be permanent American possessions" (Useem, 1945:1). This sentiment was shared by then-chairman of the Senate Interior and Insular Affairs Committee, Hugh Butler, following his visit to the islands in the early 1950s: "It should be noted that our primary title to the islands rests on force of arms, and that the United Nations Trusteeship Agreement [signed in 1947] represents little more than a *fait accompli*. I believe that it should be made categorically clear to all concerned that the United States Government must for security reasons retain absolute control of this entire area forever, or for as far as we can see into the distant future" (Butler, 1953:2–3).

In an unpublished 1972 paper, Gladwin later wrote an interesting (and workable) analysis supporting Micronesian socialism and self-reliance. By citing the socialist experiments underway in China, Cuba, and Tanzania—and warning of the problems associated with capitalism (especially the inevitable dependency relationship with the United States)—Gladwin advocated a similar economic and political path for the island people of Micronesia. In criticizing a capitalist approach for Micronesia, whereby individual gain would destructively supersede the collective enterprise inherent in Micronesian societies, Gladwin wrote that "the conclusion has emerged that self-reliance is not only possible for Micronesia, but if it is diligently pursued with careful attention to the prior experience of other Third World countries, it will most certainly provide Micronesia with a better quality of life for its people than will capitalist development as a poor client state of a foreign power" (Gladwin, 1972:44).

Unbeknownst to Gladwin, the economic future of Micronesia had already been predetermined by strategic policymakers in Washington during the previous decade. Under a Freedom of Information Act (FOIA) request, perhaps the *most critical* (and revealing) policy statement for Micronesia has emerged. Known as National Security Action Memorandum 145 (NSAM 145) and signed by President Kennedy on April 18, 1962, NSAM 145 clarified the United

States' position by stating that "it is in the interest of the United States that the Trust Territory be given a real option at the appropriate time to move into a new and lasting relationship to the United States within our political framework. This then should be our goal" (NSAM 145:1).

To implement the newly stated policy toward Micronesia, President Kennedy sent his friend and Harvard economist Anthony Solomon on a fact-finding mission to Micronesia during the summer of 1963. In what has since become known as the "Solomon Report," the author referred to his set of recommendations as "an integrated master plan" that would "make Micronesia a United States Territory" (Solomon Report, 1963:S–5).

An especially odious section of the Solomon Report, most of which remains classified to the present day, called for a capital investment program just prior to the plebiscite(s) (The U.S. subsequently succeeded in carving up the trust territory into four separate entities—see McHenry, 1975) to determine a post-United Nations trusteeship relationship with the United States. Stating the key objective of the "United States' need to retain permanent control of Micronesia for security reasons," the report baldly claimed that "the importance of those funds in influencing a favorable plebiscite result is obvious" (ibid.:11).

Using the classic formula for obtaining possession of a colonial territory by a metropolitan power, the Solomon Report delineated the following prescription for foisting economic dependency upon the Micronesian people: "It is the [Solomon] Mission's conclusion that those programs and the spending involved will not set off a self-sustaining development process of any significance in the area. It is important, therefore, that advantage be taken of the psychological impact of the capital investment program before some measure of disappointment is felt'' (ibid.:42).

When one compares the lucrative economic potential of developing Micronesia's obvious economic resource of tuna and other commercial fish (evidenced by the vast numbers of foreign fishing vessels in one of the most fertile fishing grounds in the world)—as suggested in Oliver's 1946 United States Economic Survey—with the *realpolitik* strategy of creating economic dependency in the trust territory, one sees the blatant imperial design incorporated into four decades of U.S. rule in Micronesia. That today more than 90 percent of Micronesia's economy derives from annual U.S. cash infusions bespeaks the grand success of NSAM 145 and the recommendations contained in the 1963 Solomon Report.

In addition to having created a neocolonial dependency relationship with Micronesia, U.S. rule also brought one of the world's highest suicide rates to the newly created island entities of Micronesia. Caught between two conflicting worlds, Micronesian male youths are particularly vulnerable to the stresses inherent in the collision of cultures (Hezel 1989). The Marshall Islands also now have the world's highest prevalence rate for type II (adult-onset) diabetes—27 percent—following the radical postwar shift to a Western diet. With an explosive birth rate and massive socioeconomic challenges confronting the Marshallese, their future remains dangerously precarious.

Leaving no stone unturned, the United States—as the administering authority—has taken every conceivable advantage of its Micronesian wards under a United Nations trusteeship, a trusteeship designed to foster economic self-sufficiency and eventual independence for the island people of Micronesia.

The great success of NSAM 145 and its companion blueprint, The Solomon Report, may be measured by the United States securing military rights in strategic islands just off the Asian mainland for one hundred years under a covenant with the newly created Commonwealth of the Northern Mariana Islands adjacent to Guam, itself a strategic colony since 1898.

The United States will likewise have military options (e.g., airfields to accommodate nuclear-laden warplanes, port facilities for nuclear warships, an amphibious base, a guerrilla warfare base for training counterinsurgency units, and a possible forward naval base for the Trident submarine) in Belau for half a century if the Compact of Free Association is eventually pushed through: The seventh compact plebiscite in February 1990 resulted in the lowest compact support yet.

Under separate Compacts of Free Association, the United States will maintain defense authority over the Federated States of Micronesia (The FSM consists of Pohnpei, Kosrae, Chuuk [formerly Truk] and Yap) for fifteen years (commencing in 1986), as well as in the Marshall Islands. The extremely important two-billion-dollar Pentagon missile testing facility and the ultrasophisticated Altair radar array at Kwajalein Atoll (in the Marshall Islands) will remain under U.S. control for at least thirty years, with an option to renew the lease agreement.

Adding the proverbial icing to the cake, the United States—under the Compacts of Free Association—has literally closed off the entire area of Micronesia (i.e., three million square miles of oceanic territory, an area the size of the continental U.S.) to all outside third parties under the "strategic denial" clause of the compacts. Indeed, the entire northern Pacific, stretching from the U.S. mainland to the Hawaiian Islands and westward through Micronesia to the Philippines and East Asia, is under American control.

That American anthropologists who have worked in Micronesia have been so relatively uncritical and acquiescent while the U.S. government has methodically militarized this vast territory during the past forty-five years is disturbing at best, and damnable at worst.

Conclusion

We have the trust *and the United States has the* territory.
—*Senator Ataji Balos, Marshall Islands*

Following sixty-six announced atomic and hydrogen bomb explosions at Bikini and Enewetak between 1946 and 1958, several entire Marshallese communities remain alienated and sociologically dislocated. The people of Bikini—known throughout the Pacific as the "nuclear nomads," have yet to permanently resettle on their ancestral atoll. Likewise, the people of Enewetak remain fragmented and divided as a community.

The most recent atoll community to join the ranks of the nuclear nomads are the Rongelap islanders. Because of ongoing health problems believed to be associated with their past exposure to radioactive fallout and current exposures from a contaminated environment, the people of Rongelap—with the assistance of the Greenpeace ship *Rainbow Warrior*—evacuated their home islands in May 1985. Having "temporarily" resettled on Mejatto Island in the Kwajalein Atoll complex, the Rongelap islanders are seeking congressional funding for an independent and nongovernmental radiological assessment of their ancestral atoll to determine if permanent habitation is feasible.

With an uncertain prognosis for the full extent and breadth of radiation-related damage to the health and environment of the Marshallese people, the U.S. Supreme Court ruled in mid-1989 to uphold a lower court decision to terminate all pending (and future) lawsuits by Marshallese plaintiffs in U.S. courts. Totaling more than six billion dollars, these lawsuits for health injury and property damage have now become null and void, leaving the people of the Marshall Islands without any judicial redress for claims against the United States for its nuclear weapons program.

Meanwhile, the United States—having uprooted the indigenous population of Kwajalein Island—continues to use Kwajalein Atoll in the Marshall Islands as an important Pentagon laboratory for key components of SDI ("Star Wars") research, as well as for perfecting missile warhead accuracy and antisatellite (ASAT) technology. Indeed, the "strategic" Trust Territory of the Pacific Islands has served—and will continue to serve—U.S. military interests well into the twenty-first century.

Moreover, as a contingency plan for the possible loss of the prime military bases in the Philippines, the United States has devised a "fallback arc" of islands consisting of Guam, Saipan, Tinian, Rota, and extending south to Belau.

With the world's first antinuclear constitution in 1979, the tiny island nation of Belau (population 15,000) in the western portion of Micronesia has withstood immense pressure by the United States to overturn its unprecedented and controversial constitution. Having become an international cause célèbre, the United States has forced the Belauan electorate to cast ten ballots in as many years in the attempt to overturn the antinuclear provision of the constitution.

Violence has broken out in Belau over the constitution, and the first two elected presidents have died by violent means. Following the murder of the father of two prominent antinuclear Belauan activists (attorney Roman Bedor and his educator-sister Bernie Keldermans) and the firebombing of the house of a leading female elder in September 1987, an international grass-roots network campaigned before the United Nations and congressional and Reagan administration officials to change its policy toward Belau to quell the increasing outbreaks of violence in that troubled island territory.

During a 1988 American Anthropological Association (AAA) session on the Pacific, discussant and San Francisco State University anthropologist Luis Kemnitzer—an avid supporter of the grass-roots Nuclear-Free and Independent Pacific (NFIP) movement—recounted how he attempted to solicit support for Belau's antinuclear constitution. Kemnitzer told the AAA session that when he requested support from a renowned anthropologist who has worked extensively in Micronesia, he was told that his involvement would constitute "intervention" in the internal affairs of the tiny Pacific nation!

Distressingly, there has been a conspicuous silence on the part of most American anthropologists concerning the horrific and disastrous consequences of U.S. imperial policy in Micronesia.[2] This silence contrasts sharply with those atomic scientists who, even before the atomic bomb was dropped on Hiroshima, lobbied against its use in Japan. In what has come to be known as the "Franck Report," several American atomic scientists suggested a demonstration blast over an uninhabited area of the Pacific instead of over a civilian population in Japan (Blackett, 1948[1949]:114–16). Unfortunately, precious little debate has come from the American anthropological community over U.S. hegemonic policies in Micronesia.

Although the CIMA program of the late 1940s may seem far removed from the contemporary world, the close collaboration between anthropologists and the state continues to the present day. According to a disturbing report from a New Zealand investigative periodical, the United States Information Agency (USIA)—the de facto propaganda arm of the U.S. government—has entered into contractual agreement with several American (et al.) anthropologists for the production of numerous country reports on several targeted Pacific island nations (Wellington Pacific Report 1989:1).

These reports are intended to assist the USIA for the dissemination of its "information" activities where they best support U.S. interests. One of these reports, "Issues and Interest Groups in the Pacific Islands," is intended to "analyze the major issues relevant to United States policy" in the Pacific and "focuses on the major interest groups in these countries" and their views on the problems discussed (ibid.:1). Likewise, a resident American anthropologist, Thomas Keene, is currently under contract with the U.S. Army at Kwajalein to enhance community relations between SDI personnel and the nearby ten-thousand Marshallese on Ebeye, known regionally as the "slum of the Pacific." Following numerous "Operation Homecoming" occupation protests at the missile complex, anthropology currently serves the Pentagon in helping to extinguish indigenous protest while the missiles continue to hurl into the strategic lagoon from Vandenberg Air Base in California.

That the Pacific anthropologists under contract with the USIA and the army have agreed to provide pertinent information about current Pacific island political trends should make us question the ethics of our discipline. Most assuredly, if the USIA seeks information from Pacific anthropologists, we must assume that the information collected will be used to undermine and co-opt the burgeoning NFIP movement, which is perceived as anathema to U.S. interests. Indeed, in the words of former U.S. ambassador to Fiji (and current ambassador to the Marshall Islands) William Bodde, Jr., "The most potentially disruptive development for United States relations with the South Pacific is the growing antinuclear movement in the region. A nuclear-free zone would be unacceptable to the U.S. given our strategic needs, and I am convinced that the U.S. must do everything possible to counter this movement" (*Wellington Confidential*, 1987:1).

Moreover, the fifteen member nations of the South Pacific Forum—a regional trade and political association—have consistently called for an end to French nuclear testing at Moruroa and Fangataufa atolls near Tahiti. The forum nations also have advocated independence for France's other Pacific colony, New Caledonia, in an attempt to head off an impending and bloody civil war.

The South Pacific Nuclear Free Zone Treaty (SPNFZT), known regionally as the Treaty of Rarotonga, was devised by the forum nations to denuclearize the Pacific region. That the United States, France, and Great Britain have refused to sign the protocols of the treaty (the Soviet Union and China have signed) has further alienated those nations in the eyes of most Pacific peoples.

In pursuit of its "maritime strategy," the United States stands by its policy of projecting naval power to the Asian mainland, and thus would feel constrained by entering into the protocols of the Treaty of Rarotonga (cf. *American Lake* by Hayes et al. for a fuller discussion of U.S. policy in the Pacific).

That anthropologists are conducting research on current indigenous attitudes concerning independence and nuclear related policies in the region for the USIA (including personality profiles of key island leaders) should cause some degree of alarm within anthropological circles. As Gramsci noted earlier in the century, "certain categories of intellectuals (in the direct service of the State . . .) are still too closely tied to the old dominant classes" (Gramsci, 1983[1933]:245).

With increasing violence in Fiji under its postcoup military regime, a bloody civil war threatening to break out in France's colony of New Caledonia, continued French nuclear testing near Tahiti, ongoing genocide by the Indonesian army in West Papua and East Timor, and instability in Belau over its antinuclear constitution, anthropologists must debate their role in this very troubled oceanic region.

This chapter has reviewed some of the salient elements of the larger discussion concerning the relationship between anthropology and how it has been used to further the national interests of metropolitan powers, and in particular those of the United States. The point of this exercise is not to "witch hunt" anthropologists who work at the behest of the government. Rather, my purpose is to inquire whether those anthropologists (e.g., those currently under contract with the USIA) are merely naive supplicants in a competitive job market, or instead are conscious and ideology-driven academics ("defense intellectuals") who willingly provide useful ethnographic data to the Defense and State Departments and who wish to bolster U.S. interests abroad. In either case—naive supplicant or defense intellectual—we should debate the issues in a more open and honest way than has previously been the case.

Indeed, where "ethnographic research" fades into "intelligence gathering" is obviously a subject worthy of great debate among the anthropological community (see Alcalay, 1988 for a further discussion of this debate).

The issue of "anthropological advocacy" has been rekindled in an exchange appearing in the June 1990 issue of *Current Anthropology* (Hastrup and Elsass, 1990). But even in this discussion about the role of anthropologists operating in the real world, one is struck by a glaring naivete concerning the potential (and probable) uses of ethnographic data for the furtherance of imperial objectives by metropolitan powers against the Third World.

The issue of anthropological collaboration with the state has been historically marginalized to the periphery of academic inquiry (aside from some of the notable exceptions mentioned), and it is hoped that a renewed round of debate to further flesh out this very important topic will be forthcoming within our discipline and beyond. Infusing our discipline with a renewed sense of humanism and justice should be our aim.

If we are to move our discipline beyond merely being "a child of Western imperialism," it is incumbent upon all of us to question not only the subject matter of our investigations, but also the potential (and likely) uses of our research by metropolitan powers intent on maintaining a hegemonic stranglehold on the developing nations.

NOTES

The author wishes to thank Professor Glenn Peterson of the Anthropology Department of Baruch College (CUNY) for his encouragement and sharing of an earlier paper on the CIMA program.

1. As Weaver points out, Horowitz's criticism of Project

Camelot was mixed: On the one hand Horowitz decried the elimination of the project by the government as a threat to academic freedom; on the other hand, Horowitz raised the objection of governmentally sponsored research projects that were motivated by political and military interests (Weaver 1973:138).

2. Some notable exceptions to this anthropological silence consist of the diligent advocacy by anthropologists William Alexander (Upsala College, N.J.) on the Marshall Islands, Catherine Lutz (SUNY-Binghamton) on Chuuk, Glenn Peterson (Baruch College, CUNY) on Pohnpei, and Robert Solenberger on Saipan.

REFERENCES

Ahmed, Abdel Ghaffar. 1985[1973]. "Some Remarks from the Third World on Anthropology and Colonialism." In Asad's *Anthropology and the Colonial Encounter*. London and New Jersey: Ithaca and Humanities Press, pp. 259–72.

Alcalay, Glenn. 1988. "The Ethnography of Destabilization: Pacific Islanders in the Nuclear Age." *Dialectical Anthropology* 13:243–51.

———. 1987. "Pax Atomica: U.S. Nuclear Imperialism in Micronesia." In *On the Brink: Nuclear Proliferation and the Third World. See* Worsley and Hadjor, 1987, pp. 107–21.

Asad, Talal, ed. 1985[1973]. *Anthropology and the Colonial Experience*. London and New Jersey: Ithaca and Humanities Press.

Blackett, P.M.S. 1948[1949]. *Fear, War and the Bomb: Military and Political Consequences of Atomic Energy*. London: Whittlesey House (McGraw-Hill).

Boas, Franz. 1919. "Correspondence: Scientists as Spies." *The Nation* 109 (December 20).

Bogen, Eugene. 1950. "Government of the Trust Territory of the Pacific Islands." *Annals of the American Academy of Political and Social Sciences* 267 (January): 164–74.

Butler, Hugh. 1953. "Report on the Trust Territory of the Pacific Islands." Report to the U.S. Senate Interior and Insular Affairs Committee. Washington, D.C.: GPO.

Diamond, Stanley. 1981[1974]. *In Search of the Primitive*. New Jersey and London: Transaction Books.

Dower, John W. 1986. *War without Mercy: Race and Power in the Pacific War*. New York: Pantheon Books.

Embree, John. 1946. "Micronesia: The Navy and Democracy." *Far Eastern Survey* 15, no. 11 (June 5): 161–64.

Gale, Roger. 1979. *The Americanization of Micronesia: A Study of the Consolidation of U.S. Rule in the Pacific*. Washington, D.C.: University Press of America.

Gladwin, Thomas. 1950. "Civil Administration on Truk." *Human Organization* 4, no. 4 (Winter): 15–23.

———. 1972. "Self-Reliance for Micronesia." Honolulu: University of Hawaii. Unpublished manuscript.

Goodenough, Ward. 1966. *Property, Kin and Community on Truk*. Hamden, Conn.: Archon Books. Originally published as Yale University's *Publications in Anthropology*, no. 46, 1951.

Gough, Kathleen. 1968. "Anthropology and Imperialism." *Monthly Review* 19: 12–27.

Gramsci, Antonio. 1983 [1933]. *Selections from the Prison Notebooks*. New York: International Publishers.

Hastrup, Kirsten, and Peter Elsass. 1990. *"Anthropological Advocacy: A Contradiction in Terms?" Current Anthropology* 31, no. 3 (June): 301–11.

Hayes, Peter, Lyuba Zarsky, and Walden Bello. 1986. *American Lake: Nuclear Peril in the Pacific*. New York: Penguin Books.

Heine, Carl. 1974. *Micronesia at the Crossroads: A Reappraisal of the Micronesian Political Dilemma*. Honolulu: University of Hawaii Press. This is the first published book by an indigenous Micronesian.

Hezel, Francis X. 1989. "Suicide and the Micronesian Family." *Contemporary Pacific* 1, nos. 1 and 2 (Spring and Fall): 43–74.

Horowitz, Irving L. 1965. "The Life and Death of Project Camelot." *Society Magazine* (December). New Brunswick, N.J.:
Transaction, Inc.

———. 1968. "Social Scientists Must Beware the Corruption of
CIA Involvement." In *The CIA: Problems of Secrecy in a
Democracy*. See Kim 1968.

Hymes, Dell. 1974. *Reinventing Anthropology*. New York: Vintage Press.

Joseph, George G. et al. 1990. "Eurocentrism in the Social
Sciences," *Race & Class* 31, no. 4 (April-June): 1–26.

Keesing, Felix. 1950. "The Pacific Islands People in the Post-War
World." Condon Lectures. Eugene: University of Oregon.

Kim, Young Hum. 1968. *The Central Intelligence Agency: Problems of Secrecy in a Democracy*. Lexington, Mass.: D.C.
Heath and Co.

McHenry, Donald. 1975. *Micronesia: Trust Betrayed*. Washington, D.C.: Carnegie Endowment for Intl. Peace.

Marshall, Mac, and James Nason. 1975. *Micronesia 1944–1974:
A Bibliography of Anthropological and Related Source Material*. New Haven: HRAF Press.

Mason, Leonard. 1973. "The Anthropological Presence in Micronesia." Paper presented to the Across Generations Symposium, 32d annual meeting of the Society for Applied Anthropology, Tucson, April 1973.

National Archives. 234, Boxes 234–35. Washington, D.C.

National Security Action Memorandum 145. April 18, 1962. (Obtained under a Freedom of Information Act request.)

Nevins, David. 1977. *The American Touch in Micronesia: A Story
of Power, Money and the Corruption of a Pacific Paradise*.
New York: W. W. Norton and Co.

Oliver, Douglas. 1951. *Planning Micronesia's Future*. U.S. Commercial Company's Economic Survey of Micronesia, 1946.
Cambridge, Mass.: Harvard University Press.

Ramparts. April 1966.

Richard, Dorothy. 1957. *United States Naval Administration of the Trust Territory of the Pacific Islands,* vols. I, II, and III. Washington, D.C.: Governmemnt Printing Office.

Silverberg, James. 1971. "Comment." *Human Organization* (Winter): 344–46.

Solomon Report. 1963. "Report by the U.S. Government Survey Mission to the Trust Territory of the Pacific Islands." By Anthony Solomon. October 9. Washington, D.C.

Stavenhagen, Rodolfo. 1971. "Decolonizing Applied Social Sciences." *Human Organization* 30, no. 4 (Winter): 333–44.

Tobin, Jack. 1954. "Evacuation of the Natives of Ujelang Atoll." Restricted Security Information Report for Joint Task Force Seven. January 7. Typescript.

Ullman, James. 1963. *Where the Bong Tree Grows.* Cleveland: World Publishing.

Useem, John. 1947. "Applied Anthropology in Micronesia." *Applied Anthropology* 6, no. 2 (Fall): 1–14.

———. 1945. "Governing the Occupied Areas of the South Pacific: Wartime Lessons and Peacetime Proposals." *Applied Anthropology* 4, no. 3 (Summer): 1–10.

Vidich, Arthur. 1974. "Ideological Themes in American Anthropology." *Social Research* 41, no. 4 (Winter): 719–45.

Weaver, Thomas. 1973. *To See Ourselves: Anthropology and Modern Social Issues.* Glenview, Ill.: Scott Foresman and Co.

Wellington Confidential. Discontinued newsletter from Wellington, New Zealand. Ed. Pacific researcher Owen Wilkes.

Wellington Pacific Report. Monthly newsletter by noted Pacific researcher Owen Wilkes. Available through WPR, Box 9314, Wellington, New Zealand. (WPR supersedes the former *Wellington Confidential.*

Winks, Robin. 1987. *Cloak and Gown: Scholars in the Secret War, 1939–1961.* New York: William Morrow and Co.

Worsley, Peter, and Kofi Buenor Hadjor. 1987. *On the Brink: Nuclear Proliferation and the Third World.* London: Third World Communications.

SIMIONE DURUTALO

8 Anthropology and Authoritarianism in the Pacific Islands

While people in the West dream of a Pacific Island vacation, the idea foremost in the minds of many islanders, especially the young and ethnically persecuted groups such as the Indo-Fijians, is how to get away from these same islands. They simple see no future in their countries. Most island nations cannot support their own populations and are kept afloat "on a sea of foreign aid." Today, the major export of Polynesia is people. As a result, between 10 and 50 percent of Pacific Island populations live in Australia and New Zealand, and thousands more have migrated to the United States and Canada. Many are reluctant to leave their homelands, but have either been pushed out—fleeing a brutal military dictatorship as in Fiji—or face grim prospects if they remain in the islands. Unemployment is well over 20 percent and is even higher among women and persecuted ethnic groups (Sutherland, 1987:113). Most Pacific Island states have followed the lead taken by the Fijian military dictatorship's cut of public programs and have laid off teachers, doctors, nurses, and technicians by the thousands.

The root of this widespread economic crisis can be traced to the transnational-based development model pursued by these island regimes in the last decade or so, with its overdependence on foreign capital and easy borrowing. The results of such an economy are only now coming home to roost.

The islands' ruling classes can no longer continue to persist in their claim that the Pacific islands are an exception to the general Third World experience of being swamped in a tidal wave of debt and inflation or being under the thumb of one "village tyrant" or another installed by an IMF-inspired military coup. The economic and political crises evident in the rapid militarization of island societies; the dramatic rise in unemployment, crime, and landlessness associated with urbanization; the decline and deterioration in agriculture (both subsistence and commercial); the regular resort to repression to depoliticize their population; and massive violations of the human rights of its people have brought Pacific Islanders to the realization that they are an integral part of the world capitalist economy and thus share the same problems with Third World societies everywhere. These problems take on a more acute form in the Pacific Islands due to their remoteness from the metropolitan center of the modern world economy, which aggravates the already formidable problem associated with limited land area and small population.

These concerns have more often been shunted aside, overlooked, or dismissed as the preoccupations of aberrant elements and "troublemakers" within the normally "exotic" and "happy" native island communities. The persistence of the myth of the "happy native" snoozing under swaying palm trees in an island paradise "full of sun, sand, and sex" despite present realities is linked to the cult of the "noble savage" (Howe, 1977; Said, 1978; Rokotuivuna, 1973; Babadzan, 1988). This image of the noble savage began as part of an attempt by eighteenth-century Europeans to project another as a vehicle for mental escape from the monotonous physical drudgery and alienation of their bourgeois existence. In *Coming of Age in Samoa,* Margaret Mead (1928) revived and popularized this image of the South Seas as the "last unknown" of idyllic primitive societies where people had no work to do or obligations to meet and food could be had for the asking.

The tourist transnationals and nuclear-imperialist powers have profited from these myths of "floating South Seas paradises," which have become so pervasive and institutionalized that the theoretical practice of studying these island societies cannot escape being engulfed by them. The concept of the Pacific Way (and its subsidiary the Melanesian Way) represents the most articulate expression of this sense of Pacific exceptionalism, which claims that the Pacific Islands are unique societies that have to be studied on their own terms and will therefore need a totally new methodology to understand them. The ideologues of the Pacific Way assert that although social classes may exist in other parts of the world, they are nonexistent in the Pacific Islands and any discussion of surplus extraction and exploitation in such societies, then and now, is but a futile academic exercise (Crocombe and Tupouniua, 1975; Vusoniwailala, 1978; Narokobi, 1980:x, 171). This emphasis on a traditionalism and exceptionalism can be traced to the early twentieth-century works of leading western anthropologists such as Malinowski, Firth, and Mead who have held the greatest responsibility in perpetuating a static and functionalist view of Pacific Island societies that does not fit contemporary realities (Malinowski, 1922; Firth, 1963; Mead, 1928, 1935, 1939). This was done through the elimination of innovation in their descriptions of traditional island economic and sociopolitical systems.

Through such academic sleight of hand, anthropologists have encouraged others to conceive of immutable patterns of culture and of tribal-kinship alignments that have not changed for generations. This type of anthropology tends to degenerate into colonial apologia by playing down the "West in all its guises," leaving behind an allegedly "pristine primitivity, coolly observed by the anthropologist-hero." This denial of Western imperialism results in "a bizarre contrast between unspoiled aborigines on the one hand, and hymn-singing mission children on the other." Anthropology will only be able to unravel this paradox if it begins "to abandon its obsessive concern with the 'primitive' and concern itself more with the study of change or becoming modern" (Mintz, 1985:xxvii). Within the context of the Pacific Islands, Mintz's admonition means that it is time to put a stop to the use of these islands as an ethnographic zoo, an anthropological laboratory where trainee Western anthropologists go to "win their academic spurs" while Pacific Islanders are reduced to the role of ethnographic commodities to be studied and written about without their making any input into the exercise.

Anthropological studies carried out "on us, between us, and without us," laid the intellectual foundation for colonial and imperialist practices that pervade the Pacific today (Jimenez, 1983:71). This "objectification" of Pacific Island people has allowed imperialist powers such as France, the United States, and Britain to maintain colonies in the Pacific that doubled as testing grounds for their nuclear bombs and sophisticated delivery vehicles. To contribute to the struggle for a nuclear-free and independent Pacific, anthropology has to move away from peddling "Otherness" and sterile debates about human nature, and strive towards an understanding of its own process in order to reconstitute itself as a liberating, intellectual practice. This requires that it be global, because the relation that lies at the foundation of the ethnographic enterprise is a hierarchical relation to the Other, not just the fact of Otherness, but specifically the hierarchical relation characteristic of the world economy implying the necessary silence of the Other, of whom the anthropologist speaks.

What all this means is that anthropologists will, in their intellectual practice, have to integrate reciprocity in their outlook in relation to their studied subjects. They will have to be prepared to view their discipline from the point of view of others, from the point of view of other possible anthropologies. This puts the discipline in a dilemma. Is a disengaged, detached, disinterested (in the critical sense of the word), neutral anthropology possible? Within the contemporary reality of a heavily nuclearized and militarized Pacific, the answer is clearly in the negative. The Pacific practitioners of historical social science urgently need a shift towards what Wallerstein (1977:3) calls "a wider and fresh vocabulary" to help them "rethink received social science" with its historically limited categories. The transition of the Pacific Islands from colonies to "independent" states (i.e., from primitive tribes to new nations) implies that the hegemonic European-North American social science can no longer ghettoize its analysis into segmented "ethnological" or "Oceanic" studies. Furthermore, the activities of nuclear imperialist powers in the region clearly call for island intellectuals to take cognizance of separable cases, moving through and beyond them and transforming them as they proceed. To do otherwise is to risk being ahistorical by falling into the trap of examining ideas and institutions in isolation from their economic and social mainsprings. The production of historical and anthropological knowledge is a political question. Knowledge is not only a product of contemporary social reality, and in some sense a reflection of it, but also contributes to the molding of that social reality. A dialectical relationship exists between the two processes of reflection on the one hand, and intervention on the other. Significantly different forms of historical and anthropological knowledge are produced on the basis of different methodologies. Methodology is also then a political question. Only when Island intellectuals confront the legacy of anthropologists like Mead with their "Garden of Eden" view of Pacific island innocence and optimism will the process of social liberation of these Island societies be advanced. The study of imperialism—particularly nuclear imperialism—is a good place to begin.

Nuclear War as Living Reality

To most Pacific Islanders, nuclear war is not something abstract, but has been part of their experience since 1945 with the bombing of Hiroshima and Nagasaki, followed by the U.S. atmospheric atomic and hydrogen bomb testing program in the Marshall Islands from 1946 to 1958. Then came the British nuclear tests at Christmas Island and in the Australian outback, the French testing program at Moruroa and Fangataufa since 1966, more U.S. testing at Johnston Atoll in the 1960s, ICBM test flights, antisatellite and "Star Wars" weapons tests fired from Vandenburg Air Force base in California and landing thousands of miles away at the Kwajelein Missile Range in the Marshall Islands. Thus, apart from the population of the two Japanese cities destroyed by the U.S. nuclear bombs in 1945, the island people (including the Aborigines) have been the vast majority of the people to experience the direct and negative impact of nuclear weapons on their lives.

In the nuclear history of the Pacific, colonies and bomb tests go together. The United States, Great Britain, and France all chose Pacific island colonies as places best suited for the biggest mushroom cloud and the most fallout. Colonial control enabled the western imperial powers to use the Pacific as a nuclear garbage can and nuclear weapon and missile testing range using island people as nuclear guinea pigs on which to test the effects of various levels of radiation. The sad truth is that the Anglo-American and French imperial states have used the islands as their nuclear playground largely because the islands have no choice.

> If the people of the Marshall Islands had not been under the political control of a foreign power in the 1940s and 1950s, atomic testing would probably not have taken place there; if Kiribati had been among the first rather than the last British colonies to gain independence, Christmas Island would have been spared the British H-bomb; if French Polynesia had not been a colony in the 1960s, there is no doubt that France would have had to explode its weapons elsewhere; an independent New Caledonia of the kind wanted by most of the Kanak population would follow the example of Vanuatu and keep nuclear vessels out of its ports, just as an independent Belau would not compromise its nuclear free constitution. (Firth, 1986:215)

The colonial status of much of the Pacific islands gives the imperial powers a free hand to use the region to perfect their weapons of mass destruction and annihilation that forms the central coercive core in their global strategy of intimidating the socialist bloc (minus China) and to strengthen their continued domination of the Third World. Solidarity and courage are only a part of the resources we need to bring about a nuclear-free and independent Pacific in the fight to end the peril that threatens to engulf and destroy us. These must be complemented by the correct analysis of what lies at the root of our nuclear malady in order to help us fashion the best and least costly way to combat it. This calls for a debate in one of the most neglected areas of scholarship: how the nuclear-military buildup in the Pacific is interlinked and interwoven with the exploitation and oppression associated with capitalist and imperialist penetration. Most liberal scholarship in the West is uncomfortable with terms like "capitalism" (the Free World), "imperialism" (interdependence) and "exploitation" (comparative advantage). Yet for Pacific island people and those all over the Third World, these are realities, and one cannot understand the dynamics of Pacific island societies and what makes them tick without first understanding the nature of their penetration by imperialism and capitalism.

This differing perception explains the frustration of some Third World activists with the myopic vision of the Western peace movement and its failure to grasp the indissoluble link between the maintenance of imperialism and the preparation for nuclear war. Instead, the Western peace and disarmament movement displays an "ahistorical, techno-centric, nuko-centric, ethno-centric and phobo-centric view of the world" (Ahmad, 1985:37–46) that apes those of their adversaries, the defense intellectuals who have made the modern national security state the temple of their devotion. The result is a distorted view based on the ethnocentric and pseudoscientific construct of this "priesthood of action intellectuals," which tends to see the adversary as implacably hostile and imputing to him a view of politics as a zero-sum game, promoting a very limited understanding of U.S.-Soviet relations (Gough and Gardezi, 1986). The theorizing by these defense intellectuals has effectively depoliticized war and militarized politics, leading to an excessive abstraction of warfare and strategy. Defense intellectuals have fostered illusions of control over war and ill-founded claims of rationality by decision makers. Furthermore, by holding that nuclear issues are so esoteric that only specialists can cope, the intellectuals have tended to discourage public discussion (Kolkewicz, 1987:190). These defense intellectuals assume that war in the nuclear context is merely the "continuation of management by other means," reducing the complexities of international politics to a matter of means-ends techniques. Overabstraction, scientism, numerology, and technical jargon are all part of the legacy of this professionalism (Kolkewicz, 1987:190). In sum, the Western peace and disarmament movement and their opponents, the defense intellectuals, tend to underestimate what Galtung has termed *structural violence:* the vertical dimension of war and peace. To Galtung, these are two sides of the same coin, where the former evokes images of economic factors, the latter of freedom being crushed. Any theory of liberation from structural violence presupposes an understanding of the dominance system against which the liberation is directed, particularly the species called imperialism in the general genus of dominance and power relationships.

The Nasty Side of Paradise: Caribbeanization of the Pacific Islands and Low-Intensity Warfare

The militarization of U.S. foreign policy in the Third World and the Pacific islands in particular has increased with particular rapidity in the last eight years. This policy emphasis is expressed in the dramatic rise in U.S. security assistance funds in its overall foreign aid budget. Foreign security assistance now claims 66 percent ($8.5 billion) of the total U.S. foreign aid program, as compared to only 50.7 percent ($5.7 billion) in 1979—the highest level reached under the Carter administration. The overall U.S. foreign aid budget increased by 52 percent from 1980 to 1985, and by 26 percent from 1980 to 1987, but that increase has gone almost totally to military and security programs. Despite the Gramm-Rudman cuts, security assistance, including military programs and the Economic Support Fund (ESF), has risen from $4.4 billion in 1980 to $8.5 billion in 1987. It is instructive that over the same period, U.S. bilateral and multilateral development assistance declined from $5.2 billion to $4.4 billion (Sewell and Contec, 1987:1015–1036). This increase in the military (hardware and technical assistance) component of U.S. foreign aid is an attempt to shore up the country's role as the chief military policeman of the world capitalist economy. It also reflects a major new U.S. obsession with low-intensity warfare (LIW). This reflects the concern of an influential current of thinking in the U.S. ruling power bloc, which has been arguing that the rest of this century is not likely to witness an all-out, "face-to-face" superpower nuclear and military confrontation, but rather will be a period of "greater power projection," one in which the United States will tend toward "aggressive preservation" of what it considers to be its "vital interests" abroad (Ilke, 1986:63–70;

Weinberger, 1986:42; Shultz, 1986:15–17). A U.S. Army training and command report anticipates that the period up to the year 2000 will be full of small conflicts: "wars of oppression and liberation, wars fueled from within or as proxies of larger powers," conflicts below the level of war but "with the power to topple nations or cripple governments (Miles, 1986). Low-intensity warfare is not just a scaled-down version of conventional war but can more accurately be described as revolutionary and counterrevolutionary warfare. The term "low intensity" is misleading, as it describes the level of violence strictly from a military viewpoint, when in fact it involves "political, economic and psychological warfare, with the military being a distant fourth in many cases." It is total warfare at the grassroots level (Miles, 1986:76; NACLA, 1986).

Fiji and Papua New Guinea have been earmarked by the United States (and France) as key regional states around which the policy of "strategic denial" and therefore low-intensity warfare is to be focused. The amount of U.S. AID money to the region has increased from $2.4 million in 1977 to $9 million in 1987 (Mediansky, 1987:277). Under the U.S. Military Assistance Programme (MAP) and IMET (International Military Education and Training Program), the Fijian, Papua New Guinean, and Tongan militaries are being prepared for their role in internal defense, that is, how to wage war efficiently on their own people to facilitate a more intensified process of capitalist accumulation. For this purpose the Fijian military received $300,000 in 1986 while the rest of the Pacific islands received a mere $275,000. Fiji's allocation was justified on grounds of "internal defense"; Papua New Guinea's because of its "size, strategic location and resources"; Tonga was a "reliable friend" and hailed for its hospitable welcome of U.S.

nuclear warships when other countries were reluctant to do so; and the Solomons was favored because of "its size and pro-Western foreign policy" (Wolfowitz, 1985:67–70). Non-aligned Vanuatu was a notable exclusion from these recipients of U.S. largess. Former Prime Minister Mara of Fiji had been the first Pacific island leader to be given the red carpet welcome at the White House (in November 1984) for his strong support of the Israeli bombing of the Iraqi nuclear reactor in 1981, the U.S. invasion of Grenada in 1983, its troop contribution to the U.S.-sponsored Sinai Multinational Observer Force, and denouncing New Zealand's Lange and his increasingly muted criticism of French nuclear imperialism in the South Pacific. Even the CIA-linked Foundation for the Peoples of the South Pacific declared Mara to be its 1984 Pacific Man of the Year.

The particular slant of LIW arises from U.S. recognition that the greatest danger to its Third World client regimes comes from within and not from an external threat from other nations. Thus, the main aim of the Economic Support Fund (ESF) is to stop a client's state economy from collapsing and to maintain the minimum level of political and economic stability without the use of force. Indeed, two thirds of the ESF is provided through direct cash payments or the Commodity Import Program (CIP), which can render balance of payments support to debt-ridden underdeveloped countries or those facing balance of payments problems. In CIP or cash transfer form, the ESF frees up domestic resources for the army to purchase military hardware or services. The "Freedom of Maneuver" given by ESF funds allowed the Fijian military to circumvent the constraint presented by Fiji's financial paralysis after the May 14 (1987) coup. It allowed the Fijian colonels to increase the size of their force from 2,500 to

6,500 with increased salaries while other government personnel were forced to take a cut. They drew most of their new recruits from the ranks of the little-educated, young, unemployed indigenous Fijians who formed the main battering ram of the racist *Taukei* (Fiji for the indigenous Fijians) movement. The ESF monies also allowed the former Alliance Prime Minister Mara to lead the Fijian colonels on a global military shopping spree, for new arms intended chiefly for counterinsurgency and low-intensity warfare. Among their purchases have been sophisticated telephone monitoring equipment, patrol boats, and military helicopter gunships from the Indonesian Aircraft Industries (IBTN) (Callick, 1987). The ESF has been quite an efficient mechanism in transforming Fiji from a relatively pluralistic civilian democracy into a highly militarized island society with its associated characteristics such as increased level of armaments, military authoritarianism, the increasing resort to force, and a militarized culture.

Regional Destabilization

The Israeli presence in the South Pacific is represented in the influx of Israeli experts on LIW tactics (innocuously called ''rural development advisers'') into post-coup Fiji and the sale of its Arava military aircraft to Papua New Guinea (Hunter, 1989). These developments represent an escalation of low-intensity warfare that will now become an increasingly normal feature of Fijian and Pacific island life (*News Grid,* 1991). The Israeli-South Pacific connection follows a familiar pattern found in global troublespots like Central America, Sri Lanka, and the Philippines, where one finds Israeli officers advising governments that are fighting their own people using counterinsurgency and low-intensity warfare methods. Like its Latin American and Sri Lankan counterparts, the Fijian military class are unabashed admirers of the invincible Israeli war machine.

The investigations into the Iran-contra arms deal by the joint committee of the U.S. Congress clearly revealed the use of Israel as a proxy to advance U.S. interests in the Third World when the mother country cannot perform this function due to diplomatic or public relation reasons. Recently, an Israeli author and others have carefully documented the charge that Israel systematically supports repressive regimes in their battles against their own peoples, often at the behest of the United States (Beit-Hallahmi, 1987; Hunter, 1987; Multinational Monitor, 1987). The spreading South Pacific tentacles of the Israeli intelligence and military machinery means that this small, (Middle Eastern) white-settler nation's interests now gird the globe from Managua (helping the contras) to Manila, from Suva to South Africa. Together with Taiwan and other pariah regimes with which it collaborates and has a high degree of intimacy, Israel realizes that conflict has now become internationalized and is very worried about the radicalization of the Third World. It is therefore unlikely that the Fijian military coup will be the last to be seen in the South Pacific. This is underscored by the introduction of U.S. Special Forces to conduct joint-training and wargame exercises with the Papua New Guinean military in the wake of the Fijian coup. Thus, a reverse domino theory, in which one island nation after another falls into the lap of a home-grown military dictator indoctrinated by U.S. Special Forces ideology, seems to be the likely future for the Pacific islands.

The Christian fundamentalist Fijian military strongman, Brigadier Rabuka, has (like his one-time Guatemalan counterpart, General Ríos Montt) claimed that his coup "was divinely ordained and sanctioned" and therefore will brook no opposition or criticism to its strong procapitalist policies. The claim that his regime has a monopoly on divine blessing also represents a thinly veiled attempt to try and nullify the populist appeal of Fiji's overthrown civilian coalition government. All this is part of the Fijian military state's hegemonic mission to create an ideology of order that seeks to legitimate its recourse to repression to maintain order. In today's Fiji, the free expression of opinion that fails to conform to the prevailing nuances of the state's ideology of order is no longer an expression of legitimate political difference; it has become a criminal offense. The "militarization of politics" and "criminalization of dissent" becomes the order of the day. Brigadier Rabuka has now introduced an Internal Security Decree that allows him to put somebody away in prison for twenty-five years without parole. The Fijian strongman wants to base his new apartheid constitution on that of Malaysia with its draconian Internal Security Act. He also wants to imitate Malaya's bankrupt New Economic Policy (NEP) by which the indigenous Malayan aristocracy wants to transform itself into a new, indigenous-based capitalist class. Singapore's passive trade unions serve for Rabuka as an example for labor in Fiji, and he sees a parallel between the entrenched Indonesian army and future role of the military in Fiji (Witcher, 1987:1).

The destabilization and overthrow of the Fijian labor coalition government is only the latest example of a low-intensity warfare that is being launched against small Pacific Island microstates and movements that dare to assert their sovereignty and right to self-determination. These developments are the direct result of the United States (and France)

raising their profile by formulating "strategic denial" as the
linchpin of the Western alliance's posture in the Pacific.
Strategic denial ensures the protection of what Chomsky
calls "the Fifth Freedom," understood to mean "the freedom to rob, to exploit" and dominate, to undertake a
course of action to ensure that existing privilege is protected and advanced. The Fifth Freedom is the main tool
used to "protect and advance existing privilege" from a
government that threatens its destabilization (Chomsky,
1985:47).

> Destabilization is a comprehensive concept and refers to all
> kinds of effort on the part of a powerful actor, short of open
> invasion, to weaken and eliminate another actor that for
> economic and political reasons is unacceptable, even if not
> constituting a direct security threat. Not a Vietnam-type
> approach, which involves full-scale bombing and warfare,
> destabilization seeks to destroy the government from within,
> to render a country ungovernable. It is implosion. To appear
> legitimate, sabotage is done by nationals of the target country
> or from neighbouring countries, not by the army of the
> destabilizer. (Thompson, 1988:22)

The main targets are governments that want to experiment in social reform and social transformation, like Bavadra's Fijian government. The main goal of destabilization is
to destroy any attempt by the new government to take
control of the economy. To maintain the market and production relations under the old patterns of dominance, the
regional power has to show Fijian nationals that the new
system cannot work. Social and economic transformations
are threatening examples in the region, which consists of
colonial New Caledonia and the feudal aristocracies of
Tonga and Western Samoa. The Fijian labor coalition gov-

ernment of Prime Minister Bavadra made it clear that the workers (*tamata cakacaka*) and peasants (*lewe-ni-vanua*) would now receive the fruits of their labor as workers and peasants emerged to assert their rights. The ILO (International Labor Organization) conventions governing the basic rights of workers and their working conditions that had been abrogated by the aristocratic Alliance Party were to be brought back into force and debate and criticisms of work conditions were encouraged. For the first time the people of Fiji had the first nonracial government and one that really cared for their conditions. The main priority of the Fijian labor coalition was to provide their citizens with services to improve the quality of life. It was boldly moving along this line in its first few weeks in government until destabilization escalated U.S. hegemony demands that economies remain open to investment, maximizing private production with "free" competition and "free" trade.

The economic factor is important but must not be overstated. To the Reagan administration, maintaining ideological hegemony was equally or even more important. Though not a threat to the national security of the United States, Fiji under a labor coalition government was a serious threat to the ideological hegemony of the United States and France in the region. Therefore, its lessons, its example had to be "neutralized." Destabilization begins with a propaganda campaign, for it determines the success of the whole policy. Nationals of both the target and perpetrating countries must be convinced of the necessity to reverse the policies of the new government (Thompson, 1988). Systematic denigration of the Bavadra government was aimed to convince Western audiences and Pacific island people that such a Fijian government was an "enemy," and tagging this government as Indian-dominated and Libyan- (or Soviet-) influenced goes a long way to achieving that goal. The first offensive, therefore, is literally a war of words. The language must relate however tenuously to events so disinformation campaigns are conducted. Arms shipments are "discovered" in Australia, while Indo-Fijian sugar cane fields and shops are reported by "the authorities" to be littered with Czech-made AK-47s. Propaganda directed inside the target country is well organized and financed. Probably the most successful campaign, because it takes advantage of the mistakes the Fijian Labor Party made in joining with an Indo-Fijian dominated party, was the accusation that the Bavadra government was Indian-dominated.

The propaganda campaigns in the 1980s had reached new levels of international coordination and sophistication. Right-wing groups organized to roll back communism have existed since the 1950s, but they had gained importance with the resurgence of conservative governments in the 1980s. All of them disseminated their views through the media, but some had become right-wing think tanks, providing analysis directly to governments. For example, the Heritage Foundation's Asian Studies Center put out a number of policy briefing papers that formed the basis of the Reagan administration's policy for the Pacific islands. The Honolulu-based Pacific Islands Developments Program (PIDP) prepared a South Pacific briefing paper for the U.S. State Department and financed a consultancy team led by a former Australian colonial official that recommended the return of the colonial Fijian Native Administration with its harsh penalties to the Fijian villages. In Europe, the Hans Seidel Foundation of the conservative Christian Democratic Union in Germany footed the bill for the training of *turaga-ni-koro* (village headman) crucial to the successful control of the Fijian village population in their proper position of docile political submissiveness. Former Fijian British Army veterans are to run this revitalized native colonial administration. The Taiwan-based World Anti-Communist League (WACL) has held several meetings in Fiji and Tonga and can boast that the membership of its South Pacific branches include a bulk of the influential political and business leaders of the region. World Vision, the CIA-connected, Bible-translating organization, has its tentacles all over the Pacific and one of its Fijian officers is the loudest mouth and most intransigent of the *Taukei* (landowner) movement that was created to destabilize and finally overthrow the Bavadra government. Then there is the Pacific Democratic Union (PDU), an association of right-wing parties in the Asia-Pacific region that includes the U.S. Republican Party and the Australian National-Liberal Parties. Australia's former Liberal prime minister, Malcolm Fraser, was attending a PDU meeting at a luxury hotel in Fiji chaired by Fiji's former Alliance prime minis-ter, Mara, on the very day of the Fijian military takeover. Mara has disavowed any involvement in the Fijian coup and his attendance at the PDU meeting gives him a degree of "plausible deniability." The proliferation of these organi-zations worldwide and into the Pacific Islands goes beyond legal lobbying or international networking. With funds for counterrevolutionaries threatened in the elected parlia-ments, these organizations represent the "privatization of roll back." A second important reason for the organization is that as private entities, they are not subjected to as much public scrutiny as government administration (Thompson, 1988).

The Logic of Strategic Denial vs. the Logic of Liberation

The increasing contention of the superpowers and the ANZUS policy of strategic denial means that the Pacific is to be maintained as "a closed ocean in an open world" that will continue to be used as a testing ground for nuclear weapons and delivery vehicles and as a dumping ground for nuclear waste, where the escalating militarization of the region parallels the arming of client states with no regard for the safety and livelihood of the people living there. The flickering light of democratization is now being put out beginning with Fiji, the most servile U.S. client state in the region. The callous attitude of imperialist powers toward the use of Pacific islanders as nuclear guinea pigs and toward their destiny was summarized by former U.S. Secretary of State Henry Kissinger, commenting on the danger posed to the people of Micronesia by missiles being test-fired from Vandenburg Air Force Base in California to the Kwajalein Atoll test range in the Marshall Islands: "There are only 90,000 of them out there. Who gives a damn?" (Hickel, 1971:208).

From a Pacific island perspective the underlying logic of "strategic denial" can be summed up as follows: To be exploited by their ANZUS masters through pro-Western leaders like the King of Tonga or the Fijian military dictators Mara and Rabuka is better than allowing in the Soviets (or Cubans or Libyans). The islanders are being offered a choice between "the devil and the deep blue sea"; there is no recognition of their potential for autonomous development and decision making—"if you are not with us you must be with them"—and thus become proper targets for destabilization. The paternalism and racism inherent in such warped logic is too obvious to need comment. When

Vanuatu leaders urged their fellow islanders to keep the Pacific an "open ocean in an open world" by reducing their excessive pro-Western alignment and allowing socialist states (apart from China access to the region as a counter-balance, the Western response was immediate and hostile. The attack on this call by Vanuatu to "diversify dependence" was spearheaded by the defense intellectuals, one of them pontificating on the "naive and mischievous sophistry" of such a foreign policy position (Herr, 1984:185). Hence, the fuss kicked up by the U.S., Australian, and New Zealand governments over Kiribati's decision to sign a competitive fishing agreement with the Soviets (Neemia, 1986). A Vanuatu foreign affairs official laid this argument to rest when he observed that if Australia and New Zealand are concerned about "Libyan terrorism" spreading to the Pacific, then they had better double-check to identify who was responsible for the state-sponsored terrorism already in the region. The carnage in New Caledonia, the genocide in West Papua and East Timor, and the blowing-up of a Greenpeace protest ship in New Zealand's Auckland Harbour had nothing to do with Libya but a lot to do with Western powers, who are the self-proclaimed protectors of Pacific island people (Sawyer, 1986).

The strategic-denial doctrine is buttressed by a forward-based offensive military strategy constituting the Pacific ring of thermonuclear fire, which comprises strategic/nuclear and conventional weapons as well as logistical, environmental/biological, covert, advisory, coast guard, and sea-lift capabilities. The system is highly interconnected and stretches from Hawaii to Guam, Japan, and South Korea; from Hawaii to Australia and Antarctica; and from the Philippines to Diego Garcia and the Persian Gulf (Hayes et al., 1986; Arkin and Fieldhouse, 1985). It seems highly ironic that the pinnacle of technological achievement, the most interdependent and developed system unifying the Asia-Pacific region, is a military one, designed not to coordinate the logistics and production for human development but to repress human potential and, in the worst case, wreak nuclear devastation on the region in one final act of fear and domination.

The Task of the Pacific Island Intellectual

What does this intensification of economic super-exploitation, militarization, and forward/offensive strategy mean for the practice of the Pacific island intellectual? We must begin by asserting that the Pacific islands are part and parcel of the underdeveloped Third World, which is integrated into the world capitalist economy. As such, Pacific island societies are no exception to the general rule that the prevailing social scientific ideology and history always are constructed with an eye to the interests of the ruling class. These ideologies and histories must conceal the exercise of power (and the enjoyment of privileges and wealth) by the islands' aristocratic/"big man"/capitalist class, projecting its interests as universal interests, making it seem natural that representatives of this class should determine socioeconomic policy in the general interests. The aim here is to blur and conceal social division in order to provide, like the Pacific Way ideology, a condition of false unity among potentially conflicting groups, principally wage labor and capital, followed by chiefs/*tonwais* ("big man") and commoners, landlords and tenants, and different ethnic groups. Bourgeois and aristocratic ideology in this case function to render social power as self-evident, as beyond question and therefore outside history (Chomsky, 1978).

One of the basic tasks of the Pacific island intellectuals is therefore to discover their historically defined role not only as social critics, but even more so as cartographers involved in mapping out the structure and mechanism sustaining domination. This will entail a struggle against the long and well-established position adopted by most Pacific intellectuals in both the colonial and neocolonial phase of our history, in which they functioned as upholders of authorized world views—as mere bootblacks and propagandists for whomever happened to be in power. To accomplish this task of challenging or reorienting the dominant colonial and neocolonial consciousness (Constantino, 1978; Sivandan, 1977), we need committed intellectuals who are not going to join the uncritical chorus singing high praises to *Vakaitaukei* (Fijian Way of Life), *Fakatonga* (Tongan Way), *Fa'aSamoa* (Samoan Way), and the Melanesian Way without being aware of the contradictions these idealized and romanticized ways of life have with the realities governing the socioeconomic conditions in the capitalist-oriented and dominated societies of the South Pacific (Durutalo, 1983).

This is a time of widespread socioeconomic and political turmoil in the islands, and there is a real danger that conditions will push most Pacific island intellectuals into a kind of "realism." They may begin to feel that they must be realistic because in the present situation, attention to what ought to be done rather than what is done will, in Machiavelli's words, bring ruin rather than preservation. Such a realism, by its narrow focus, biases the reflection of issues to be studied in favor of an interpretation of reality based on fear and hate, upon the limitations of possibilities, emphasizing what cannot be done. The difficulty with this Machiavellian type of realism is not that it rejects the easy optimism of an utopian dream world, nor that it focuses on what *is*, but that it unnecessarily constricts the focus. In Lynd's wonderful prose, the shortsightedness of this realism is that

> it does not take *what is* in its full dimensions, which includes what can be. Realism which excludes the as-yet unrealized possibilities of the future inherent in the present, realism which excludes the larger, enduring purposes of [human beings], is less than full realism. Full realism includes [people's] dreams. Dreams need not be illusions. If utopianism which ignores what is brings ruin, it is also true that realism which denies dreams of what may be will not bring preservation. Where there are no dreams, people perish. (Lynd, 1952:24)

This is why it is crucial that Pacific island intellectuals, no matter how great the danger or how exigent the immediate situation in which they find themselves, should not abdicate to others, particularly to the counter-intellectuals, the scope and nature of intellectual inquiry (Constantino, 1978; Sivandan, 1977). When intellectuals resign their traditional position of independent thought to support unquestioningly the "national interest," they are accepting issues that are defined by others and thereby become mere instruments of national policy. Is it not precisely the obligation of the intellectual to extend the realism of the immediate, to constantly reexamine events to restore historical depth and range, to avoid the use of activity as an anodyne?

An intellectual's activity does not have to become a total prisoner of its historical situation. This demands a realism that refuses to stop with issues as given, but that insists on examination of the complex phenomena subsumed under stereotypes. But the reliance on stereotypes, which blocks intellectual inquiry at the start, is precisely the method that military and political realism, with the increasing support of the counter-intellectuals, currently employs. In this, there is a tendency to use wider and looser categories with less and less precise meaning, and to use less and less critically such terms as "democracy," "communism," "peace," "aggression," "freedom," "ethnicity," and "tradition," as if they were the end of the analysis and have become self-explanatory instead of what they should be for the intellectual: the impetus to continue investigation of what is happening in the Pacific islands and to search for fresh ways of approaching present problems.

A time of crisis such as now, with economic and political turmoil sweeping the shores of the Pacific, need not be a time of paralysis or defense. In such a period, the business of the intellectual is to attempt to discover what new forms of new values are coming into being, to try to distinguish the valid from the specious, and to bring those charged with hope to fulfillment. In such "times of trouble" we need intellectuals who will hazard all they have in order to discern not only the limitations but also the possibilities in the present, to widen the area of choice and to help bring about a productive and constructive future. Such exercise of the function of the intellectual is never more important than when it demands the greatest courage.

REFERENCES

Ahmad, E. 1985. "Cracks in the Western View: Questions for the U.S. and Europe." *Radical America* 19(1), pp. 37–46.
Arkin, M., and R. Fieldhouse. 1985. *Nuclear Battlefields: Global Links in the Arms Race*. Cambridge, Mass.: Ballinger.
Babadzan, A. 1988. "Kastom and Nation-Building in the South

Pacific." In R. Guideri, F. Pollizi, and S. J. Tambiah (eds.), *Ethnicities and Nations: Process of Interethnic Relations in Latin American, South West Asia and the Pacific.* Austin: Rothko Chapel Book (distributed by University of Texas Press).

Beit-Hallahmi, B. 1987. *The Israeli Connection.* New York: Pantheon.

Callick, R. 1987. "Fiji Rebels Ready to Break Royal Link." *The Sunday Observer,* September 27.

Chomsky, N. 1978. *Intellectuals and the State.* Baarn, Netherlands: Vereldvenster.

———. 1985. *Turning the Tide.* Boston: South End Press.

Constantino, R. 1978. *Neo-Colonial Identity and Counter-Consciousness in the Philippines: Essays on Cultural Decolonization.* London: Merlin Press.

Crocombe, R., and S. Tupouniua (eds.). 1975. *The Pacific Way.* Institute of Pacific Studies, University of the South Pacific, Suva, Fiji.

Durutalo, S. 1983. "The Liberation of the Pacific Island Intellectual." *Review (SSED)* 10, pp. 6–18.

Firth, R. 1963. *We, the Tikopia.* London: George Allen & Unwin.

Firth, S. 1986. "The Nuclear Issue in the South Pacific." *Journal of Pacific History* 21(4), pp. 202–16.

Gough, K., and H. Gardezi. 1987. "The 'Soviet Threat' in the Pacific." *Bulletin of Concerned Asian Scholars* 19(2), p. 67.

Hayes, P., L. Zarsky, and W. Bello. 1986. *American Lake: Nuclear Peril in the Pacific.* New York: Penguin.

Herr, R. 1984. "The American Impact on Australian Defense Relations with the South Pacific Islands." *Australian Outlook* 38(3).

Hickel, W. 1971. *Who Owns America.* Englewood Cliffs, N.J.: Prentice-Hall.

Howe, K. 1977. "The Fate of the Savage in Pacific Historiography." *New Zealand Journal of History* 11(2), pp. 154–317.

Hunter, J. 1987. "The Israeli Role in Guatemala." *Race and Class* 29, pp. 35–54.

———. 1989. "Papua New Guinea: Bees and History." *Israeli Foreign Affairs*, March.

Ilke, F. 1986. "Taking Sides in Small Wars." *Defense/86* (March/April), pp. 63–70.

Jimenez, G. 1983. "Anthropology in My View." In M. C. Howard, (ed.), *Anthropology: A Brief Critical History*, pp. 69–76. Suva, Fiji: University of the South Pacific.

Kolkewicz, R. 1987. "The Strange Career of the Defense Intellectual." *Orbis: A Journal of World Affairs* 31(2), 190.

Lynd, H. 1952. "Realism and the Intellectual in a Time of Crisis." *The American Scholar* 1(21), pp. 221–32.

Malinowski, B. 1922. *Argonauts of the Western Pacific*. New York: E. P. Dutton.

Mead, M. 1928. *Coming of Age in Samoa: A Psychological Study of "Primitive" Youth for Western Civilization*. New York: Morrow.

———. 1935. *Sex and Temperament in Three Primitive Societies*. London: Routledge & Kegan Paul.

———. 1939. *From the South Seas: Studies of Adolescence and Primitive Societies*. New York: Morrow.

Mediansky, F. 1987. "The Security Outlook in the Southwest Pacific." *The Australian Quarterly*, Spring and Summer, pp. 266–77.

Miles, S. 1986. "'US' New Strategy in the Third World—The Low-Intensity Conflict." *Ampo* 18(1), pp. 72–4.

Mintz, S. 1985. *The Sweetness of Power: The Place of Sugar in Modern History*. New York: Penguin.

Narokobi, B. 1980. *The Melanesian Way: Suva, Fiji and Port Moresby, Papua New Guinea*. Institute of Pacific Studies, University of the South Pacific, Suva, Fiji.

Neemia, U. 1986. "Russophobia and Self-Determination in Kiribati." *South Pacific Forum* 3(2), pp. 136–49.

News Grid. 1991. "Fiji Asks Israel for Military Aid." August 2. CompuServe, Columbus, Ohio.

North American Committee on Latin America. 1986. *Special Issue on Low-Intensity Warfare* (April/May).

Rokotuivuna, A. 1973. *Fiji: A Developing Australian Colony.* International Development Action, Melbourne.

Said, E. 1978. *Orientalism.* New York: Pantheon Books.

Sawyer, S. 1986. "Rainbow Warrior: Nuclear War in the South Pacific." *Third World Quarterly* 8(4), pp. 1325–1336.

Sewell, J., and C. Contec. 1987. "Foreign Aid and Gramm-Rudman." *Foreign Affairs,* Summer, pp. 1015–1036.

Shultz, G. 1986. "Low-Intensity Warfare: The Challenge of Ambiguity." *The U.S. Department of State Bulletin,* March, pp. 15–17.

Sivandan, A. 1977. "The Liberation of the Black intellectual." *Race & Class* 17(4), pp. 329–42.

Sutherland, W. 1987. "Fiji." In C. Clarke and T. Payne (eds.), *Politics, Security and Development in Small States,* pp. 113–24. Sydney: Allen & Unwin.

Thompson, C. 1988. "War by Another Name: Destabilization in Nicaragua and Mozambique." *Race & Class* 29, pp. 21–44.

Vusoniwailala, L. 1978. "Communicating a Pacific Model for Human Development." In A. Mamak and G. M. McCall (eds.), *Paradise Postponed: Essays on Research and Development in the South Pacific,* pp. 115–25. Sydney, Australia: Pergamon Press.

Wallerstein, I. 1977. "The Task of Social Science" (editorial). *Review.* Fernand Braudel Center, State University of New York, Binghamton.

Weinberger, S. 1986. *Report of the Secretary of Defense, Fiscal Year 1986.* Washington, D.C.: U.S. Department of Defense.

Winkler, J. 1982. *Losing Control: Towards an Understanding of Transnational Corporations in the Pacific Islands Context.* Pacific Conference of Churches, Suva, Fiji.

Witcher, S. 1987. "Fiji's God-Appointed Colonel Seeks to Lead His People Back to Paradise." *Asian Wall Street Journal,* October 19, p. 1.

Wolfowitz, P. 1987. "FY '86 Assistance Requests for East Asia and the Pacific." *U.S. Department of State Bulletin,* May, pp. 63–70.

JOHN D. WAIKO

9 *Tugata:* Culture, Identity, and Commitment

In Binandere a *tugata* is the introduction of a speech while the person stands in his *arapa*.[1] In his *tugata* a speaker establishes himself, his identity, and his social position in the clan, and gives a brief outline of his subject. He would be embarrassed if someone introduced him: in the village a man speaks for himself, staying put on his *arapa* and, having attracted attention by rattling his spatula against his lime gourd and clearing his throat, he says: "I am a grandson of so and so, my father is x of the y clan and I live at z village. No one but me is about to talk." In this way the speaker introduces himself through his grandparents, from whom his knowledge is derived, and through his parents and relatives who are his mentors.[2] The *tugata* is important in two ways. The audience must know from the beginning the identity of the speaker and the sources of his information because without that they will turn their backs on him, a certain sign that they think he knows little about his topic. He has failed to establish his authority over his subject and his right to a hearing.

My *tugata,* for the purpose of this paper, is twofold. It includes first, my village roots and my Binandere identity. And then, because my lifetime and my work span both village and nation—including my long-established Binandere identity as well as a newly emerging Papua New Guinea identity—my *tugata* as a western-trained, national academic figure also is presented.

Arapa: Village Roots and Binandere Identity

Here, then, is my *tugata.* I am a grandson of Tariambari; my father is Dademo and the clan members descended from Danato, the ancestor of Ugousopo clan. I was the third person born at Tabara in a family of five children, three boys and two girls. This was the fifth time the Bosida clan had called their village Tabara, but after a huge flood destroyed it my father and mother moved to Boide. At this place, there was a cluster of five houses. Three were *mando,* women's houses belonging to the two wives of my uncle, Dumbu, and one for my mother; two were *oro,* men's houses, one for Dumbu and his sons and the other belonged to us. An *arapa,* a kind of wide street, was in between the *mando* and the *oro.* We were a community of 5 adults and 12 children.

The Binandere, to which I belong, see themselves as located within a family and among a small group with whom they have built strong bonds. In turn, a Binandere views others on the basis of their kin associations and the alliances they might have fashioned in the past through war and trade, or today through business or politics. Much Binandere behavior is determined by obligations and enmities within a close network of people. All are judged on how they fulfilled their obligations to others. This aspect of my Binandere identity has been carried over into my actions and reactions to national academic and political events and decisions.

Binandere are also very conscious of their location by place, for the Binandere have looked out on the world from a house and a village that they see as surrounded by three concentric circles: *rorobu* (gardening land), *taote* (breeding forest), and *toian* (hunting ground) (see Waiko, J.D., 1985:12–17). My own roots are anchored at the *arapa* of Boide hamlet, where I grew up and to which I have made conscious and constant reference in later life.

The significance of the *arapa* is that this physical space holds all people who reside on it as a single entity. Its members enter into a kind of contractual obligation with one another, which requires that, if and when one of them is affected by something else, then another member is expected to act in response to or as a consequence of it. For instance, in a *tai pamo duduno,* or a clash, the *arapa* is zealously guarded so that no outsider enters it. Should any outsider set foot on it, then that act provokes angry reaction from the residents of this section of the village. In times of conflict, everyone must attempt to stay put in their *arapa,* even if challenged by their opponent. Another example is that if a member of the *arapa* residence dies, all the other members must go into mourning. A man of another *oro be* (clan) hunts for a wild pig, kills it, ties its front and hind legs, put a stick through them, carries the corpse to the village, and hangs it on the side of the house belonging to the next of kin of the dead person. This act requires that when the mortuary feast is held the hunter is given a whole domesticated pig or the best part of the one slaughtered for the final ceremony in honor of the deceased.

The *arapa* could be the area between the *mando* (women's house) and the *oro* (men's house), both of which face each other, or just the front space of a house in a particular section of the village. Thus the physical charter of a community contains the idea that one belongs to a fixed place or *arapa*. From there one is linked in a web of networks of relationships that underlie rights and obligations within the confines of the *arapa*. Although the area is bare ground usually swept by women, the *arapa* is a highly respected place. This sense of honor is expressed in the killing of a pig whenever an adult falls in an *arapa* as a result of slippery ground. On a rainy day, everyone grips the ground tightly with their toes to avoid falling. Even if the fall is an accident, the owners of the *arapa* make absolutely certain that relatives of the fallen do not accuse them of having set up a snare to trap intruders with evil intent from entering other people's *arapa*. The pig killing is a declaration that the owner is innocent and that the fall is in fact an accident.

The center of the *arapa* in the village is marked by *ni sisi,* the fireplace in front of and underneath each house within the rows of *mando* and *oro*. For the women, their *ni sisi* is for the fire to cook lumps of vegetables (taro, banana, potatoes, pumpkin, greens) with pieces of meat and fish in large clay pots of conical shape, whose sizes range from 20 cubic meters to 5 cubic millimeters. It is also a place where women gather for gossip. I cherish my mother's *arapa* with fondness. She cried out in a beautiful and poetic singing, which was a vivid description of happiness, sadness, or pain to express whatever mood moved her emotions.

In the morning or in the evening, the women shift their fire under the eaves of the roof or *aewa,* the ash place inside the *mando.* For men, the *ni sisi* is a hall without walls where both formal and informal meetings take place. Social interaction among male members of the nuclear family occur here everyday at early dawn and at dusk, except when it rains and the fire burns underneath the house. No big cooking is done here, although male children may reheat the leftover food from the previous night. They may also bake bananas or sago to eat for breakfast, without depending too much on their sisters and mother to provide it daily, particularly during lean times. This is also a place of informal learning as the male elders teach codes of behavior, family history, legends, and other traditions. Almost every day this knowledge is told and repeated. By the time children reach the age of initiation in older times or become teenagers nowadays, they must have heard these various testimonies a thousand times. Thus, from about the age of two, it was my duty to learn to make fire at the *ni sisi* and every afternoon I collected twigs to feed it constantly. Among my daily chores was to light the fire, place woven mats of coconut leaf around it, and stake a lance with an arrow end upwards, for the senior elders to lean against when they came to take their seats to transmit knowledge. My responsibilities also included collecting bunches of nuts from betel trees about 200 feet in height, and picking sticks of pepper or mustard leaves to be placed near the fire place for evening chewing. If these duties were performed every day without complaint, the child was regarded as undergoing a proper upbringing according to the custom of the clan. Elders pour wisdom and power through the words they speak at the *ni sisi,* so that obedient children tend to grow up learning to be wise and to have power of the knowledge. Binandere earn their way to knowledge. Having done so myself over many years, I question whether knowledge gained by outsiders over weeks or months or even a year or two can ever accurately reflect Papua New Guinean reality.

The *arapa* is also a formal gathering place where important meetings occur. Men come together to discuss issues of general concern and of warfare, in particular. Formal feasts and major ceremonies are conducted in this area, where the sponsors are received, entertained, and fed, and from which the distribution of pig meat and vegetables is done. In times of disputes or conflicts, the parties stay put on their own *arapa* and speeches are delivered from them; decisions are handed down here after the big men have made their public statements. In some ways it is possible to think of national institutions such as national and provincial parliaments, chambers of local government councils, or even the National Research Institute and the University of Papua New Guinea as national *arapa*.

Formal negotiation about marriage and bride price also occur on the *arapa*, as well as the exchange of bride wealth. Late in the evenings, two elders might meet there to discuss sorcery. Nowadays, village committees and councillors use the *arapa* to discuss community matters and business concerns. My own Australian National University doctoral dissertation was presented at such an *arapa*.

During the *bondo,* a final feast to honor a recently deceased relative, the *guru* dance took place at night when men gathered at the *arapa* of the family holding the feasts (Waiko 1985:19–22). The young men beat the *euku* drums and blew the conch shell, joining in the chorus of songs while the elders dramatized and recited them as the men moved to and fro within the *arapa*. The sounds of the instruments to the rhythm of the *guru* echoed the singing of birds, frogs, insects, and the crowing of cocks at dawn and dusk. All these were a natural orchestration of music and drama in the theater of the *arapa*.

Tatoro da Badari: *Growing Up Under the Armpit*

The power, authority, and indeed the effectiveness of the right to belong to an *arapa* are articulated most pointedly when members of a household or clan discuss matters to do with payback, for the charter rights and obligations of an *arapa* member are often brought out in time of war and peace. Only as a member of the *arapa* entity can you act in a conflict, engage in a hostile killing action, or propose a peaceful resolution if your family or any member of your group is affected. Because direct personal responsibility must be involved, it is not acceptable for one member of an *arapa* to take action on serious matters on behalf of another, for that may lead to grave consequences. Personal action and the rationale for hostility is justified when a member of your group is hurt and thus individual rights are violated. That very act affects you personally, and also your rights to be a member of the same entity, be it household or clan. The charter for individual action is that the hostile act toward another person also affects you. In terms of vengeance, complaint can exist only if there is a personal loss, including loss of a close relatives, land, or valuable items. For instance, in warfare or through sorcery, the killing of a woman of marriageable age requires revenge. In addition to the loss of that person, a member of the household or clan also loses the right of access to a share of the bridewealth. This arouses such emotion that the urge or impulse is felt to initiate action to exact vengeance or equivalent loss. Yet the use of violence is strictly controlled. it is a group-sanctioned right, not an individual right, and applies only against another person who has done wrong or harm to someone who is personally close. The victim of revenge is not necessarily a person who is disliked. The *arapa* provided the forum for both private conversation and the public debate to arrive at a consensus with which the majority of people present feel comfortable. A decision reached collectively is capable of holding together those present, at least temporarily until the decision is implemented. If those present do not hold together, then the decision, at least, contains (or comprises) the basis for any further debate. Thus consensus is a kind of an *obada,* a lid that is imposed on further talk either by agreeing or, in many cases, by apparently accepting the implementation of a decision by most members present during a particular discussion.

The right to be an integral part of the *arapa* entitled household members to benefit from the fruits of one another's labor, whether in sharing garden produce, a big catch of fish, rendering service, or raising a pig for another close kin. Each member is regarded as a resource person and is expected to contribute something towards the well-being of the *arapa* as a corporate entity, whether economic or emotional. Everyone relies upon each other as a source of material and moral support in good times and bad. As such, the household as a unit is a capital resource when any kin undergoes a lean period. Whenever an *arapa* member is in need of a valuable item such as a pig that is not easily available, then other members provide it. That is the art of *arapa* interdependence embedded in the charter. Simply put, every member regards the other as *ujiwo,* a capital resource from which assistance of any kind comes forth at good and bad times through the obligation of kinship.

The underlying principle that embodies the ideal value of the concept of *arapa* is goodness. Although Leo Hannett used the concept of "tribe" in a loose manner, he nonetheless described this value well. "It is manifested in that personal humane concern for other, that sense of oneness, and that feeling of brotherhood which flows in the blood of every member of the tribe. Why must such good qualities be thrown away? Isn't the world today yearning with anguish for just such qualities? I would rather be a tribalist, feeling at one with, and being loved by, many than be an individualist who is more likely to be shipwrecked with the inhumane disease of loneliness" (Hannett, 1978:99).

In the absence of the state, the ethical system of the Binandere emphasized the importance of reciprocity among people. The cultivation of sympathy and cooperation must begin in the family, as defined by *arapa*, and then extend by degrees into the larger areas of the village, clan, and tribe.

Just as reciprocity and a mutual sense of belonging exists among members of the *arapa* in the temporal world, so its boundaries extend to include the dead kin in the spiritual universe. At dawn and at dusk, the fire is lit in the *ni sisi* or the hearth of the *arapa*. At the same time, fire is also made under the *oro* and *mando*, all of whose floors are raised from the ground. It is believed that, while the family gather around for warmth and other social reasons, close relatives among the dead also come to the fire in the place beneath the houses where the Binandere used to bury their dead in the old days. The living and dead share the fire. Binandere feel that if the fire is not lit under their own house, then dead kin are insulted and will go to the *arapa* where there is one.

If the family members of an *arapa* have not had a good taro harvest or been unsuccessful at hunting, this is because dead kin have turned their backs on them. For it is close relatives among the dead who are a capital resource to provide and protect the growing taro and other vegetables in the food gardens, as well as to make wild animals easily available to hunters in the nearby forest for a quick kill. In fact, whenever an *arapa* member has a good harvest, some vegetables are cooked with fish or animal meat in a clay pot and offered to the dead kin. When a huge wild pig is killed and distributed, some of the best pieces are cooked and offered on small sticks as thanksgiving to the dead by tucking them into the sago roof inside the house. I recall vivid sights. Often, as I lay on the black palm floor with my face upwards, I could see where fat from the pig meat had oiled the roof. The constant smoke from the fireplace turned the thatched leaves black. so that glowing rays of fire from underneath the house shone or glistened against the roof.

Thus, the *arapa* is the starting point of both the living and the dead. What the *arapa* at Boide knew to be true of myself, I have imposed on the rest of the temporal and spiritual world that is important to me. Often I thought of the spirits of the dead, the animals, even the rocks and plants as living within a complex set of family and other relationships, all sharing the hearth of an *arapa* with the living kin. It was warm and comforting to grow up feeling that I was cared for and protected by the closely knit family of both present and past—to remember my father's household was the sponsor of feasts and that clan members often supported us by providing food and other services. The nurture received as a child and my upbringing from such a background has remained as a strong, constant pull toward my *arapa* of Boide hamlet.

Wider Identity: Provincial, National, International Tugata

Briefly, I must now turn away from my village roots to give more details about myself. I do this so that my perspective is known, so that people may gauge how I know some of the things that I write about.

I remained a child of the village until I was about 12 years old. The formal initiation ceremonies that marked the transformation of the young Binandere from youth to manhood had been discontinued by the time I was growing up, and also I did not have the chance to perform some of the tasks that the Binandere see as being measures of adulthood. I never cut, chopped, and collected sago on my own but always helped my father, and I have never hunted and killed a pig on my own. These were the activities and distinctions of an older youth. A couple more years in the village would have enabled me to accomplish those tasks of the adults. By the time I was 10 years old I must have heard the legends, accounts of warfare, and other stories a thousand times. I had absorbed much of the oral tradition and other customs and my clan history before I entered a formal system of western education.

One evening I made a fire in front of the *oro* and my mother came and placed her *tero,* a mat woven from coconut palm, and sat on it. She told me of a decision that she and my father had made, and her words were like fish bones in my throat; I was to go to school at Tabara.[3] I felt uneasy because this was the beginning of leaving my parents' protection. There were some members of my clan at Tabara, and Kove, my uncle, was the evangelist in charge of the school; but nothing could drive out my feeling of insecurity about going to school. Apart from stories that the evangelist teachers were beating some pupils, my main worry was that my going to school would break the life I had grown accustomed to in the village.

In the evening the fire was lit in front of the *oro* as usual, but instead of the adults telling legends and other stories my brother told me what would be expected of me when I started school. He taught me how to drill so my first words of English were, "fall in," "right dress," "left turn," "right turn," "about turn," "stand at ease," "attention," and "quick march." "Do not try to understand the meaning of these words," he said. "But you must learn to make the right movement as the teacher calls them." He gave me a couple of lessons on the river beach where he acted like a teacher and I as the pupil. Thus began my "parrot memorizing" instead of learning through experience and examples from the parents.

The day came when I was to go to school. Traveling to and from school, lessons in Binandere, playing in the breaks, and working in the teachers' gardens became the routine in and out of school for the rest of 1955.

After school we returned to Boide. Sometimes we helped our parents in the garden. If it was the trapping season we set traps to catch birds and animals. We checked the shares early in the morning before going to school. In the evening we lit fires both in front and underneath the *oro* and the elders taught us traditions and customs. In other words I began to acquire *kiawa* (white) skills and *kiawa* knowledge to graft on to the continuing education from my society. (The Binandere do use a literal term for white man, *parara embo;* but the common term, *kiawa,* comes from the word for the first type of steel axes introduced to the Binandere, an axe with a fluted blade. The foreigners were the *kiawa embo,* the steel axe men.)

The Tabara village mission school was the first in a succession of institutions which were to take me further and further away from my father's *oro.* In 1956 I entered the Anglican Mission primary school at Manau, and shared with other boarders a life ordered by the ringing of bells.

From Manau I went to Martyrs' Memorial secondary school on the Buna-Kokoda road in Orokaiva territory. I was moving to the edge of the lands that a Tabara man could know through his knowledge of clan migrations and alliances. My last year of secondary school, at Madang, took me well beyond the world known to the older Binandere. In 1967 I went to the University of Papua New Guinea and in 1973 I completed the M.A. in African history, at the School of Oriental and African Studies of London University.

It was while I was a student at the University of Papua New Guinea (UPNG) that I encountered Margaret Mead. My reaction to her helped to inform my subsequent education, particularly my doctoral dissertation, and my activity as director of the Institute of Applied Social and Economic Research (now the National Research Institute), which among other tasks responded to requests by foreigners to do research in this country.

Although the thrust of Mead's confrontation at the University of Papua New Guinea with the grandchildren of the people she studied in Manus remains emotionally powerful for me, others—particularly Leo Hannett and Elijah Titus—will have to speak to the specifics of their charge that she had inaccurately depicted their culture, and her dismissive response. As one who had grown up learning the words of the elders and being steeped in Binandere tradition and knowledge, I was offended that people my own age from Manus, people with similar knowledge of their own traditions, were dismissed because of their age. Mead told them in strong terms that this outsider's knowledge was more valid. Elders said it was more valid.

I determined at that time to explore the issue of validity of historical knowledge and to include my own people, the

Binandere, in any study I produced through Western ways of knowing and from the base of my second *arapa*.

In 1977 I was awarded an Australian National University scholarship to do a doctoral dissertation in Canberra, Australia. I proposed to write the required thesis in my mother tongue first and then translate it into English. The head of the History Department refused it on the grounds that I would not be able to finish the study within three years. With strong support from my supervisor, I insisted that I had a moral obligation to write the thesis in the vernacular even if there was no precedent.

One of the obvious questions was, "Who is going to examine the work in the vernacular?" My simple answer was, "That is not my problem!" And I demanded that the thesis be submitted in two languages. A compromise was reached in which literate historians would examine the study in English and Binandere oral historians would assess the material in my language. This appeared to be an easy way out. Accordingly, I produced 270 pages of the study in Binandere and translated most of it into English with 478 pages. Thus, the Binandere version formed the integral part of the "text" while its English translation was the "appendix" consistent with literate academic traditions.

The reason behind the compromise was that after the completion of the study, three copies would be sent to literate historians who were familiar with the subject matter for an examination. Their assessment would be translated into Binandere to be passed on to the Binandere elders who were also knowledgeable on their history.

It was relatively easy for the thesis examination in English. For the Binandere elders, however, the process of their assessment was difficult as they did not know how to read the written word. As a result, the "text" was to be read and prerecorded on a tape recorder and given to three persons who would be proficient in Binandere. These persons were to be given the copy of the tape with the thesis and two recording devices. Each person would carry the machines to the three separate villages of the Binandere assessors. The aim was that the carrier of the machine would play the contents of the prerecorded tape and at the same time turn the second machine on in order to record any comments from the elder upon hearing the thesis from the other tape. The instant remarks and the final assessment on the study were to be transcribed, translated, and dispatched to the examiners of the English version of the thesis. If there were any disagreement(s) about whether to pass or fail the candidate these would have to be cleared when the literate and oral historians met together.

The examiners of the English translation may have read the thesis under the neon light, perhaps in an air conditioned room or while sitting on a comfortable couch in a lounge with a glass of whisky, or while sitting on a chair placed next to an ebony table. In contrast, the Binandere elders passed their verdict in a different environment. They were to listen to and examine the thesis in a customary setting, where each family—grandparents, mother, father and children—would sit around a fire in the front or *arapa* of their house, while the selected elder would sit on a woven coconut mat, lean against a staked lance with an arrow end upwards. The listening and recording were to go on until late at night and when the fire was moved under the raised-floor house, the family entered the house to sleep. In the early dawn the fire was again taken out to the *arapa*. Before going to the garden the elder would listen and discuss the study. Thus, the examination of the thesis would have been the customary art of telling and learning by listening to *Be Jijimo: A History According to the Traditions of the Binandere People*.

The examination of the English translation was straightforward. The registrar of the University dispatched the copies of the thesis. By comparison, the process of the assessment by the Binandere was cumbersome and unprecedented. For the examiners nominated by the university, the overall cost was less than for their counterparts in the Binandere community who were isolated by physical distance and by the complicated process. One Australian examiner kindly gave a small amount of money towards securing the assessment from the elders.

The process of examination by oral historians was short-circuited when Graceford Genene, a perceptive and critical historian and elder of the Buiekane clan, Uaudari village, met his untimely death in November 1983. According to Binandere custom it is taboo to proceed with any project at such a time. As a mark of respect the other two Binandere examiners, Gerald Boigo of Manau village and Japhet Jigede of Bovers village, did not proceed to assess the thesis. Instead a great feast was held during which the text of the Binandere version was presented to the community. I had invited my supervisor, Dr. H. Nelson, to witness the ceremony on behalf of the Australian National University. The celebration, which was filmed, was released under the title *Man Without Pigs*.

I sat for the oral examination for the assessors of the English translation in February 1983 and I graduated from the university three months later. Some elders have heard the draft of the Binandere text and they made perceptive but critical comments on their history. It is expected that the Binandere text, *Be Jijimo,* is to be published in its own right in the vernacular.

This autobiographical aside should help place my life within two cultural contexts. Among the Binandere, I am old enough to have known people who grew to manhood in the days before the arrival of the *kiawa*.

Now, if I were speaking before my own people and I had established my identity, I would declare strongly, in a voice and style conveying a confidence I might not feel: it is I who is going to present the history of the Binandere community. The people sitting around might see my skin glistening with perspiration and my stomach muscles quivering, but I would have to continue in a firm voice.

The writing of Binandere history from immediately before the arrival of the *kiawa* through the period of contact and into the colonial times, presents special difficulties. These are not simply problems of methodology, but also of historiography. The *kiawa* has his own culture with its own chronological system.[4] And of course the Binandere has his own way of viewing time and sequences of events. His perspective is guided by his own system of values and interests. That system influences his actions and helps him give meaning to an event when he looks back on it. Since contact, each of the two cultures—the Binandere and the *kiawa*—have embedded their separate histories in their distinctive cultures, each having its sequential account and interpretation. The *kiawa* have looked at their own documents and have written, and that writing has in turn become something to be consulted by those working in the literary tradition. At the same time the Binandere have taken their memories of the events of contact and expressed them within the constantly changing repertoire of their own oral tradition.

Those who made the first written reports—the government officers, missionaries, the adventurers—inevitably interpreted what they saw in the light of their own beliefs. The historians take those prejudices and consider them within another set of values, sometimes correcting and sometimes adding to the distortions of the first observers. Frantz Fanon put it well when he said, "The history which he (the colonizer) writes is not the history of the country which he plunders, but the history of his own nation in regard to all that she skims off, all that she violates and starves" (see Zahar, 1974:37). Even where the *kiawa* have tried to read the documents to see what was happening to the colonized, and have talked to the villagers, they have still found it difficult to cross from one culture to another. The *kiawa* have looked at the villagers with the cultural techniques of the *kiawa* and they have presented their findings about the villagers within the *kiawa*'s cultural forms. The *kiawa* have always taken a lot and given little in return. Mead, during the aforementioned confrontation with Manus students at the university, agreed that she had, indeed, received both status and money as a result of her work in Papua New Guinea. Her justification was couched in terms of the broadening of *kiawa* knowledge. I believe that *kiawa* researchers continue in this tradition vis-à-vis Papua New Guinea. This makes it necessary to have a policy for foreign research that forces more accountability toward Papua New Guinea people. This belief formed an important part of my former role as director of the Papua New Guinea Institute of Social and Economic Research, and as current professor in the History Department at the university.

Leaving economic, political, and social deprivation aside, I want to illustrate cultural theft with accounts of the removal of artifacts from Papua New Guinea. Sir William MacGregor, the first lieutenant-governor of British New

Guinea (later Papua), collected 11,476 objects between 4 September 1888 and 1 September 1898. The artifacts were dispatched to the Queensland Museum in Brisbane where some of them were transferred to the Australian Museum in Sydney, the National Museum of Victoria, and others were sent to the British Museum in London. Today the Queensland Museum retains 8,825 artifacts, which the lieutenant-governor removed during the decade of his rule in Papua.[5]

These artifacts have now become an integral part of both the aesthetic and scholarly tradition of the foreign culture. *Kiawa* observe, describe, and write about the artifacts in their scholarly journals. The publications inform western audiences and contribute to foreign aesthetic traditions. By now, the artifacts may even be completely forgotten by the descendants of the people from whom they were taken in the first place. When the descendants of the people who once made the artifacts see them in a foreign display they feel that they have been the victims of cultural theft: their past was taken and is still being consumed by others. Sometimes they are humiliated by the sight of objects that were once specific and revered now being identified by the careless labels of the foreigners. The carefully guarded clan design becomes just something from the "South Seas" or "Melanesia." The removal of artifacts is but a small part of the complex concept and practice of cultural theft.

In the same manner the nonmaterial culture has been taken away from the people. When foreigners write history, for example, they of course write in a language unknown to the people who came into contact with the *kiawa*. Even in the last decade hundreds of foreign scholars have conducted research among the various communities in Papua

New Guinea, but most if not all of the finished products have appeared in print in the languages of the foreigners and not in the vernacular.[6] Lately some foreign scholars have collaborated with members of the local community, but even then the writing usually appears in print in a foreign language. Perhaps the foreigners seek to rid themselves of their guilt. Within anthropology, for example, there has been a scholarly dialogue with fellow members of their discipline only, as they aim to illuminate each other's understanding of society. They see this effort as essential to making contributions to knowledge among western scholars: they do not aim to illuminate the world and the knowledge of those people whom they have studied. Stephen Feuchtwang takes this point further.

> Literacy has been one of the main criteria of social classification in Anthropology and what is central to its study: preliterate peoples. It has another side in the development of anthropological theory besides defining its subject matter, and that is the lack of challenge by its subjects unable to read the finished work. Surely this lack of challenge has encouraged notions of immutable and unconscious structures and left unraised in social anthropology the question and the theory of the state of consciousness and the internal transformation of society and social production of its own knowledge. (Feuchtwang 1973:79)

Yet notice that Feuchtwang here is still talking about the state of anthropology in terms of western scholarship. He seems to say no more than that the lack of challenge by colonized cultures themselves leads outsiders to lie to themselves and others. Indeed, not until I read Charles Valentine's descriptions of so-called "cargo cult" did I come to accept that the field of anthropology might provide an intellectual example for Papua New Guineans (Valentine 1963, 1965, 1968, 1979). My concern is also with the contribution that the various disciplines can make to the cultures of the peoples studied.

The distance kept between the anthropologist and the colonized people is based on, inter alia, the inequality of intellectual tools; this corresponds to the distance between the colonized and the colonizer in the economic field— something that is again based on an inequality of technology. This gap is even widened by the members of the colonized community when they use foreign documents as their authority. They adopt and adapt to the models and methods and even the language of the colonizing *kiawa*. Even if the colonized scholar attacks the colonizer's work he does it in the latter's language, depriving the people— the subjects of the studies—of an opportunity to engage in the debate. That is to say, the colonized literate members do not begin the dialogue between the colonized elite and the subject peoples: the knowledge they obtain does not filter through to the common majority and thereby engage them in an enriching of their cultures.

It seems that if people wish to recover their lost heritage, they must learn the language and follow the scholarly rules of the foreigners. But in doing so they enter the foreigners' cultural tradition. They are alienated from their own tradition and it is difficult for them to transfer anything back to their own people. If the person who has acquired a western language and knowledge of the methods of western scholarship writes about his people, then he extends the boundaries of the foreign culture. Ironically, the black scholar who points to gaps in the works of foreign writers and offers alternative explanations is adding a richness to the foreign culture. Still nothing is being returned to the people who are the subjects of the scholarship.

The black scholar's inability to communicate with the people of the culture in which he was born is obviously partly a result of the language that he now uses and the more general alienation that has followed from his many years in foreign educational institutions. But the black scholar also becomes trapped in the enclave of the foreign colleges and universities. He has built his reputation within the enclave, and he believes that he has obligations to see that the ways of the enclave continue. Thus, he is accepted by the intellectual community of the foreign community but not necessarily by his own people.

I try to avoid cultural theft in the following way. I present part of the thesis in my mother tongue, the language of the community of which I am active member. I take this stand because I want my work to become immediately open to criticism by those best equipped to judge it, and so initiate a dialogue between the educated elite and the villagers. I am convinced that if my work is presented in the vernacular, then it will contribute to the vulnerable but persistent oral forum that is capable of criticism in its own way but does not withstand the hazards of changes in the human memory over a long time. I hope that the dialogue between the villagers and the foreign-trained scholars will gain a momentum of its own with both cultural traditions emerging the richer. The oral culture certainly has the flexibility to absorb and exploit new content and new forms.

Even had I wanted to I would have found it very difficult to present my thesis entirely in English. I had set myself the task of writing about the Binandere intellectual tradition. I tried to say how the Binandere perceived their world, how this perception has changed over time, and how the Binandere now look back into their own past. The Binandere culture has been oral or displayed: it has been spoken or sung or acted or danced. It also has been a culture without the divisions that westerners have been able to impose on their cultures. The Binandere do not separate the religious from the secular, or the social from the political, or even the past from the present. Actions are all at the same time customary, meeting immediate practical needs, religious, social, and political. Words used by the Binandere carry inferences and associations that cut through orderly boundaries between sections of knowledge. The words that express Binandere values assume that the listeners already share those values. The Binandere vocabulary is not used to define Binandere values: the values are embedded within the language. As others have found, the problems of translation are immense (see, for example, Beekman and Callow 1974). Something is always lost. At best it is just a flavor, an additional association that a word may carry, and at worst the very essence of an idea completely evades all attempts to trap it within an English vocabulary. I have therefore written in Binandere for three reasons: so that the people who are the subject of this study may know what I have had to say about them, so that there may be an exchange between those Binandere who have been educated within the western tradition and those who have sustained the old culture, and so that I can make accurate and evocative statements about what the Binandere believe and value.

If I have succeeded I will have made a contribution to two cultures. I will have taken from and given to both cultures. My work is meant to present "a corrective approach to Eurocentric documentary history and perhaps even helping the people to come to terms with social change and the disruption of traditional life" (*The University This Week*, 1983).

Before I end my *tugata* I must once again rattle the bone spatula against the lime gourd to attract attention to another problem. I am conscious of my role as a participant in a community, and as an observer of it. My informants are also aware of my two functions. The old people know what I am doing when I sit with them, my tape recorder and microphone obvious on the woven mat. As I prepare to ask them for the sort of evidence that western scholarship expects they may speak of my grandfather, refer to incidents in my childhood, and ask me about recent political events. They know that I share much oral culture with them; they need not explain allusions or point out the obvious. Generally they are willing to shift the conversation to the sort of detail that I require from them. They want their history preserved and they want it to be full and accurate. But some knowledge gives prestige; to share it with others is to devalue it or risk it being used irresponsibly. Also the members of some clans might see me as the representative of rivals; and they are therefore reluctant to be completely frank with me. Such occasions are rare although there is knowledge of some practical value that old men are reluctant to give away easily.

An outsider would not necessarily find the old people any more ready to reveal their knowledge; the outsider is just as likely to be perceived as unworthy or as an enemy agent. On balance, I trust that my education in two cultures has given me advantages that are not available to foreigners dependent on limited time in the field. Very few outsiders have gained the degree of familiarity with a Melanesian language to allow them to penetrate the metaphors and the words charged with sentiment because of their association with past events.

My systematic attempt to record Binandere culture

began in 1966 even before I went to the university. I continued this work in my B.A. honors thesis. But in spite of my familiarity with Binandere culture I have still had to do the same sort of fieldwork that would be expected of a foreign scholar. I have had to travel to other villages, quietly ask around to find the names of the men and women considered to be the custodians of clan histories, and then sit down with them, and record their narratives. When possible I have taken advantage of events such as feasts and land disputes to record claim and counterclaim about the past. After the excitement of the moment has declined I have returned to the central actors to check whether words used to belittle or flatter can be substantiated. At the end of my fieldwork in 1979, I had over 100 hours of tapes of songs, legends, clan histories, and reminiscences requiring indexing, cross-checking, and translating. In addition I had notebooks I had used in conjunction with the tapes. Sometimes I was able to play back tapes to informants and allow them to make amendments and additions to their testimony. Even so, a massive amount of oral recording and cross-checking not immediately required for the writing of this thesis remains to be done. Having completed transcribing and translating the relevant material I have written the history in the vernacular, the part I present in the language. Earlier drafts were read to a few selected elders to get criticism and some feedback from the knowledgeable oral historians. In this way I could check some of the accounts based on the *kiawa* records and contrast these with those of the surviving oral sources.

Most of the old people who knew the pre-Christian community are now dead or dying. Slowly but steadily some Binandere are regarding me as a worthy custodian of their traditions. Just as a father transmits his knowledge to his trusted son so that he in turn can preserve the family's special learning, I find myself in the position of being the carrier of Binandere traditions. Already the old and the young alike are demanding from me oral traditions dealing with customary land rights.

My work as a collector of the people's history has been changing my role within the community. At times I have been expected to give my knowledge as though I were a disinterested outsider. I just answer questions, and others use the information as they think fit. But in some cases I have gone further: I have stated my beliefs and joined the action. I feel that I have to make up my own mind over issues that concern the Binandere, and sometimes this forces me into conflict with either village or national authorities. This can lead to a hectic confusion of scholarly, personal, and communal roles.

While doing fieldwork in June 1978, for example, I planted a large area of garden and built a fence around it. In early November when the taro was growing, several pigs belonging to a "big man" from Taire, the next village, broke down the fence and destroyed the taro. I mended the fence only to have it broken again. I got a spear and killed one pig. I reported the case to a village *komiti,* a representative of the Tamata local government council. He carried the dead pig to its owner. I heard that a lot of young men brandished their steel axes in the air, threatening to cut me up because I had killed the pig.

Other pigs kept uprooting the garden. My warning to the big man had been ignored. So I speared another pig in mid-December. This time I sent word for the big man and his young men to come to the garden, cut me up and carry away their pig. Some of my own young men and I remained in the garden, but no one turned up except the big man's wife. She said that the pig was earmarked for another man from Tubi village, and we carried the pig there.

On New Year's Day 1979, both national and provincial politicians called a meeting to discuss a proposal from a transnational corporation to buy timber rights. It was scheduled to take place in Taire village and in front of the *arapa* of the house of the big man whose pigs I had been killing. Tamata council president Clive Youde was in the chair and the politicians explained the benefits that would flow to the village people from the investment. Some leaders opposed the politicians, while others supported the proposal. I spoke last, pointing out the weakness of the politicians' case and the advantages and disadvantages of the investment. On balance I strongly opposed selling the timber.

The big man whose pigs I had killed has a lot of land and forest. He said that he wanted nothing from the politicians and the companies. He refused to agree to sell the timber rights from his land, and other land owners followed his example. The politicians, with their uniformed police escort, left the village in disgust on the next day. Their belief that the big man would use the occasion to oppose and shame me had proved false.

I do not think that I could sit and watch large corporations exploit Binandere resources any more than I could watch the pigs uproot my garden. Nor could I sit aside and just observe the villagers mount their opposition against the authorities who regard them as naive and irrational, or even label them as cargo cultists. In this sort of situation I have to declare where I stand (see also Waiko, 1981b:33–41).

I therefore end my *tugata* by admitting to what may appear to be contradictions. I am both observer and participant; and I am a custodian of tradition while I take part in events that will change the Binandere. But these are really the different obligations that flow from being both a student of western social sciences and a member of the Binandere community. They are not contradictions to invalidate conclusions that I might present either to a villager or a *kiawa* scholar. An anonymous *kiawa* observer has this to say about my study:

> Waiko has provided keen insightful analysis into a people's past and into the cultural values that have helped shape that past. While some might characterize as too narrow an in-depth look at one small group of people among the many in Papua New Guinea, I find particular merit in Waiko's ability to show the depth, complexity and richness of Binandere culture and history. His work should serve as a thoughtful caution to those obsessed with the "bigger picture." In many ways, the eventual publication of this work certainly will enrich the field of Pacific Studies. Those scholars committed to the use of cultural analysis as a necessary prerequisite to understanding the complex dynamics involved in culture contact and culture change will applaud Waiko's approach. The author's exhaustive consideration of Binandere oral art forms bear directly upon the larger issues surrounding the use of oral traditions in the writing of history. Through his extensive examination of Binandere culture, Waiko shows quite convincingly the chasms of cultural misunderstanding that can separate peoples from very different worlds. Being presently involved in writing the history of another Pacific Islands people, I learned a great deal from my review of the Waiko thesis.[7]

What is, then, the characteristic difference between documents and oral traditions as bases for history? It is not, I believe, that the document is "possibly true" while the oral narratives are "not true." The difference is, I suggest, that written and oral sources are embedded in different cultural traditions. They are meant to be judged by quite different traditional standards in literate and oral cultures. The problem arises when literate historians try to fit oral testimony into the method, model, and the time scale that accommodates history based on documentary sources. The reverse is also true in a situation where oral narrators attempt to adopt the written word into the complex ethos that caters to history derived from oral traditions. Yet the similarity of the approaches is striking, and a good historical methodology is equally important for both. More often than not, the undisclosed ideological motives inherent in the Western historiography tend to be carried over to the writings of the anthropologists and the historians.

Eric Schwimmer (1969), for example, said, "the Orokaiva are neither devoted or accurate historians." He made an attempt to reconstruct a community's experiences of a disastrous event that occurred about a decade before 1966, when the anthropologist conducted his study. However, his view totally contradicts my own findings about the Orokaiva: that they are devoted and actually very accurate historians. One possible explanation, other than sheer anthropological prejudice against oral history, might be that the central fact of Sumbiripa cult belief was the 1956 eruption of Mount Sumbiripa (Lamington). Schwimmer's informants, who were predominantly missionary-influenced, may have denied knowledge in order to deny belief in the cult. Thus, the choice of one informant of one persuasion can make inaccessible an entire area of oral tradition. In the same way, a literate historian reading documentary sources on colonial contact in Papua New

Guinea, which contain *kiawa* biases and distortion of historical facts, can only have access to one area of knowledge; but it also may be, in this instance, that the oral
traditions are changing in *kind*.

Nevertheless, a good historical method is required for
the study and writing of oral history. My own work among
the Binandere is a small beginning to develop methods to
analyze Melanesian material in the same way that other
scholars have attempted in the analyses of European
(Thompson 1982), African (Miller 1980; Vansina 1969), and
Polynesian history (Sorrenson 1979; Mercer 1979).

NOTES

1. Throughout this chapter, words are in the masculine gender for simplicity, but discussion is meant to include women and
men (except for descriptions specific to men or women).

2. It is a standard practice among the Binandere to introduce
oneself through the grandparents. It is assumed that the latter are
more likely to be known than the parents or the grandchildren.

3. My parents did not see any value in all their children going
to school. But they tolerated Gaiari and Mendode, my elder sister
and brother, acquiring the *kiawa*'s knowledge. They insisted that
their three other children including myself should grow up in the
village and learn the traditions and customs of the clan. This
arrangement was disrupted about 1955 when a *kiap* (colonial
district officer) by the name of Mr. Johnson visited Boide. He
declared that the collection of houses was too small to be a village
on its own, and that the residents must move to join the bigger
village. Both my father and Dumbu, his clan brother, refused to
obey the order. As a result the *kiap* jailed them for disobedience.
I have written this traumatic experience in a dramatic form.

4. There are innumerable works that deal with the question
of time and chronology. I found it useful to read S. Toulmin and

J. Goodfield, *The Discovery of Time* (New York: Penguin Books, 1965). Although the book is Eurocentric, it shows how contemporary Western historiography is just one aspect of the sense of processes of change through time.

5. I spent a week in the Queensland Museum in Brisbane, in April 1978 when I carried out the research. I am grateful to Dr. Michael Quinell who assisted me with the location and identification of the artifacts. There is now an agreement between this institution and the National Museum of Papua New Guinea to return about 4,000 to 5,000 items over the next four years. I also conducted some research in the Australian Museum in Sydney in August 1977. I am thankful to Dr. J. Specht and his staff for their kind cooperation. I have filed for the museum "My Preliminary Impression Regarding Various Items from the Oro Province, P.N.G. held in the Museum."

6. Leaving aside other social and natural sciences researchers, Morauta says nearly one hundred anthropologists alone entered Papua New Guinea in 1977 to carry out research. But I do not know how many have written in the vernacular of the community in which they conducted research (see L. Morauta, "Indigenous Anthropology in Papua New Guinea," *Current Anthropology* 20 (3), 1979, p. 561).

7. The quotation is from an anonymous reader who reviewed a revised version of my Ph.D. thesis. I submitted the revision for consideration and publication by the University of Hawaii Press in 1986. The press declined to publish it.

REFERENCES

Beekman, J., and J. Callow. 1974. *Translating the Word of God.* Michigan: Zondervan.

Encyclopedia of Papua New Guinea. Melbourne: Melbourne University Press.

Feuchtwang, S. 1973. "The Discipline and Its Sponsors." In T.

Asad (ed.), *Anthropology and the Colonial Encounter*, p. 79. London: Ithaca Press.

Mercer, P. 1979. "Oral Traditions in the Pacific Islands: Problems of Interpretation." *Journal of Pacific History* 14, pp. 130–53.

Miller, J. (ed.). 1980. *African Past Speaks: Essays in Oral Traditions and History*. London: Shoe String.

Powell, K. 1978. "The First Papua New Guinean Playwrights and Their Plays." Master's thesis, University of Papua New Guinea, Port Moresby.

Schwimmer, E. G. 1969. *Cultural Consequences of Volcanic Eruption Experienced by the Mount Lamington Orokaiva*. Department of Anthropology, report no. 9. University of Oregon, Eugene.

Sorrenson, M. K. P. 1979. *Maori Origins and Migrations: The Genesis of Some Pakeha Myths and Legends*. Auckland, New Zealand: Auckland University Press.

Thompson, P. (ed.). 1982. *Our Common History: The Transformation of Europe*. Sydney, Australia: Pluto Press.

University This Week. 1983. "Another Doctorate for Papua New Guinea." May 6. (Newsletter of the University of Papua New Guinea.)

Valentine, C. A. 1963. "Social Status, Political Power, and Native Responses to European Influence in Oceania." *Anthropological Forum* 1, pp. 3–55.

———. 1965. "The Lakalai of New Britain." In P. Lawrence and M. Meggitt (eds.), *God, Ghosts, and Men in Melanesia*. Sydney: Oxford University Press.

———. 1968. "Social and Cultural Change in New Guinea." In P. Ryan (ed.), *Encyclopedia of Papua New Guinea*. Melbourne: Melbourne University Press.

Valentine, C. A., and B. Valentine. 1979. *Going Through Changes: Villagers, Settlers, and Development in Papua New Guinea*. Port Moresby: Institute for Papua New Guinea Studies.

Vansina, J. 1969. *Oral Traditions: A Study in Historical Methodology*. London: Routledge & Kegan Paul.

Waiko, J. D. 1970. "The Unexpected Hawk." In L. Hannet et al. (eds.), *Five New Guinea Plays*. Brisbane, Australia: Jacaranda Press.

———. 1977. "The People of Papua New Guinea: Their Forests and Their Aspirations." In J. Winslow (ed.), *Melanesian Environment*, pp. 407–27. Canberra, Australia: National University.

———. 1981a. "The Binandere Oral Traditions: Their Sources and Problems." In D. Denoon and R. Lacey (eds.), *Oral Traditions in Melanesia*, pp. 1–30. Port Moresby: University of Papua New Guinea and Institute for Papua New Guinea Studies.

———. 1981b. "Land, Forest, and People: Villagers Struggle against Multi-National Corporation in Papua New Guinea." *Kabar Seberand: Sulating Maphilindo* 8–9, pp. 33–41. Queensland: James Cook University.

———. 1982. *Be Jijimo: A History According to the Tradition of the Binandere People of Papua New Guinea*. Ph.D. thesis, Australian National University, Canberra.

———. 1985. "Na Binandere, Imo Averi? We Are Binandere, Who Are You?" In M. Chapman (ed.), *Pacific Viewpoint* 26(1), pp. 10–29.

———. 1986. "Oral Traditions Among the Binandere: Problems of Method in Melanesian History." *Journal of Pacific History* 21(1), pp. 21–38.

———. 1989. "Australian Administration Under the Binandere Thumb." In S. Latukefu (ed.), *Papua New Guinea: A Century of Colonial Impact, 1884–1984*. Port Moresby: University of Papua New Guinea Press.

———. 1990. " 'Head' and 'Tail': The Shaping of Oral Traditions Among the Binandere in Papua New Guinea." In R. Finnegan and M. Orbell (eds.), *Oral Tradition* (special issue on South Pacific), vol. 5, no. 2/3, p. 334.

———. n.d. "Binandere Values: A Personal Reflection." In R. May and H. Nelson (eds.), *Melanesia Beyond Diversity*. Forthcoming.

Williams, F. E. 1969. *Orokaiva Society*. Oxford: Clarendon Press. First published 1930 by Oxford University Press.

Zahar, R. 1974. *Frantz Fanon: Colonialism and Alienation Concerning Frantz Fanon's Political Theory*, W. F. Feuser (trans.). London: Monthly Review Press.

ANGELA GILLIAM

10 Papua New Guinea and the Geopolitics of Knowledge Production

On December 2, 1986, the United Nations voted on whether to reinscribe the South Pacific island country of New Caledonia on the United Nations list of non-self-governing territories. The vote was 89 for reinscription, 24 against, with 34 nations (including the United States) abstaining. The occasion signified acknowledgement by the international community that New Caledonia was indeed a dependent territory, and not part and parcel of the Republic of France. The preparation for this vote also signalled the heightened international visibility of South Pacific nations—and for the purposes of this chapter, Papua New Guinea—in their thrust to gain recognition for a major diplomatic initiative surrounding a nuclear-free and independent Pacific. Moreover, the campaign prepared the terrain for Pacific nations to actively link environment, development, nuclear disarmament, and decolonization.

To understand the significance of this effort, one has to

juxtapose this historic achievement against the heritage of Pacific ethnography, the lens through which much of the world views the region. If the image of Pacific diplomats jars the reader, it may be because it does not correspond to the ethnographic descriptions popularized by Margaret Mead and other anthropologists. Speaking about the Pacific region in general, Papua New Guinea's ambassador and permanent representative to the United Nations, Renagi R. Lohia, maintains that "the literature and the pool of information about the people and their way of life has imprisoned them in the anthropologist's . . . 'primitive paradise' . . . created as the exotica that the 'civilized' world must enjoy . . . [making] it difficult for them to be . . . liberated from this intellectual colonialism [and] domination" (Lohia, 1989).[1] United States anthropologists have a special responsibility as both the inheritors and practitioners of the legacy left by the early social scientists in the Pacific. They are also nationals of the country that is a principal actor in the geopolitics of the region.

For many Pacific leaders and intellectuals, a nuclear-free and sustainable ocean is part and parcel of the domain of academic inquiry. It is within this context that Pacific peoples are in a battle to redefine themselves in relation to the rest of the world. In the struggle between the representatives of powerful nations who perceive of the Pacific as a nuclear testing ground and those who are increasingly concerned about the damage to their genetic heritage and environment, scholarship is a fundamental component of the contest.

Pacific scholarship has by and large remained unchanged and explicit in the past 60 years of research, incorporating the descriptions of Pacific peoples as "primitives." Anthropologists could not only aid Pacific peoples to appreciate the ethnographer's enthusiasm for polities in which kinship is central to social organization, but also come to share the Pacific vision of the region as home to modern nation-states. In order to assume this double role, the legacy of exotification must be recognized.

Hierarchical Exotification as Methodology

That anthropologists have been the primary channels through which nation-states in the Pacific communicate with societies outside the region contributes to a situation in which the geopolitical concerns of Pacific peoples are usually not analyzed within the field of anthropology. Career legitimacy and economic status is based on how "different" or "primitive" are the objects of research in one's area of expertise from people in metropolitan, Western societies. Anthropology has sometimes posed the notion that "contact" and progress forward from the Stone Age has been as a result of interaction with Europeans. And, ethnographic data has traditionally represented capital for both the Western researcher and his/her government (Pandian, 1985:90).

In addition, status in the profession is enhanced by having established an expertise in a location that is distant. Central to exotification is the implied possibility of danger in the field. Exotification also focuses on difference and conflict within the communities to be studied.

Hierarchical exotification has been particularly burdensome for the Melanesian peoples of Papua New Guinea, the Solomon Islands, New Caledonia–Kanaky, and Vanuatu, and is distinct from what one Samoan journalist has called the heritage of "happy-go-loving, simple, untroubled South Sea waifs and nymphs' that engulfed Polynesians (Lelaulu,

1986). For Melanesians, anthropology has represented a veritable crisis. Indeed, the "Melanesia-Polynesia division" invites a reexamination of the analyses of hierarchy in Pacific societies (Thomas, 1989).

The principle of conflict becomes the primary prism through which social scientists have gauged the cultural particularities of Papua New Guinean Melanesians especially. It was the late Ralph Karepa (1983), a Papua New Guinea diplomat from Erave in the Southern Highlands, who suggested the interrelationship between professional standing as an anthropologist and the emphasis on conflict in Papua New Guinea cultures. He maintained that though traditional interclan and intertribal conflicts in the Highlands were basically elements of struggles for regional influence, they had been exaggerated by Western scholars. Hau'ofa, a Tongan social scientist, warned that fellow anthropologists had insufficiently redressed "the distorted image of Melanesians. . . . We have neglected to portray them as rounded human beings who love as well as hate, who laugh joyously as well as quarrel, who are peaceful as well as warlike, and who are generous and kindly as well as mean and calculating. . . . It is these ignored qualities of the people which have enabled us to enter unsolicited and live among them. . . . Have the models, for example that of conflict, which we have taken to the field, blinded us to these?" (Hau'ofa; 1975:287).

Much of the hierarchical exotification of the peoples of Papua New Guinea has rested in their enclosure within a "sex, savages, and spears" subtext. These three categories are often linked in ethnographic research and serve to reinforce each other. Thus, sexual behavior and values are seen to be an integral part of the overall struggle for resource and kinship exchange, which in turn are inextricably linked to the presumed primary causes for conflict in Melanesian cultures (e.g., Feil, 1984; Godelier, 1982; Knauft, 1985; Koch, 1974). According to some analyses, conflicts become formalized in clan warfare, which remains the organizing ethos of Highlands Melanesian cultures (Hallpike, 1977; Meggitt, 1977). Thus, many later scholars have continued the preoccupations of Mead (1928, 1930, and 1935) and Malinowski (1927, 1929), using a functionalist discussion of sexuality or warfare that overlooks the broader Pacific world and the interlocking relationships with the more powerful countries of the region. For many anthropologists, the study of violence and conflict is necessary if it is to be eliminated. But the historically popular themes of pacification, headhunting, and cannibalism are viewed as external to the colonial wars of domination and the concomitant appropriation of labor. They also are removed from the effects of participation in the two World Wars and they ignore contemporary nuclear threats. Some recent work has epistemologically challenged perceptions of Melanesian societies. Buck asserts that "a set of filters which force the user to see a wide variety of phenomena," identically including Melanesians' resistance to colonialism, contributes to a "cargo-cult discourse," and creates "cargo cults" as objects of analysis (Buck, 1989). Others have attempted to move beyond Western assumptions about conflict and assess the deeper cultural meanings of "straightening out" or "disentangling" interpersonal dilemmas in Pacific societies (Watson-Gegeo and White, 1990). Rodman and Cooper (1983:15), albeit using conventional conflict discourse, nonetheless point out that "indigenous fighting was suppressed as a result of Melanesians' awareness that Europeans' coercive and military power was far greater than their own."

Contemporary Conflict and Cultural Evolution

Pacific ethnography has been characterized by analyses that imply a cognitive context of a cultural evolutionary scale. On this scale, some Pacific peoples offer a key to understanding the distant, European past. Paul Mercier (1966:54) has critiqued this model and warns against the labeling of certain cultures as representing "contemporary ancestors" of Europeans. Undergirding this frame of reference is that of a modern civilization witnessing the struggles of "ancient" peoples who have remained presumably little touched by time or the travails of colonialism. This results in a hierarchy in which that which is modern resides in the more "recent" society. Thus, modernity is measured by new and continual transformation in the direction of Westernization and progressively more material accumulation. Stocking elucidates the power of this construct. "In sharp contrast to the evolutionary period, when the characteristic posture of anthropologists toward surviving primitive peoples was one of progressivist assimilationism, a romantic preservationism with strong undertones of 'Noble Savagery' became the attitudinal norm of sociocultural anthropology. Despite a questioning of relativism in the aftermath of World War II and despite the involvement in the postwar period, this romantic tendency to view the societies they study as outside the historical processes of modern civilization has continued strong until the present" (Stocking, 1987:289).

By framing Pacific societies as being outside history, it is thus possible to engage the subject of warfare in a way that avoids any mention of contemporary geopolitical concerns of Pacific peoples. Hierarchical exotification becomes in and of itself a part of warfare, and is frequently used by nonanthropologists. A classic example of an attempt to use this discourse can be found in one of the 1954 Atomic Energy Commission (AEC) propaganda films that was incorporated into *Half-Life* (1986), Dennis O'Rourke's incisive examination of the long-term genetic effects of nuclear testing on Marshall Islanders. The narrator in the AEC film explains a trip to Chicago by seven Marshallese for radiation testing. "These are fishing people, savages by our standards. . . . John [the mayor of Rongelap] . . . a happy, amenable savage . . . goes first. A savage governs his life by ritual and he understands this because he thinks of the Iron Room [a radiation detector for human beings] as a new ritual. . . . Sitting alone inside the room—outside a strange kind of priest in a long, white coat—a long lonely wait inside. . . . It was all very interesting and worth talking about. When the Ritual of the Iron Room was over for John, it began for the others . . . as each finished, he was . . . given apples and other good things to eat . . . and would . . . return to Rongelap . . . in the middle of the Pacific Ocean where hardly anybody lives (*Half-Life,* 1986).

If a people are continually portrayed as backward, how can their anti–nuclear war position be grounded in the twentieth century? More than anything, their views about the future are dismissed as irrelevant, unimportant, and unsophisticated. They are the stuff of National Geographic magazine covers—quaint, timeless, and incapable of modern political discourse. The contemporary impact of the nuclear and military accumulation on Pacific societies receives little attention. The intellectual inquiry of Melanesian societies has helped to establish a popularly held view that the more localized the process of conflict is, the more likely it is that the culture in question represents peoples who are backward—"primitive" or "savage." These intraregional conflicts in the "ethnographic present" have been deemed dangerous and therefore worthy of study, especially those that involved traditional weapons such as spears. On the other hand, the society that is technologically capable of killing hundreds or thousands in warfare is often deemed to be a more advanced culture than the former type. Theories of cultural evolution and its directionality are partly grounded in the capacity to produce death.

In the international arena, such a "killability ratio" has become the basis for the hierarchy of military decision making. This is suggested by the operations in international organizations such as the United Nations, where authority in international conflict and dispute resolution is often rooted in just such technological capacity. Indeed, it has been the implied position of many of the nuclear states that countries that do not have the capacity to build nuclear weapons have no right to a say in the decision-making process about their disposition or elimination. Within the United Nations, the "balance of terror" has also meant controlling Third World access to any technology with military potential. The United Nations has been under siege by those who would neutralize the power of the body to challenge nuclear states. "The United Nations is being dismantled politically through efforts of the Western alliance to exclude the international organization from participation in global decision-making, especially conflict resolution" (Singham and Hune, 1986).

In discussing whether or not anthropology affected the way Pacific diplomats functioned at the United Nations, Harvey Feldman (1986), former U.S. ambassador to Papua New Guinea and subsequently to the United Nations, cogently suggested that this question had two aspects. One was the perception that the world had of Papua New

Guinea, and the other was the degree to which anthropological images affected the way Papua New Guineans perceived of themselves. That anthropology and self-image could reinforce each other is elucidated by the power of the still-current belief that contact with Europeans is the catalyst in Pacific cultures for leaving the "Stone Age." Such a construct contributes to a situation in which the *intellectual* input and interpretations from Papua New Guineans themselves about their society are not acknowledged.

Without the principle of reciprocity and mutual indebtedness between researcher and informant, the unequal exchange between them inevitably will lead to exotification and invention in the descriptions of other peoples. A vertical relationship between observer and observed is conditioned by the question of state power within the field situation and often consolidates hierarchy.

Geopolitics of the Pacific

The cultural images of Papua New Guinea have served subtle geopolitical functions. On the evening of September 10, 1986, the Australian Foreign Minister, Bill Hayden, confronted an astute audience at the University of Papua New Guinea in which he received criticism about the fact that much of Papua New Guinea's budget goes toward paying the salaries of Australian "experts" in Papua New Guinea. For example, Utula Samana, then premier of Morobe Province, challenged Hayden on this occasion with a question that reflected the region's concerns about Australia's authentic geopolitical identity. Australia's "aid to PNG is a clear indication of [its] strategic interests. What about the dumping of nuclear wastes? What about your selling uranium to France? Are you part of Europe or of the

Pacific?"[2] That same night, on the Australian Broadcasting Corporation's evening news (also transmitted to Papua New Guinea) came the statement that "due to pressure from the United Nations, Australia brought Papua New Guinea to independence before it was ready." The visual background for this commentary was of Papua New Guineans in traditional dancing and dress, and others holding bows and arrows.

Like Australia, New Zealand has manifested ambivalence with regard to its role in the Pacific. Pressure on New Zealand has come from the U.S. government regarding that country's refusal to allow nuclear-powered ships to make port calls. The awareness that both New Zealand and Australia are just as "downwind" from nuclear fallout as other South Pacific Forum states appeared at one time to strengthen the South Pacific Forum's resolve to forge a joint nuclear policy. But the strength of the anti-nuclear movements in both of these countries is offset by a cultural and racial identification with Europe and the political objectives of the United States.

It was the Melanesia Alliance also known as the Spearhead Group, comprised of Vanuatu, Papua New Guinea, and the Solomon Islands, that encouraged the South Pacific Forum nations to adopt a unified position for the independence of New Caledonia. Initial leadership on this issue came primarily from Vanuatu, and Permanent Representative Robert van Lierop paved the way for the New Caledonian Kanaks to make their presence felt at the Nonaligned Meeting in Harare, Zimbabwe, in September 1986.

South Pacific nations also attempted to form trade agreements based on the principles of self-reliance and nonalignment. In 1985, after Kiribati signed a fishing agreement with the Soviet Union, policy analysts in the United

States began to "redefine" the Pacific region. For example, on the same day that the Kiribati president, Ieremia Tabai, was delivering a lecture at the University of Papua New Guinea on the development issues of small, poor countries, the *New York Times* (Haberman, 1986) featured an article entitled "Challenge in the Pacific: Moscow's Growing Naval Strength." Using the anti-Soviet analysis then popular, the article mentioned the Soviet fishing agreement with Kiribati. As Lohia (1986a) noted, "only when perceptions of us change us from 'natives' into 'communist natives' are we taken seriously as human beings by Westerners." Even the international objective for a nuclear-free and independent Pacific that South Pacific countries have been promoting was often considered no more than evidence of "Soviet influence."

Papua New Guinea's participation at the United Nations has met with diverse perceptions. It was acclaimed by Girma Abebe (1986), Secretary of the United Nations Trusteeship Council, who witnessed Papua New Guinea's emergence as an independent nation. "In ten years since joining the United Nations in 1975, Papua New Guinea (1) became vice chair of the Fourth Committee in 1983; (2) chair of the Fourth Committee in 1984; (3) Vice-President of the General Assembly twice in ten years during the 34th and 36th sessions; and (4) hosted the first regional meeting of the Decolonization Committee in Papua New Guinea in 1985." In the view of a junior diplomat from Jamaica, when Papua New Guinea chaired the Fourth Committee, the supra-bloc diplomacy of Ambassador Renagi R. Lohia, the Permanent Representative of Papua New Guinea to the United Nations, was an example for younger diplomats to emulate (Wolfe, 1986). José Ramos-Horta, then permanent observer to the United Nations for the Revolutionary Front of Independent East Timor (Fretilin), on the other hand, was censorious. Papua New Guinea had been the "laughing-stock of the United Nations because it was seen as an appendage of Australia in its voting patterns, voting with Australia, New Zealand or the United States even on issues that were very minor" (Ramos-Horta 1986a).

If that was the perception of Papua New Guinea before 1983, it was modified when Renagi Lohia was appointed to the position of ambassador and permanent representative to the United Nations from Papua New Guinea in 1983. His tenure at the United Nations was marked by controversy, and was to propel Papua New Guinea into a visibility it had not previously had, and perhaps for which it was not totally prepared. If certain Western representatives maintained that Ambassador Lohia had "exceeded his brief," there were other diplomats who would agree that Papua New Guinea's statement during the decolonization debate in 1985 gave new vigor to the subject itself. It was during this debate that Papua New Guinea raised the issue of New Caledonia's independence. France, represented by Ambassador Claude de Kemoularia, interrupted noisily whenever the words "New Caledonia" were introduced. Francis Saemala (1986), then ambassador and Permanent Representative of Solomon Islands commented, "With all due respect, I thought [the French ambassador's behavior during the debate] was undiplomatic in some respects and childish in others." According to Ambassador Saemala, the decolonization debate was especially significant for Pacific people. "For the first time since joining the UN, Solomon Islands extracted a reply from France [on the question of New Caledonia]. . . . It is quite an achievement for us in the Pacific that one of our own chaired the Decolonization Committee" (Saemala, 1986).

Lelei Lelaulu (1986), UN journalist from Samoa and executive director of the Pacific Islands Association, also considered Ambassador Renagi R. Lohia's contribution to be pivotal. Lohia "was a man of action, intellect . . . [with] considerable talent, and therefore a thorn in the side of France." When the Papua New Guinea Foreign Ministry effected a reorganization of personnel at the United Nations, Lohia returned to Papua New Guinea amid speculation that France and its allies had exerted pressure to have him recalled.

Nonetheless, Papua New Guinea's geopolitical concerns had been given added impetus by the Melanesia Alliance's determination to aid New Caledonia's independence from France. The unity among island nation-states produced a singular decision at the South Pacific Forum Meeting in August 1986 to reinscribe New Caledonia as one of the non-self-governing territories through the United Nations Committee on Decolonization. In the words of the late Jean Marie Tjibaou (1986), the assassinated leader of the New Caledonian indigenous (Kanak) independence movement (Front de Libération Nationale Kanak et Socialiste (FLNKS), "Papua New Guinea is the 'elder brother' of the Melanesian nations and must take the issue of Kanak independence as far as possible." And in a renewed commitment to this issue, Papua New Guinea returned Renagi Lohia to the United Nations as special advisor on the subject of New Caledonia of the PNG delegation to the 1986 session of the General Assembly.

The Reinscription Campaign and the Emerging Image of Pacific Nations

The campaign for reinscription of New Caledonia on the United Nation's list of non-self-governing territories and the question of independence for that country must be posed within the wider context of the attempt to achieve a nuclear-free and independent Pacific. Pacific nations are convinced that France's ability to test nuclear weapons in Pacific waters is based on the colonial status of both New Caledonia and Tahiti. Repeating the admonition of Vanuatu leader Barak Sope to those attending the Nuclear-Free and Independent Pacific Conference hosted by Vanuatu in 1983, Firth notes that "the Pacific Islands will not be nuclear-free until they are truly independent. . . . The nuclear history of the Pacific arises from its lack of independence" (Firth, 1987:136). The French government has publicly declared its intention not to join any agreement between the Soviet Union and the United States to restrict nuclear weapons and to continue testing in the Pacific. France may also wish to maintain control over New Caledonia because of its mineral wealth. New Caledonia is the third largest supplier of nickel in the world, and has deposits of cobalt and manganese, all strategic or high-technology minerals.

The campaign for reinscription of New Caledonia also confronted directly the origin of the United Nations as a place where large countries, or those closely allied with powerful interests, could control the issues. In the last 25 years, the principle that all nations are equal irrespective of size or wealth, has progressively gained acceptance.

Ambassador Lohia of Papua New Guinea had been selected by the South Pacific Forum representatives at the United Nations to supervise formal enlistment of sponsoring nations for the resolution. The list of sponsors for the resolution on reinscription was an impressive coalition of East-West and North-South countries. In 1986 these included Zimbabwe (Chair of the Non-Aligned Movement), Zambia (Chair of the Council for Namibia), Ghana (Chair of the Fourth Committee), all seven South Pacific Forum nations, and all Association of Southeast Asian Nations (ASEAN) members except one.

The basis on which Forum countries were calling for reinscription was concretely defined within specifications relating to United Nations Charter obligations regarding the granting of independence to colonial peoples. Second, as the administering power presumably "preparing" a non-self-governing country for independence, France had not transmitted information since 1947 about New Caledonia as required by Article 73E of the United Nations charter. Third, Resolution 15/14 of 1960 explicated the principles under which the General Assembly could define the concept of a non-self-governing territory. Forum nations had already gained support from the Commonwealth nations in 1985 and from the Non-Aligned Movement in September 1986.

Tjibaou (1986) had insisted that the very future of the Kanak was invested in the vote. "Reinscription must happen this year because next year there is a referendum in New Caledonia on independence. If this referendum occurs within the context of reinscription, we have a chance for decolonization. If it does not, it could be another ten years before we have the opportunity to bring the issue up again."

Through planned, strategic immigration, great numbers of people—including military personnel—had traveled to New Caledonia and would be eligible to vote in the referendum. Legu Vagi (1986:7), the then Papua New Guinea Minister for Foreign Affairs noted that France's military build-up in the Pacific is "of such proportions that the French military presence in New Caledonia is approximately twice as large as the entire armed forces of all

Forum island countries combined.'' Without United
Nations involvement, a referendum could be projected as
an election by a multiracial society to remain a part of
France, 20,000 kilometers away.

December 2, 1986, was to prove historic for several
reasons. In their statements, two former administering territories, or colonizers—Australia and New Zealand—presented themselves as members of the Pacific, first and
foremost. In addition, a group of small, nation-states attempted to lobby on the basis of principle as opposed to
economic power. France's reported application of economic pressures was referred to in formal statements, such
as that by Robin Mauala (1986:5), the diplomat representing
Samoa. ''We are a region of small states . . . we cannot
threaten, cajole or bully . . . we cannot promise economic
or political advantage in return for support in this case.''

In mentioning the relationship between regional solidar-
ity and decolonization, the permanent representative of
Vanuatu, Ambassador Robert Van Lierop (1986), appeared
to appeal to anticipated ''no'' votes by African, Arab, and
Latin American states, respectively. ''For us in the Pacific,
New Caledonia is our Namibia, New Caledonia is our
Palestine, New Caledonia is our Malvinas [Falkland Is-
lands].''

The importance of the diplomatic campaign of 1986 was
matched only by the difficulty of maintaining the critical
support for the same principles of decolonization the subsequent years.

It was surmised that France used trade agreements and
other economic power to control more than one vote of
small, developing countries in 1987. On December 4, 1987,
the General Assembly voted again on the question of New
Caledonia. The vote on Resolution No. 42/79 was 70 in

favor, 29 against, with 47 abstentions. A contentious issue was the appropriate interpretation of the referendum in New Caledonia on September 13 of that year. The French government had insisted that "the people of New Caledonia . . . [had] elected to remain a territory of France" (Blanc, 1987).[3] Speaking as chairman of the South Pacific Forum, Western Samoa Prime Minister Kolone maintained that "we in the Forum cannot accept that interpretation" [because] "over 80 percent of Kanaks stayed away from the polls" (Kolone, 1987:14).

Emerging with new force in the 1987 debates was the notion that there were four aspects to self-determination: (1) integration into an independent country, (2) self-government leading to independence, (3) free association, and (4) independence. The reformulated definition retreated from sovereignty, and presupposed that self-determination could exist without a nation's control over its foreign or military policies. Some diplomats argued that the phrase "self-determination and independence" was tantamount to "predetermining the outcome of self-determination." Others denounced the "fallacious credo that self-determination can only mean independence."

As Galtung (1989) decries, "almost all territories remaining under some form of colonial rule are found in the [South] Pacific [and are used] . . . especially for nuclear testing or as potential nuclear battlefields." Most of those territories are controlled by either France or the United States, both of which have refused to sign the Treaty of Rarotonga, which calls for a nuclear-free and independent Pacific. It is the national desire to protect strategic denial, the policy of restricted international contacts for island nation-states, that has kept the United States from signing the Law of the Sea Treaty or the protocols of the Treaty of

Rarotonga. Moreover, strategic denial has been applied to trade and development issues regarding protection of national fisheries from American purse seines in both the Solomon Islands and Papua New Guinea (see Kengalu, 1988). The United States maintains that the island nations must hold a policy of "non-discriminatory access by U.S. fishermen to the region's exclusive economic zones" (Dorrance, 1980:33). The Treaty of Rarotonga took effect on December 11, 1986, within days of the 1986 vote on reinscription for New Caledonia. It represented a challenge by South Pacific Forum nations to the nuclear states, and was an explicit attempt to redefine the terms of the debate about disarmament.

That France "has refused to allow a medical survey by foreign doctors to investigate the recorded increases in the incidence of brain tumors, leukemia, and thyroid cancer" (Apin, 1989) in its Pacific colonies replicates its refusal to permit UN monitoring of compliance as administering power of a nonself-governing territory. Nuclear testing "has kept Polynesia under colonial rule long after French colonies in Africa gained independence. . . . Paris controls not only foreign affairs and defense, but also the police, justice, immigration, information, communications, foreign commerce, international air and sea traffic, currency, research, and higher education" (Danielsson, 1990:30–31).

On November 22, 1988, and December 11, 1989, the General Assembly adopted resolutions on the question of New Caledonia without a vote, which appeared to reflect a weakened momentum by Pacific nations. The Matignon Accords had been signed by Tjibaou in 1988, but rather than signal conflict-free movement towards independence, that agreement was cloaked in the memory of the massacre of 19 Kanaks by French forces in May 1988 and was a portent of continuing tragedy. The Accords were interpreted by some as primarily colonial reforms meant to maintain France's continued presence in the South Pacific (Winslow, 1990). The assassination on May 4, 1989, of the two highest leaders of the Kanak independence movement—Jean-Marie Tjibaou and Yeiwene Yeiwene—by another member of the same organization was overwhelming in its effects on South Pacific Forum initiatives. In addition, military rulers in Fiji had abandoned the nuclear-free position of the deposed and now late Dr. Timoci Bavadra in 1987. The principle of self-determination in the Pacific has coalesced with unresolved conflicts regarding ethnicity and cultural identity throughout the Pacific, including Papua New Guinea. That the Papua New Guinea government had allied itself with ethnic Fijians on the basis of ethnic or Melanesian solidarity rather than on the principles it supported in the United Nations affected the antinuclear elements throughout the Pacific.

Another challenge to the Papua New Guinea government is how to transfer the ecological concepts of "sustainable development" that it has helped South Pacific Forum nations to project at the United Nations to domestic issues such as those surrounding the Bougainville copper mine.

If the attempts by Pacific governments to reconstitute their nations within the context of sovereignty are further manipulated, it could fragment South Pacific Forum resolve around regional issues. Contrary to the Forum position, the Micronesian territory of the Marshall Islands has "accepted a scheme for an American waste disposal company to ship millions of tons of . . . waste to be used as landfill to enlarge the chain of . . . atolls [for] millions of dollars" (*Tok Blong SPPF* 1989). There are several "waste traders" who "have targeted such obscure places as the Marshall

Islands, Western Samoa, Kiribati, Tonga and Tuvalu as possible places to profitably dispose of refuse that Americans don't want" and who "disguise waste-importation schemes as development projects" (Brown, 1990:8–12). It was due to regional concern around just such ecological issues that heads of government consolidated at the 21st South Pacific Forum in Vila, Vanuatu, from July 31 to August 1, 1990. Indeed, these same leaders met with U.S. President George Bush in Hawaii on October 27, 1990, to address these concerns, especially the transportation of chemical weapons from Germany for disposal on Johnston Atoll.

The United States–Pacific Island Nations Summit demonstrated somewhat contradictorily both the invisibility of Pacific nations and evidence that Papua New Guinea had indeed wrenched itself "away from the quaint natives image" as Lohia had hoped (Lohia, 1986b). Preliminary remarks in the text by President Bush used two concepts that had been advanced by Lohia in previous lectures (see Lohia, 1989). "In the words of Ambassador Lohia of Papua New Guinea, we see an Aquatic Continent . . . reaching out from our West Coast to American Samoa and our other island jurisdictions, the United States is a co-equal member with you in the Pacific's 'extended family' " (Bush, 1990). News reports in Hawaii were essentially the only extensive coverage in the United States on the summit and attributed the concepts of "aquatic continent" and "extended familyhood" to President Bush (*The Sunday Star-Bulletin & Advertiser,* 1990:B3). Yet, the five-hour meeting continued the subtle battle over the concepts of sovereignty, self-determination, and independence that are the purview of the United Nations. South Pacific leaders were concerned that sending the chemical weapons from West Germany to

Johnston Atoll was a component of overall disarmament agreements between East and West, without consultation with governments in the Pacific. Others pondered whether it was in fact deployment of them (Wills, 1990). Moreover, equal status and title of "president" were accorded to leaders of both Micronesia and the Marshall Islands, as though they were fully sovereign states.[4] President Bush thus placed the Pacific heads of state on the same footing as U.S. regional representatives and their countries as states or territories, hence transforming the context of the relationship between sovereignty and independence. This was heightened by the fact that Hawaii Governor John Waihee was not invited and "Peter Tali Coleman, governor of American Samoa . . . [represented] Hawaii, Guam and the Northern Marianas" (*Honolulu Star Bulletin,* 1990:A4). Because Australia and New Zealand were not party to the meeting, Father Lini, then prime minister of Vanuatu, sent his regrets and did not attend.

Some in the Pacific maintain that Australia and New Zealand government policies increasingly suggest a shift in their geopolitical identities, and point to the insistence in 1989 by both countries to introduce a weakened resolution calling for a nuclear-free Pacific at the United Nations. This diplomatic initiative was made without consulting other Forum countries, which prefer that the nuclear states sign a protocol. Furthermore, an inaugural Asia Pacific Economic Cooperation meeting in Australia in November 1989 signalled further erosion of the South Pacific Forum solidarity because only Australia, New Zealand, and ASEAN countries were invited. These new partnerships contrast with other Pacific nations' participation in the Non-Aligned Movement, where interests often coalesce with those of other Third World nations, especially in their common effort for a total nuclear test ban (*New York Times,* 1989:A17).

Controlling the Image: The Quest to Redefine Anthropology

When South Pacific diplomats are asked how they view the potential contribution of anthropology to their countries, the answers are instructive. What Tjibaou had to say definitively compared the Kanak experience to the struggle against apartheid, describing anthropology in New Caledonia and likening what happens in New Caledonia to what was experienced in Zimbabwe prior to its independence. "Anthropology in New Caledonia has taken on the sharp edge of the division in that society within the context of a struggle for independence by the indigenous population. There are anthropologists who scientifically corroborate the Kanak claims to the land. Likewise, there are those who attempt to erase the Kanak past in the islands in order to eliminate the roots of legitimacy" (Tjibaou, 1986).

Tjibaou (1986) also charged anthropology with a unique responsibility to take the words and experience of dominated peoples to the international media, since people in the Pacific have little access to it.

It is Ambassador Saemala (1986) who demonstrates how the real struggle between Pacific peoples and anthropology is not only in the definition of development, but also regarding the budgetary decisions and implementation of development planning. In fact, he believes that at the United Nations few function with the backdrop of prejudices grounded in what he labels "the false image of pure culture." Where this is a problem is in bilateral aid meetings during the presentation of development projects.

[For] New Zealand, Australia, Japan, the United States, and the United Kingdom, the anthropological presentation seems to have had effect. They say to us "develop your agriculture before manufacturing" . . . they will do research in London or Washington before deciding on an aid package. Then the decisions about aid policy do become influenced by erroneous analyses. When we go to a donor with a long-term, education or boat-building project, they say, "go slowly . . . your people's simple way of life should not be disturbed." Their perception of *development for us* is based on missionaries, district officers, and anthropologists' descriptions of us as "simple." Because of what they think is best for us, they end up setting our priorities, and our list of priorities changes. (Saemala, 1986; emphasis added)

Ambassador Saemala lamented that it is in the major media that the stereotyping becomes widespread and projects the view that "we are so backward." Framing the analysis of a front page article on the conflict surrounding the colonial legacy in Papua New Guinea of mining in Bougainville, was the use of the classic vocabulary and discourse of both hierarchical exotification and Melanesians as contemporary ancestors: "tribes," "jungle," "largely uncharted and unknown until World War II," "most of the 3.7 million people live as their ancestors did," "jungle hamlets," "Highland warriors in feathers and mud now use shotguns as well as spears in traditional tribal fights," "militants have done ritual killings," "bow and arrow," and "traditional peace ceremony" (*Los Angeles Times*, 1989).

The fact that Pacific peoples do not fully control the conceptual contexts with which their societies engage the world community must be viewed within the wider context of the "geopolitics of information." As Anthony Smith

(1980:27) noted, "To be imprisoned inside the misinterpretation and misunderstanding of others can be a withering form of incarceration." His perceptive judgment replicates Ambassador Lohia's statement at the beginning of this chapter. This struggle over who controls information is not unique to the Pacific and is shared by many who have confronted pressure as they attempt to redefine development, reconstitute the expertise, and remake science to fit their people's requirements. As such, scholarship is a fundamental aspect of information. As one Fijian scholar notes, "knowledge and information scarcity are related to a crucial lack of capacity to deal with many issues . . . [and can] lead to devastating decisions [regarding] sea-bed mining, protection of the ocean ecosystem, conservation of living marine resources, and telematics" (Anthony, 1988:xv).

Ramos Horta (1986b:84) intimates that a new social science—especially for Papua New Guinea—is irrevocably tied to government policy. "In view of PNG's vulnerable position [vis-à-vis Indonesia] . . . its only defense is a visible international posture, diversification of its international relations, and some serious mobilization." Part of this visibility would be reinforced by modifying the *invisibility* brought about by foreign social science.

Thus, the Papua New Guinea government and anthropologists alike must recognize that scholarship and information are strategic. The reproduction of data that presents Melanesians as having entered the twentieth century as a result of "contact" with Europeans affords those who disagree with a nuclear-free and independent Pacific the opportunity to dismiss their geopolitical concerns. It also influences multilateral relations within international organizations, even as cognitive constraint by Pacific peoples themselves. Moreover, transference of talismanic anticommunism to the nuclear-free and independent Pacific movement will add complexity to diplomacy. In this regard, Robie cites one former U.S. ambassador to Fiji, who concluded that the "most potentially disruptive movement for U.S. relations with the South Pacific is the growing antinuclear movement in the region. . . . The U.S. Government must do everything possible to counter this movement" (Robie, 1989:20). Thus, the conflict in the Pacific of most importance does not embody usage of varying types of spears. Ahistorical analyses of regional conflict, weaponry, and so-called tribal fighting are divorced from the contemporary reality of genetic alteration of Pacific peoples and of the living organisms that sustain them. As Lucas and Vatin (1975) demonstrate, a "scientific" description as savages (*l'ensauvagement*) of those who espouse independence from metropolitan control of their lands is a form of "military ethnography."

And, as Papua New Guinean and other Pacific scholars redefine the categories of appropriate academic inquiry, they will aid those Western scholars whose commitment to equality is often entrapped within intellectual reference points that reinforce hierarchy.[5] Anthropologists would do well to begin to conceptualize Pacific peoples in the global context within which they would see themselves. Ambassador Lohia (1986a) puts the issue in a long-range perspective. "World War II was created outside but fought on our island. It destroyed a lot of our land, crops and people. . . . Anthropologists and missionaries came to our country and said that our regional disputes were 'clan warfare', that we should put down our bows and arrows, which we did. And . . . we islanders are being drawn into one hell of a 'clan fight' in the Pacific by the so-called civilized world. . . . The

question is, what can we from the Pacific do to get everyone
to live like truly civilized, human beings?''

NOTES

Acknowledgments: Excerpts from this chapter were previously published in "Anthropology, Geopolitics, and Papua New
Guinea," *Central Issues in Anthropology* 8 (July, 1988).

The assistance and time provided by country representatives
and U.N. personnel are hereby gratefully acknowledged. The
author recognizes that interviews with diplomats and ambassa-
dors often involved discussion of sensitive policy issues, and
their trust and recognition of the importance of this research
project are greatly appreciated. Data was also generously provided by U.N. personnel Girma Abebe and Lelei Lelaulu.

In addition, the author respectfully acknowledges the help of
the late Ralph Karepa, who was interviewed in 1983 while Acting
Ambassador from Papua New Guinea to the United Nations. The
substance of that interview first appeared without acknowledg-
ment (at Mr. Karepa's request) in "Language and 'Development'
in Papua New Guinea" (Gilliam, 1984).

The author also thanks Karen Watson-Gegeo and Gerald
Horne for their assistance with this chapter.

1. These words by Ambassador Lohia were part of his keynote address, "Search for Genuine Security in the Aquatic Continent of the Pacific," at the conference entitled, *The Pacific
Community: A Common Security Agenda for the Nineties,* but
were not excerpted for publication (see Lohia, 1989). The complete address can be obtained by contacting the Institute for
Global Security Studies, 225 North 70th Street, Seattle, Wash.
98103.

2. This question was raised by Utula Samana from the audience on the occasion of Bill Hayden's speech at the University of

Papua New Guinea in Port Moresby, during the 1986 Waigani Seminar, *The Ethics of Development,* at which I was in attendance.

3. On two occasions, while representing the International Women's Anthropology Conference (a nongovernmental organization with consultative status at the U.N. Economic and Social Council), I presented petitions on behalf of New Caledonia. On October 16, 1987, France used the right of reply in the Fourth Committee to respond to me, insisting that "the French of Melanesian origin are free French citizens" (Document no. A/C.4/42/SR.14) (see Gilliam, 1990).

4. The Compact of Free Association defines the relationship between both the Federated States of Micronesia (FSM) and the Republic of the Marshall Islands with the United States. This complex treaty stipulates that certain features of domestic, foreign, and defense policy are to be constructed partly by the United States, and represents an intermediate position between colonial and independent status. Within the United Nations, the Security Council terminated the trusteeship agreement in 1986, thereby precluding the United Nations Trusteeship Council from ever listing those two countries as non-self-governing territories. Both FSM and the Marshall Islands became full members of the South Pacific Forum in 1987 and have established "bilateral" agreements with many nation-states.

5. In 1982, I raised a related question as discussant for the symposium entitled "The Relevance of Melanesia for Anthropology and the Relevance of Anthropology for Melanesia" at the Northeastern Anthropological Association's meeting. On that occasion, it was pondered whether one day, Papua New Guineans, like some Africans, might say that there is only room for sociology in Papua New Guinea, because the latter investigates social and cultural processes in *modern* society. Annette Wiener (1976), who has investigated the issue of gender in the Trobriand Islands, in her defense of anthropology appealed to Kubulan Los—then ambassador from Papua New Guinea—who was in the

audience, to take a position on the relevance of anthropology for Melanesia. He declined.

REFERENCES

Abebe, G. 1986. Interview with author at the United Nations, May 6.

Anthony, J. 1988. "Introduction." In R. Walker and W. Sutherland (eds.), *The Pacific: Peace, Security and the Nuclear Issue,* pp. xi–xviii. Tokyo: United Nations University.

Apin, T. 1989. "Nukes, Not Liberty." *Third World,* no. 22, October.

Blanc, P. L. 1987. France, quatrième commission, point 18, "Intervention," prononcée par S. Exc. M. Pierre-Louis Blanc, Ambassadeur, Représentant permanent de la France auprès des Nations Unies, 21 octobre 1987, New York. Permanent Mission of France to the United Nations.

Brown, T. 1990. "Islands at Risk." *Pacific Magazine (The Seattle Times/Seattle Post-Intelligencer).* September 2.

Buck, P. 1989. "Cargo-Cult Discourse: Myth and Rationalization of Labor Relations in Papua New Guinea." *Dialectical Anthropology* 13, 157–71.

Bush, G. 1990. Text of remarks at opening of the United States-Pacific Island Nations summit, October 27, 1990. East-West Center, Honolulu.

Danielsson, B. 1990. "Poisoned Pacific: The Legacy of French Nuclear Testing." *The Bulletin of the Atomic Scientists,* March, pp. 22–31.

Dorrance, J. 1980. "Oceania and the United States: An Analysis of U.S. Interests and Policy in the South Pacific." National Security Affairs Monograph Series 80–6. Washington, D.C.: National Defense University Research Directorate, U.S. Government Printing Office.

Feil, D. K. 1984. *Ways of Exchange: The Enga Tee of Papua New*

Guinea. St. Lucia, Australia: University of Queensland Press.

Feldman, H. 1986. Interview with author in New York, May 9.

Firth, S. 1987. *Nuclear Playground.* Honolulu: University of Hawaii Press.

Galtung, J. 1989. "The Pacific: A Poisoned Nuclear Lake." *The Contemporary Pacific: A Journal of Island Affairs* 1(1, 2).

Gilliam, A. 1984. "Language and 'Development' in Papua New Guinea." *Dialectical Anthropology* 8, pp. 303–18.

———. 1990. "Representing IWAC at the UN: The Story of Two Petitions." *IWAC Newsletter,* issue 13, June.

Godelier, M. 1982. *The Making of Great Men: Male Domination and Power among the New Guinea Baruya.* Cambridge: Cambridge University Press.

Haberman, C. 1986. "Challenge in the Pacific: Moscow's Growing Naval Strength." *The New York Times Magazine,* September 7.

Half-Life: A Parable for the Nuclear Age. 1986. Distributed by Direct Cinema Limited, P.O. Box 69799, Los Angeles, Calif. 90069.

Hallpike, C. R. 1977. *Bloodshed and Vengeance in the Papuan Mountains.* Oxford: Oxford University Press.

Hau'ofa, E. 1975. "Anthropology and Pacific Islanders." *Oceania* 45(4), pp. 283–89.

Honolulu Star Bulleton. 1990. "OHA Trustees Upset Over Non-Invite." October 27.

Karepa, R. 1983. Interview with author in New York, November.

Kengalu, A. M. 1988. *Embargo: The Jeanette Diana Affair.* Bathurst: Robert Brown.

Knauft, B. 1985. *Good Company and Violence: Sorcery and Social Action in a Lowland New Guinea Society.* Berkeley: University of California Press.

Koch, K. F. 1974. *War and Peace in Jalemo: The Management of Conflict in Highland New Guinea.* Cambridge: Harvard University Press.

Kolone, V. 1987. Statement by Honourable Va'ai Kolone, Prime

Minister of Western Samoa and Chairman of the South Pacific
Forum, to the 42d session of the United Nations General
Assembly, October 9, New York. Permanent Mission of
Western Samoa to the United Nations.

Lelaulu, L. 1986. Interview with author at the United Nations,
April 29.

Lohia, R. R. 1986a. Interview with author at the United Nations,
October 13.

———. 1986b. Interview with author, December 2.

———. 1989. "Search for Genuine Security in the Aquatic Con-
tinent." Keynote address at the Institute for Global Security
Studies conference, *The Pacific Community: A Common
Security Agenda for the Nineties,* September 6–9, Seattle
University. Excerpted in *Pacific Security Report* 2(3), pp. 2–
4.

Los Angeles Times. 1989. " 'Mine of Tears' Conflict Imperils
Papua New Guinea." December 17.

Lucas, P., and J. C. Vatin. 1975. "L'Algerie des anthropologues."
Paris: François Maspero.

Malinowski, B. 1927. *Sex and Repression in Savage Society.*
New York: Harcourt Brace.

———. 1929. *Sexual Life of Savages in Northwestern Melanesia:
An Ethnographic Account of Courtship, Marriage, and Fam-
ily Life among the Natives of the Trobriand Islands, British
New Guinea.* London: George Routledge & Son.

Mauala, R. 1986. Statement by Ms. Robin Mauala, chairperson
of the delegation of Samoa, before the 41st session of the
United Nations General Assembly, 1 December, Item 19.

Mead, M. 1928. *Coming of Age in Samoa: A Psychological Study
of Primitive Youth for Western Civilization.* New York: Morrow.

———. 1930. *Growing Up in New Guinea: A Comparative Study
of Primitive Education.* New York: Morrow.

———. 1935. *Sex and Temperament in Three Primitive Societies.*
New York: Morrow.

Meggitt, M. 1977. *Blood Is Their Argument: Warfare among the*

Mae Enga Tribesman of the New Guinea Highlands. Mayfield.

Mercier, P. 1966. *Histoire de l'anthropologie*. Paris: Presses Universitaires de France.

New York Times. 1989. "Nonaligned Nations Seek Total Nuclear Test Ban." November 15.

―――. 1989. "Pacific Economic Group Makes Progress at Meeting." November 13, p. D2.

Pandian, J. 1985. "Anthropology and the Western Tradition: Toward an Authentic Anthropology." Prospect Heights: Waveland Press.

Ramos-Horta, J. 1986a. Interview with author, July 22.

―――. 1986b. *FUNU: The Unfinished Saga of East Timor*. New Jersey: Red Sea Press.

Robie, D. 1989. *Blood on Their Banner: Nationalist Struggles in the South Pacific*. London: Zed Books.

Rodman, M., and M. Cooper. 1983. *The Pacification of Melanesia*. ASAO Monograph no. 7. University Press of America.

Saemala, F. 1986. Interview with author at the United Nations, May 6.

Singham, A., and S. Hune. 1986. *Non-Alignment in an Age of Alignments*. London: Zed.

Smith, A. 1980. *The Geopolitics of Information: How Western Culture Dominates the World*. London: Oxford University Press.

Stocking, G. 1987. *Victorian Anthropology*. New York: Free Press.

The Sunday Star-Bulletin and Advertiser (Honolulu). 1990. "Pacific Summit: Bush Reassures Assembled Leaders from the 'Aquatic Continent.' " October 28.

Thomas, N. 1989. "The Force of Ethnology: Origins and Significance of the Melanesia/Polynesia Division." *Current Anthropology* 30(1), pp. 27–31.

Tjibaou, J. M. 1986. Interview with author in New York, September 26. Interpreted by D. Winslow.

Tok Blong SPPF. 1989. "Garbage Imperialism Rears Its Ugly Head in the Pacific." No. 28, July.

Vagi, Legu. 1986. Statement by the Honourable Legu Vagi, MP, Papua New Guinea Minister for Foreign Affairs, to the 41st session of the U.N. General Assembly, October 10.

Van Lierop, R. 1986. Statement by Permanent Representative of Vanuatu, delivered in session, December 2.

Watson-Gegeo, K., and G. White. 1990. *Conflict Discourse in Pacific Societies.* Palo Alto: Stanford University Press.

Weiner, A. 1976. *Women of Value, Men of Renown: New Perspectives in Trobriand Exchange.* Austin: University of Texas Press.

Wills, P. 1990. *Chemical Weapons at Johnston Atoll: Deployment or Disarmament?* Centre for Peace Studies, University of Auckland, Auckland.

Winslow, D. 1990. "Kanaky Since the Matignon Accords." Paper presented at 7th Annual Nuclear Free Pacific conference, April 6–8, Crescent Beach, British Columbia.

Wolfe, R. 1986. Interview with author at the United Nations, December 2.